The B.C. Fact BOOK

The B.C. Fact BOOK

Everything YOU Ever Wanted
To Know About British Columbia

Mark Zuehlke

Whitecap Books
Vancouver/Toronto

The information in this book is true and complete to the best of our knowledge. All recommendations are made without guarantee on the part of the author or Whitecap Books Ltd. The author and publisher disclaim any liability in connection with the use of this information. For additional information please contact Whitecap Books Ltd., 351 Lynn Avenue, North Vancouver, BC V7J 2C4.

Edited by Linda Ostrowalker
Cover design and illustration by Rose Cowles
Interior design by Warren Clark
Typeset by Warren Clark
Printed and bound in Canada by D.W. Friesen and Sons Ltd., Altona, Manitoba.

Canadian Cataloguing in Publication Data

Zuehlke, Mark.
    The B.C. fact book

    ISBN 1-55110-227-3

    1. British Columbia—Handbooks, manuals, etc.   I. Title.
FC3807.Z83   1995   971.1'003   C94-910960-6
F1087.Z83 1995

Contents

S

T

V

W

Y

Acknowledgements

Completion of this book would have been impossible without the assistance of literally dozens of people in federal departments, government ministries, Tourist Infocentres throughout the province, National Park and Provincial Park staff, and many others who helped in the tracking down of sometimes obscure information. Everyone at the environment ministry was particularly helpful, especially Syd Cannings and the gang in the Conservation Data Centre, and carnivore specialist Sean Sharpe who patiently fielded many return calls for further clarification on one subject after another. The staff at the B.C. Archives and Records Service (BCARS) were, as always, a great help.

Dr. Elizabeth Vibert at the University of Victoria and Cheryl Coull developed my understanding of the emerging mosaic of First Nations Peoples' cultural and tribal-identity issues. Various experts at the Royal British Columbia Museum also contributed much useful advice and information on a variety of subjects.

Thanks also go to the following people who made suggestions of gave helpful advice: Maggie Kerr-Southin, Rosemary Neering, Diane Swanson, Peter Grant, and Louise Donnelly.

Special thanks to Fran Backhouse, who opened up the wealth of information found in her wildlife and environment files, and was endlessly supportive—a true friend.

Introduction

The title of a book like this and the subject listings the book contains pretty much speak for themselves. This is a book that attempts to encapsulate as much factual information about the province's landscape, wildlife, its peoples, their history, culture, and present economic and social experience as is feasible in one easily used and read volume. Through this process, it is hoped, the book will help give some understanding of how British Columbians have been shaped by the environment in which they live and of who they are as a people. That's the big-picture purpose behind this book, but it's also hoped that the facts it contains will make for some enjoyable and informative reading on a subject-by-subject level that will enhance both residents' and visitors' understanding of this endlessly fascinating Canadian province.

It should be noted that there was no attempt to list every community in the province. The decision to include one community and not another was, however, not completely arbitrary. Communities listed and the details in their descriptions were selected on the basis of what that information contributed to the sense of who British Columbians are and how they live now, or have lived in the past.

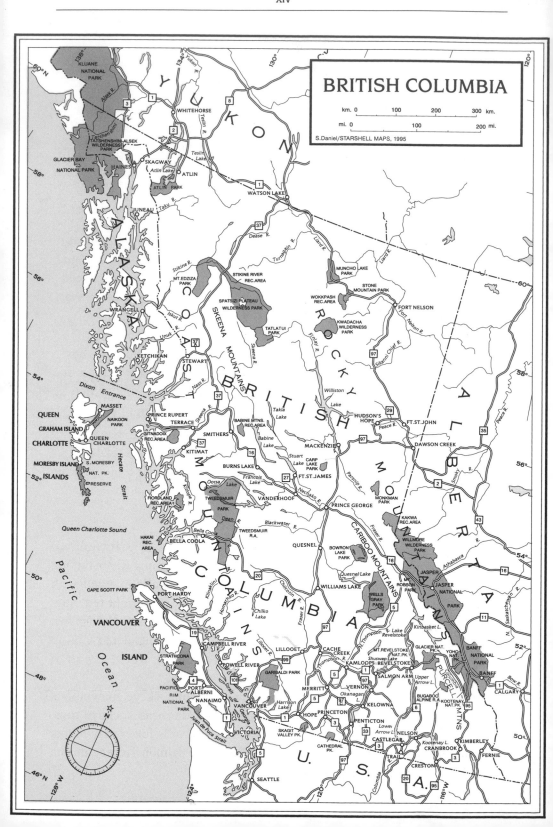

Abbotsford International Airshow

Held annually on the second weekend of August, this is North America's largest airshow, drawing more than 300,000 people daily. Military and civilian precision aerobatic teams from around the world perform; historical and experimental aircraft are displayed and flight-tested; and stunt flyers put on thrilling shows. Among those performing are always the Canadian Armed Forces Snowbirds' nine-plane aerobatic team, flying the Canadian-designed and -built Canadair CL-41 Tutor jet painted red, white, and blue. The airshow is held at Abbotsford International Airport, located on Mt. Lehman Road in the Fraser Valley city of Abbotsford.

Active Pass

Running between Mayne and Galiano islands into Georgia Strait, Active Pass is travelled by more than five million ferry passengers yearly. Currents run quickly in this channel and there is always a lot of boat activity. Many people believe the name derives from one or the other of these facts. The pass, however, is named after the U.S. survey ship *Active*, a 750-ton paddle steamer with two guns, which entered the channel a month before the British Royal Navy's own HMS *Plumper* arrived in 1858. As the American ship got there first the British recognized the American name designation.

Adams River

Site of the continent's largest sockeye **salmon** run. Every four years millions of sockeye return to the eleven-kilometre length of the Adams River linking Adams Lake to **Shuswap Lake**. The river becomes literally clogged with spawning salmon that have changed from a silver colour to a bright red. Several thousand chinook and hundreds of coho and pink salmon also spawn here. Because of the large numbers involved, the river is considered vital to sustaining B.C.'s sockeye salmon population and is now protected as part of Roderick Haig-Brown Provincial Park.

In the years between dominant runs the number of sockeye spawning is much lower but still outnumbers most other North American sockeye runs. There was a dominant run in 1994, which was significantly lower in numbers than anticipated, contributing to fears that the entire salmon fishery on the West Coast may be threatened.

To get to Adams River the sockeye set out in early fall on a seventeen-day, 485-kilometre odyssey that takes them from the Pacific Ocean up the **Fraser**, **Thompson**, and South Thompson rivers, through Little Shuswap Lake, Shuswap Lake, and finally into the Adams River.

Agricultural Land Reserve

Prior to 1973 nearly six thousand hectares of prime agricultural land were lost throughout the province each year to urban and other development. This happened despite the fact that only about 17.5 percent of the province's land base had agricultural capability and, of this, only about 1.1 percent was considered prime agricultural land.

In 1973, the provincial government moved to stem this loss of agricultural land by creating the Agricultural Land Reserve (ALR). About 4.7 million hectares of land, representing 5 percent of B.C.'s land mass, were included in the reserve. Although a further 12.5 percent of the province was deemed to have some agricultural capability, these lands were either excluded due to their extreme isolation and consequent safety from urban pressure or due to their marginal commercial agricultural value.

Land falling into the reserve is subject to land-use restrictions with most non-agricultural usage prohibited or strictly controlled. Applications for non-agricultural use of land within the ALR are considered by the Agricultural Land Commission (ALC). The ALC's commissioners are drawn from throughout B.C. for their experience in agricultural and land-use issues.

Since it began operations in 1974 the ALC has been effective in slowing the loss of arable land to non-agricultural uses. From a loss of six thousand hectares annually in the early 1970s, the prime agricultural land base is now reduced by about 750 hectares per year. This is despite the fact that more than thirty thousand applications to exclude land from the ALR have been filed with the commission since 1974—an average of sixteen hundred per year.

Although the ALR has proven a successful strategy for preserving the province's small agricultural land base, it remains a controversial solution. Municipalities and land developers often complain that it restricts their ability to accommodate and undertake urban development and growth in an orderly and affordable manner. Many farmers—especially in sectors that are increasingly facing declining prices and rising operational costs, such as the Okanagan fruit-growing industry—complain they are held hostage to a government policy that denies them the right to develop their land as they choose, but simultaneously provides little assistance or subsidization during times when prices are depressed.

Agriculture

Each year British Columbian farmers produce over two hundred commodities valued in excess of $1.3 billion. The province's nineteen thousand farms provide direct employment for about twenty-nine thousand people, and as the farm yields move down the province's food chain to local and export markets another five B.C. jobs are created in relation to each farm job.

As the majority of the province is non-arable due to its rugged mountainous terrain and high altitudes, agriculture is concentrated primarily in narrow valleys.

The Fraser Valley alone contains almost half of B.C.'s farms and generates more than half of the province's farm revenue. Dairy products, poultry, eggs, hogs, vegetables, floriculture, and nursery products are the main commodities. These same commodities are produced on a smaller scale on **Vancouver Island**'s Saanich Peninsula and east coast.

The heartland of B.C.'s cattle industry is found in the central interior. One-third of the province's 600,000 beef cattle and calves graze on pastures and rangeland here.

The Okanagan region produces over 96 percent of B.C.'s tree fruit crops and nearly 100 percent of its premium wine grapes. Additional Okanagan agricultural pursuits include raising cattle, hogs, and poultry.

The Kootenay region produces mainly cattle, tree fruits, forage, grain, and Christmas trees.

Eighty-five percent of the province's grain production occurs in the **Peace River** region. Canola, cattle, forage, and honey are also major commodities of this area.

Outside these regions of the province agricultural activity is limited, although there is a small amount of arable land found in the **Skeena River** area inland from the northwest coast and in isolated pockets on the **Queen Charlotte Islands**.

Dairy production—the province's largest agricultural sector—is worth about $260 million annually. It is followed by the beef and veal production sector at $234 million, poultry and eggs sector at $209 million, vegetable sector at $157 million, and floriculture and nursery sector at $141 million.

The value of agricultural products increases substantially after it has been transformed into various food products by the province's processing industry. Dairy products, for example, are valued after processing at about $616 million. The value of total agricultural products after processing is about $3.11 billion.

More than 60 percent of B.C.'s agricultural products are consumed within the province. Only about $464 million of agricultural primary and processed products and $98 million of beverages are exported beyond Canada. Inter-provincial exports are valued at about $750 million.

The value of crops bears scant relationship to the quantity of land used. B.C.'s floriculturists, producing potted plants, cut flowers, bedding plants, and foliage plants, realize annual sales of $80 million from a land base of only ninety hectares.

To sustain the province's profitable dairy industry, B.C. dairy cows produce about 510 million litres of milk each year, enough for each person in the province to be able to drink half a litre of milk a day. B.C. chickens lay nearly 720 million eggs annually. Berries are grown in quantities that could supply every person in the province with eighteen kilograms of berries annually. Twelve million kilograms of blueberries alone are grown annually and, of these, two million kilograms are sold to U-pick customers. B.C. is also the largest producer of fresh mushrooms in western North America, producing a total of fifteen million kilograms annually. One of B.C.'s most highly prized commodities is its apples, which are exported to more than thirty countries.

Ainsworth Hot Springs

Near Kootenay Lake, these hot springs are reputed to have the highest mineral content of any in Canada. Of the province's ninety-five documented hot springs, Ainsworth's are the only ones heated by molten rock boiling up from the earth's core. This feature is known as an intrusive spur. Other B.C. hot springs result from surface moisture seeping underground, being heated by the earth's core, and then bubbling back up to the surface.

Ainsworth's water temperatures vary from 29° to 45° Celsius. Air temperature in the cave ranges from 40° to 45° Celsius. The horseshoe-shaped cave was originally a mine shaft. When the miners discovered mineral-rich hot water instead of ore they abandoned the operation.

Air Disasters

The first death in Canada resulting from a plane crash occurred at Victoria, B.C. on August 6, 1913, when American barnstormer John M. Bryant was killed in the crash of his Curtiss seaplane.

The nation's first major air disaster also took place near Victoria, on August 25, 1928, when a B.C. Airways Ford Trimotor plunged into Puget Sound en route from Victoria to Seattle during bad weather. All seven people aboard were killed.

On April 27, 1947, Trans-Canada Airline (TCA) flight No. 3, en route from Lethbridge to Vancouver, disappeared without a trace. The Lockheed Lodestar was presumed crashed and all fifteen passengers and crew aboard dead after the most extensive air and sea search in B.C. history to that time failed to find the wreckage. Authorities concluded the plane must have strayed off the flight path of its approach to Vancouver airport, and disappeared after crashing into the ocean. But in September 1994, a hiker, who had actually first discovered the plane's wreckage two years earlier and presumed it to be a known crash site, led authorities to the plane in the Mount Seymour watershed near North Vancouver. The plane was buried beneath a half-metre of dirt and undergrowth in a creek bed surrounded by thick woods. In 1947 there was little population in the North Vancouver area, explaining why no-one witnessed the plane's crash.

Four years later, on October 17, 1951, a Queen Charlotte Airlines' Canso struck Mount Benson near Nanaimo. Twenty-three people perished.

On November 24, 1952, a Royal Canadian Air Force plane went down at Comox, killing twelve.

On December 9, 1956, B.C. had its worst air disaster when a TCA North Star CF-TFD slammed into Mount Sleese in the Nesakwatch Valley near Chilliwack. All fifty-nine passengers and three crew died in the fiery crash. Among those aboard were Canadian Forces peacekeepers coming home from overseas duty and five Canadian Football League players returning from an all-star game. The wreckage was not discovered until May 14, 1957, despite an intensive search. A 2.5-kilometre off-limit zone declared by provincial Order in Council extends outward from the crash site to protect the area as a memorial to the dead because many of the bodies were never recovered.

In June 1957 two planes crashed. A Pacific Western Airlines' (PWA) DC3 crashed at the Port Hardy airport killing fourteen, and a Canadian Pacific Airlines (CPA) flight went down at Mount Cheam near Chilliwack resulting in thirteen deaths.

On July 8, 1965, CPA DC-6B, the *Empress of Buenos Aires,* on a flight from Vancouver to Winnipeg, was at an altitude of about forty-five hundred metres when a bomb exploded in the cargo bay and ripped its tail off. The plane was about 240 kilometres north of Vancouver over Dog Creek, near 100 Mile House. All fifty-two people aboard perished.

On February 11, 1978, a Pacific Western Airlines' Boeing 737 crashed during landing at the Cranbrook Airport when it took evasive action to miss colliding with a snowplow operating on the runway. Six people in the rear of the plane managed to escape before it burst into flames. The other forty-two passengers and crew perished.

On January 11, 1995, a Learjet, privately contracted by the provincial government to serve as an air ambulance, crashed into the sea during an approach to Masset airstrip in the Queen Charlotte Islands. Everyone aboard—

the two crew, two paramedics, and a doctor—died. The plane had flown from Vancouver to pick up a pregnant woman experiencing fetal distress after a helicopter crew earlier refused the flight because of bad weather conditions.

Airports

With more than nine million passengers passing annually through its terminals, Vancouver International Airport is British Columbia's busiest and largest airport. It is also the only airport in the province linked into major international routes and serviced by non-Canadian international carriers.

A network of airports serviced by the two major Canadian airlines or affiliated companies provide air transport links throughout the province. Victoria International Airport and Nanaimo's Cassidy Airport are Vancouver Island's primary airports. Besides Vancouver International, Abbotsford International Airport serves as the Lower Mainland's secondary air transportation link. In the Okanagan, Kelowna Airport is the area's primary airport, with Penticton Airport providing secondary service. Major carriers land in the East Kootenays at Cranbrook-Kimberley Airport and provide limited service into the West Kootenays at Castlegar Airport. The Thompson Valley region is serviced through Kamloops Airport. The major airport in the north-central region of the province is Prince George Airport. Main northwestern coastal airport links are at the Terrace-Kitimat Airport and Prince Rupert Airport. Major Canadian airline carriers flying into the northeastern part of the province use Fort St. John.

Most B.C. communities either have a small airstrip for emergency, recreational, and local transportation purposes or are within a short drive of such a facility. Many of these smaller airports are serviced by local air charter and airline companies flying between them and the nearest major airport.

Akamina Pass

B.C.'s most easterly point is found in the extreme southeastern corner of the province. Part of the Akamina-Kishinena Provincial Recreation Area, this narrow pass through the **Rocky Mountains** into Alberta is very isolated, accessible mainly by logging roads. The region is largely unpopulated. Before taking a trip into these mountains travellers should get road condition information locally at such communities as Elko. Carrying topographical maps is recommended. Akamina is a Kutenai First Nations word meaning "mountain pass."

Alaska-Canada Boundary

The Alaska-Canada Border parallelling British Columbia runs from 54° 40' north latitude, just north of the mouth of Portland Canal, up the canal to

56° north latitude, then traverses the mountain summits in a ragged line parallelling the coast as far as 60° north latitude, where the border continues between Alaska and Yukon Territory.

The area of Alaska bordering B.C. is known as the Alaska Panhandle and its boundary with the province was the subject of a major dispute between Canada and the United States that waxed and waned throughout the late 1800s and was resolved only in 1903. In 1825, Russia, then possessing Alaska, and Great Britain agreed on a boundary between their two colonies. The Russian concern was access to fjords and inlets for fishing and whaling purposes and marine access to native communities for fur and other trading; the British were little interested in the coastline but for the fur trade wanted control of as much inland terrain as possible. Creation of the Alaska Panhandle resulted from their negotiations, known as the Convention of February. Under the agreement Russian territory would never extend inland more than ten leagues—about forty-eight kilometres.

When the United States purchased Alaska from the Russians in 1867, it inherited the Russian position. Canada, however, had just attained confederation and with British Columbia's joining Canada in 1871 they attempted to rationalize the boundary with Alaska by having the panhandle merged into the new Canadian province.

It quickly became apparent that the United States had no intention of surrendering this land and the two nations entered into lengthy and controversial negotiations. Complicating the negotiations was the fact that Canada did not yet have full treaty negotiating power—that authority being retained by Great Britain until 1919 when the British government agreed to Canada's signing the Treaty of Versailles because of its contribution to the successful fighting of World War I.

The U.S. position was that it controlled the coastline continuously despite the fact that many deep fjords and inlets on the coast penetrated far inland. Canada argued that the ten-league rule applied and that it consequently controlled the heads of many of these fjords. The dispute smoldered for nearly thirty years without resolution until 1897 when the sudden influx of thousands of miners bound for the Klondike Gold Rush led to both sides vying for control of the heads of inlets, which were being used as jumping-off points to the Yukon gold fields.

Two years of negotiations in the Joint High Commission failed in 1899. In 1903 an international tribunal, composed of three Americans, two Canadians, and Lord Alverstone, the Lord Chief Justice of England, was convened to resolve the dispute once and for all. The Americans and Canadians were inflexibly partisan in favour of their respective nation's position. Lord Alverstone, in what many Canadians thought a blatant sell-out of Canadian interests to improve American-British relations, cast the deciding vote in favour of the U.S. claim rather than deadlocking the tribunal by siding with the Canadians. The two Canadian judges refused to sign the agreement, but, as Britain and not Canada had the power to make treaties at the time, the border was confirmed on October 20, 1903.

Today the 1,434-kilometre border between Alaska and B.C. is a six-metre cleared swath—three metres to each side.

Alaska Highway

The 2,288-kilometre-long Alaska Highway extends from Dawson Creek, B.C. to Fairbanks, Alaska. Of the total length, 1,009 kilometres lie within British Columbia, stretching from Mile 0 at Dawson Creek to twelve kilometres south of Yukon Territory's Watson Lake, a point astride 60° latitude north, which denotes the B.C.-Yukon boundary. The British Columbia section of the Alaska Highway is officially designated as a section of Highway 97, which runs through the province's interior from the southern boundary with the United States to its northern border with Yukon Territory.

Construction of the highway is considered one of the most spectacular engineering feats of the twentieth century, primarily due to the speed with which the long road running through incredibly rugged terrain was constructed. The decision to build the Alaska Highway was made by the United States after the Japanese bombing of Pearl Harbor in December 1941 and subsequent Japanese capture of two Aleutian islands led to fears that Alaska was vulnerable to invasion by Axis forces. A land link was deemed essential to sustain the military garrisons established to defend Alaska.

Work on the highway began in February 1942 and in eight months and twelve days a mostly one-lane dirt track barely wide enough in places for a military truck to travel was completed. About eleven thousand U.S. soldiers and sixteen thousand civilians (including thirty-seven hundred Canadians) were involved in the project, which required crossing eight mountain ranges, countless streams, and cutting a road through seemingly endless forests. More than eight thousand culverts and 133 bridges had to be installed or constructed. The United States bore the construction cost of $147.8 million, and Canada provided right of way.

Following the conclusion of World War II the Canadian government took over the 1,954-kilometre Canadian section on April 1, 1946. It paid the United States $108 million for adjacent airfields, flight strips, buildings, telephone systems, and other assets, but not highway construction costs. It was opened to unrestricted civilian traffic in 1947, but continued to be maintained by Canadian army engineers until 1964 when the federal department of public works took over maintenance.

Today the highway serves as the major link for many of B.C.'s northern communities. While the northeastern section of the province through which the highway crosses has undergone significant development and exploitation of mineral, oil, and gas resources, areas to the west of the highway remain lightly settled, remote, and undeveloped. Although some of the Alaska Highway remains unpaved and construction and reconstruction work is almost continuous, the entire highway from Dawson Creek to Fairbanks can now be travelled in three to four days.

Alert Bay

Alert Bay is located south of Port Hardy on the northeast coast of **Vancouver Island**. Until 1994 this village was home to the world's tallest **totem pole**. The fifty-three-metre pole was carved by six Alert Bay natives. Its images relate the history of the Kwakwaka'wakw people.

The world's tallest totem pole (fifty-five metres) was raised in August 1994 on Songhees Point in Victoria, as part of the 15th Commonwealth Games celebrations. Alert Bay, however, has pledged to build one that is even taller to regain its claim to being home to the world's tallest.

Alexander Mackenzie Heritage Trail

In 1793 Scottish fur trader and explorer Alexander Mackenzie became the first European to cross the North American continent, preceding the Lewis and Clark expedition by more than twelve years. On the last stage of his journey, Mackenzie and nine companions were guided to the Pacific by natives who led them along an overland route that proved more easily travelled than his original plan to follow what would later be named the **Fraser River**.

The overland route he followed was 420 kilometres long and stretched from the mouth of the West Road (Blackwater) River's confluence with the Fraser River between **Prince George** and Quesnel to Dean Channel, northeast of Bella Coola on the Pacific coast.

Much of the route was a main trading trail used by the Bella Coola, Chilcotin, and Carrier peoples. The coastal tribes traded **oolichan** grease or oil with the interior tribes for moose and beaver hides, and obsidian. The last few kilometres of Mackenzie's journey were made by boat to the tidewater at Dean Channel. Here, on July 22, 1793, Mackenzie mixed vermilion with melted oolichan grease and inscribed on a large stone that had served as the party's bed the night before, "Alexander Mackenzie, from Canada, by land, the twenty-second of July, one thousand, seven hundred and ninety-three."

In 1982, under an agreement between B.C. and the federal government, the Alexander Mackenzie Trail (often referred to as the Grease Trail in memory of the oolichan grease trade) was proclaimed and protected as a historic corridor. In 1988 it became a Provincial Heritage Site, with work beginning to mark the trail with historical signs and interpretation notes. Much of the trail remains in its original condition and is a very rugged hiking route. About three hundred kilometres of the trail has been built for recreational use; the remainder is aboriginal footpath. Some of the trail crosses First Nations land or private property and hikers are asked to respect the rights of these private owners.

The trail takes between eighteen and twenty-four days to hike. Hiking the entire route is considered an undertaking suitable only for experienced backpackers. Although it can be travelled either direction, most hikers travel it east to west to follow in Mackenzie's footsteps. Best hiking season is late summer or early fall, after the worst of the mosquito and blackfly hordes have dissipated from the stretches of low swampy land. Rivers are also easier to ford during this time of year.

From West Road River to **Tweedsmuir Provincial Park** the trail follows relatively flat terrain that crosses several streams. The eighty-kilometre Tweedsmuir section is the most popular part of the trail; many hikers elect to fly in by floatplane just to hike this section, which passes through dense forests, and provides access to the many alpine lakes and meadows of the Rainbow Mountains. Beyond Tweedsmuir, the trail passes through west-coast forests and eventually reaches the ocean.

Amphibians

Of the forty amphibian species native to Canada, eighteen are found in British Columbia. The province also has two introduced species. Seven of the province's amphibian species are salamanders; the remainder are frogs. The highest concentrations of amphibians in the province are found in the coastal rainforests and the interior valley grassland regions.

No amphibians survived the glaciation of Canada so their existence in the province dates back no further than eighteen thousand years. B.C. amphibians are small predators, feeding primarily on invertebrate species—especially insects—and consequently serve as a significant biological control.

The following amphibians exist naturally in British Columbia: rough-skinned newt, long-toed salamander, northwestern salamander, tiger salamander, pacific giant salamander, western red-backed salamander, ensatina salamander, clouded salamander, Coeur d'Alene salamander, tailed frog, great basin spadefoot toad, western toad, pacific treefrog, striped chorus frog, red-legged frog, spotted frog, northern leopard frog, and wood frog. The American bullfrog and green frog have been introduced.

Animal Life. *See* Biodiversity.

Annual Events and Celebrations

Throughout the province most communities have at least one major annual event that gives a sense of the community's area, pace and structure of daily life, and its ethnic composition. Other events focus on athletic, recreational, dramatic, or artistic pursuits.

Some of the most notable annual events held within the province are listed here according to the time of year in which they occur.

The Cariboo Cross-Country Ski Marathon held in February at 100 Mile House is usually considered the largest such event to be held in the province. Competitors come from across North America.

In April, the communities of Parksville and Qualicum Beach on the east coast of **Vancouver Island** celebrate the return of the once rare small black Brant goose. Thousands of the birds stop off here en route to northern destinations and their stopover is celebrated by a large number of birdwatchers.

Cloverdale holds the Cloverdale Rodeo in May. This rodeo is rated number one in North America because it usually draws about five hundred of the world's top rodeo contestants and the stands only seat seven thousand—meaning everyone has close to a front-row seat.

In late May, there is the Swiftsure Yacht Race in **Victoria**. With about 350 sailboats participating annually, the city becomes clogged with sailors and boating enthusiasts. There are many opportunities to view sailboats of all types.

In June, the Canadian International Dragon Boat Festival routinely draws crowds in excess of 100,000 to watch about two thousand paddlers race on the waters of False Creek in **Vancouver**. Multicultural entertainment at Pacific Place Plaza of Nations on the former **Expo 86** site occurs at the same time.

The most varied ethnic performances to be seen in B.C. occur on July 1, Canada Day, at the Royal BC Museum in Victoria. This event is witnessed by more than 150,000 people each year.

In early July, at Mission, the Annual Mission Indian Friendship Centre Powwow draws native Indian dance troupes and dancers from across North America.

Also in early July, the world-famous Williams Lake Stampede is held; often on the same weekend as the Vancouver Folk Music Festival at Jericho Beach, featuring music from Latin America, Asia, England, and Eastern Europe, as well as major Canadian folk singers.

Successfully putting itself on the map by developing an unusual event, the Vancouver Island city of Nanaimo continues to host the Nanaimo Bathtub Festival. This event sees several hundred contestants transforming bathtubs into vessels and then racing them from Nanaimo to Vancouver.

The province's largest sandcastle-building competition, which attracts about forty thousand people, is held in Parksville in mid-July. Other sandcastle competitions occur at Christina Lake and at Harrison Hot Springs.

In late July, Seabird Island in the Fraser River is home to one of the largest open-air gatherings in North America, known as the Earth Voice Festival. This music festival is a continuation of the Voices for the Wilderness gatherings that were held to bring attention to plans by the provincial government to allow logging in the **Stein River Valley**.

In early August, the Vancouver Symphony Orchestra holds a popular concert high atop **Whistler** Mountain, while the Victoria Symphony hosts its Symphony Splash aboard a barge tied up in Victoria's Inner Harbour.

More than 300,000 people descend on Abbotsford for the **Abbotsford International Airshow** in mid-August. Also in early to mid-August, the First Peoples Festival at the Royal BC Museum in Victoria is the largest celebration in Canada of aboriginal tradition, art, and culture. Average attendance runs about 400,000.

In late summer, two **Okanagan Valley** communities host athletic events known as exercises in sheer endurance and physical stamina. The **Kelowna** Apple Triathlon serves as a good warm-up to Penticton's Ironman Canada Triathlon. This last event pits athletes against each other in a one-day combined four-kilometre swim, 180-kilometre cycle, and forty-two-kilometre marathon.

During the last two weeks of August the Pacific National Exhibition (PNE) offers the largest agricultural show in the province. It is held at the PNE grounds in Vancouver.

Aquaculture

The first commercial farming of fish in British Columbia started in 1912 with the opening of a shellfish farm. It would not, however, be until the early 1970s that the potential of aquaculture as a way of supplementing the wild fish harvest began to capture the imagination of entrepreneurs and received encouragement from the provincial and federal governments. What followed was a fish farming boom focused primarily on **salmon**, rather than shellfish.

Since 1972, when the first salmon farms were established on the province's coast, the B.C. aquaculture industry has grown rapidly, both in terms of fish harvested and value of sales. From 1972 to 1981 commercial salmon farming underwent a lot of ups and downs as farmers and researchers sought to determine the ideal farming conditions, fish pen sizes, and structures. They also worked on developing market acceptance for their product. By 1981, salmon farms were producing 176 tonnes of salmon per year worth $985 million. Production and the number of farms then see-sawed for a number of years due to the rapid expansion in the number and size of farms depressing prices until a reorganization of the industry was undertaken in the late 1980s.

The 1987 harvest—which reached 1.93 million tonnes and sales of $12.872 million—was the beginning of salmon farming's rapid rise in importance to the province's fishing industry and established salmon as the king-product of B.C.'s aquaculture industry. This was an increase in value over the previous year's sales of $10.14 million. The total value of other fish farm products in the same year did not exceed $3.3 million, continuing a trend of gradual growth in the other fish farming sectors that persists today.

Salmon farming yields and values continued to rise rapidly to a 1991 high of 24.4 million tonnes valued at $110.9 million. By the early 1990s, however, the B.C. salmon farming industry, numbering about 120 farms, started meeting stiff competition from Chilean producers of Atlantic salmon. Both the province's and Chile's industry concentrate their sales on the U.S. market. Consequently, by 1993, salmon harvests were stabilized at 24 million tonnes and the value was little higher than that of 1991 at $115 million.

The period of rapidly increasing harvests and values also corresponded with a gradual shift from farming Pacific salmon varieties, mainly chinooks, in favour of Atlantic salmon. By 1992, 52 percent of salmon farmed were drawn from Atlantic stocks. The primary reason for this shift is that Atlantic salmon are larger than Pacific varieties and may be less susceptible to diseases and other problems arising from raising salmon in compact areas.

Cultivating Atlantic salmon in Pacific Ocean waters has resulted in some environmental concerns. Although penned, there are always some Atlantics that escape from the farms and it is feasible that these introduced species may begin to compete with Pacific salmon stocks—perhaps in time coming to displace them. Fish farms are also criticized for increasing pollution and nitrogen levels in the sheltered coastal bays in which they establish operations due to the heavy use of nitrogen-based foods to stimulate rapid fish development and landing weights.

Besides salmon, the province's aquaculture industry produces oysters, Manila clams, and rainbow trout grown in freshwater farms. Research and farm development is also taking place to produce Japanese scallops, geoduck clam, abalone, sea urchins, and sea cucumbers. In all, there are about 670 operating fish farms in the province, of which 380 are shellfish farms.

Aquarian Foundation (Brother Twelve)

In 1927 Edward Arthur Wilson, a former sea captain and self-declared mystic, established an occult society and utopian community outside Nanaimo on **Vancouver Island** that was variously known as the Aquarian Foundation or The Great White Lodge. Wilson called himself Brother Twelve, claiming to be the twelfth Master in an occult Brotherhood that guided the evolution of the human race. He also claimed to be the reincarnation of the Egyptian god Osiris and that he had come to the Nanaimo area after a series of revelatory visions led him to a picturesque nob of coastal land to the community's south, known as Cedar-by-the-Sea.

From here, Brother Twelve sounded his "first trumpet blast of the New Age" by sharing his visions and, along the way, accumulating a vast sum of money drawn from his more than two thousand followers—many of whom were from wealthy families. A series of sensational court cases soon followed his creation of the community, as family of his followers and the provincial government sought to stop his activities. Brother Twelve was accused of misusing foundation funds and advocating free love. The court cases resulted in the breakup of the colony, but Brother Twelve formed a new settlement, the "City of Refuge," which he first established on nearby Valdes Island and, later, on DeCourcy Island. Here, he and his disciples waited to survive Armageddon, which he assured the remaining followers was imminent.

Conditions in the new colony became increasingly harsh as Brother Twelve and his sadistic mistress, known only as "Madame Z," reportedly treated the followers as slaves. They also were alleged to have attempted to murder their enemies, including high-ranking government officials, with black magic. Ultimately, the followers revolted, fleeing the colony and successfully suing for recovery of their money. By the time the court writ came down, however, Brother Twelve had wrecked the colony buildings in vengeance and supposedly fled to Switzerland with a reported $400,000 in gold and notes hoarded in mason jars. Some reports indicate that Brother Twelve may have died in Switzerland in 1934 but other evidence suggests he later fled that country with his ill-gotten fortune for an unknown new refuge.

Today, little remains of the DeCourcy or Valdes island colonies, but a number of the original Cedar-by-the-Sea buildings remain as private residences.

Arbutus

The arbutus, which is found only on the West Coast of North America, is Canada's only evergreen hardwood. In the United States it is known as the Pacific madrone. Within B.C., arbutus is concentrated in the southwest corner of the mainland, the **Gulf Islands**, and on **Vancouver Island**, especially the east coast and the southern tip around **Victoria**. The favourite habitat of arbutus is dry, upland sites. In such locations it can grow to diameters of one metre or more.

With their red bark and glossy green oval-shaped leaves, arbutus trees are visually distinctive. The leaves' shape and glossiness allow heavy rainwater to run easily off their surface. Arbutus sheds its paper-thin bark in a natural peeling process. In the spring it is adorned with milky white flowers that by fall evolve into clusters of orange-red berries.

Archaeology

There are about fifteen thousand archaeological sites scattered throughout B.C. that have been officially recorded, but it is believed that tens of thousands remain to be found.

To date, archaeological findings confirm the probability of human habitation in the province twelve thousand years ago. Water-rounded stones, referred to by archaeologists as pebble tools, discovered near the Fraser River at Yale are believed to be about eleven thousand years old. These tools are fist-sized river stones with flakes knocked off one end to form a steep, strong cutting edge, while leaving the naturally smooth surface of the rest of the stone to fit the hand. They were used to scrape, cut, or chop. Water-rounding of pebble tools could only have occurred during times of high sea levels—during the period of glacial melt which ended about eleven thousand years ago in the Yale area.

The oldest archaeological site so far uncovered in the province is at Charlie Lake Cave, near **Fort St. John** in the **Peace River** region. Archaeologists have slowly dug their way into four-metre-deep pits that offer a stratum of artefacts telling the tale of a people's occupation of the area for 10,500 years. The oldest layers include bison bones that are larger than those of historical bison. Some of the bones carry cut-marks left by human butchering. Scattered among the bones were a few stone artefacts, including a heavy adze-like tool, possibly used to chop through joints; a flaked-stone spearhead, still carrying microscopic residues of human blood; and a small perforated stone bead, which might once have decorated a magic hunting shirt.

The Charlie Lake site lies deep between two massive sandstone outcrops which, more than ten millennia ago, is believed to have faced out over a narrow arm of glacial Lake Peace where animals could have crossed. Such water-crossings would have been favoured by historical **First Nations peoples** as reliable places to ambush game.

Another significant archaeological site was unearthed near Kamloops on the shoreline of Gore Creek. Here, a human skeleton radiocarbon-dated to about eight thousand years ago was discovered. Archaeologists believe the man was trapped and drowned by a mud flow that swept down a gully of the South Thompson River valley. Gore Creek Man, as the skeleton was named, was found by chemical analysis to have eaten mainly land animals rather than ocean-run **salmon**, in contrast to the subsequent residents of the area. No artefacts were discovered with the skeleton.

There are sites on the **Queen Charlotte Islands** that indicate the presence of human life, however, as far back as ten thousand years. Radiocarbon dating of artefacts found at the Lawn Point site on the east coast of Graham Island test to about seventy-two hundred years ago.

At the mouth of Burke Channel on the central mainland coast, the small isolated fishing community of Namu is believed to be the oldest continuously inhabited settlement with cultural deposits in Canada. Found beneath its crumbling boardwalks and bunkhouses are artefacts dating back almost ten thousand years. Here, a small spherical pebble with a pecked encircling groove, possibly a net or line sinker, has been dated to about nine thousand years.

Archaeological sites and historic objects are protected under the Historical Objects Preservation Act of British Columbia and should not be disturbed or removed under any circumstances without approval.

Archives. *See* Cultural History.

Arrow Lakes

Upper and Lower Arrow lakes owe their present-day size to the **Hugh Keenleyside Dam** near **Castlegar**. They extend 220 kilometres between Castlegar and Revelstoke with a width that never exceeds two kilometres.

Originally they were two smaller lakes joined by thirty-two kilometres of river. When the dam was completed in the summer of 1969, the lakes were backed up to their present size. The lakes' water levels are altered regularly by the dam operation, resulting in wide stretches of sandy beach.

To create the lakes, several small communities, houses, and some excellent farm land were flooded. Fauquier, Burton, and Edgewood were moved to higher ground. Needles, serving now only as a ferry dock, was abandoned.

Art Galleries. *See* Cultural History.

Avalanches

Of all forms of natural disasters snow avalanches have, since 1900, killed more people in British Columbia than any others. Most winters do not pass without at least one avalanche-related death. In fact, with increasing numbers of skiers flying into remote areas by helicopter and more snowmobilers the annual rates of deaths have increased since the 1980s over the preceding portion of the 1900s.

Snow avalanches within the province occur mostly in the Coast, Columbia, and Rocky mountain ranges, although they can happen in any area where sufficient snow pack combines with a suitable degree of hill or mountain slope. An avalanche is triggered when the bonds holding the snow pack together break due to additional stresses created by such factors as precipitation, wind, sudden temperature rises, and the added weight of new snow. Usually, slope steepness exceeds twenty-five degrees in at least one section of the avalanche area. Snow or ice released from the starting point pours into a track that is either an open slope or, more commonly, a gully which confines and directs the flowing mass. As the avalanche accelerates, additional snow, ice, water, rock, soil, and vegetation are swept up and added to the downward flow. Maximum avalanche speed depends on steepness, length, shape, and roughness of the track; the height of the avalanche; and the material involved in it. Maximum speeds of large dry-snow avalanches in **Rogers Pass** have been tracked at about fifty metres per second.

In terms of human lives lost, the worst avalanches in Canadian history have all occurred in British Columbia. The worst of these resulted in sixty-six deaths when a work train in the Rogers Pass was derailed and buried March 4, 1910. In 1915 the Britannia Mine was struck by an avalanche, killing thirty miners. Two avalanches in 1965 resulted in thirty-three deaths—twenty-six miners died at the Granduc Mine, north of Stewart, and seven people died when the community of **Ocean Falls** was struck by an avalanche. Another seven people died at the North Route Cafe, near Terrace, on January 22, 1974, when snow crashed down upon the business establishment and its parking lot. This avalanche prompted the provincial government to establish the Department of Highways Avalanche Task Force (now known as the Snow Avalanche Section of the Ministry of Transportation and Highways). A complex avalanche indexing system is used by the task force to predict avalanche likelihood and preventive action is taken to control and restrict damage if the avalanche site is near highways or buildings.

Although this program has been highly effective in limiting avalanche damage, the rate of deaths from avalanches has continued to be significant each year due to recreational use of back country regions where snow pack and avalanche likelihood are not measured. Between 1900 and 1979 there were a total of 267 avalanche-related fatalities in B.C. for an average of about three per year. Almost half—136—occurred, however, in five avalanches so the true average death rate was only a fraction of the generalized average of three per year. Between 1980 and 1994, however, there were seventy-two deaths with no more than three people usually dying per avalanche. The annual death rate during this period averaged four per year despite the introduction of the avalanche safety program.

Of the seventy-two casualties during this period, only two—a woman killed in her Telegraph Creek home in the winter of 1988–89 when she refused to leave it after being advised by authorities that the house was in the pathway of an imminent avalanche, and a railroad employee—were not involved in recreational activities at the time of their deaths. All other deaths from avalanches in B.C. during this period involved skiers, snowmobilers, snowshoers, climbers, or back country hikers.

Snowmobilers and skiers have been most at risk. Forty-six of those dying in avalanches during this time period were skiers, including seven heli-skiers killed in a single avalanche near Blue River in 1987 and nine skiers killed in the Bugaboos by an avalanche in 1990. Seventeen snowmobilers were also killed between 1980 and 1994.

Avalanche control techniques used by the highways ministry Snow Avalanche Section involve the use of explosives to trigger an avalanche before it becomes large enough to constitute a serious threat to public safety. Usually a gun, known as an "avalauncher," is used to fire a gas-propelled explosive into the avalanche path. In the avalanche-prone Coquihalla and Kootenay Pass regions, 105-millimetre recoilless rifles with an effective range of five kilometres are deployed. Helicopter pinpoint bombing is frequently used as well. Explosives can also be placed at the foot of short slopes by safety teams and the shock waves resulting from the explosion can trigger an avalanche. By using these techniques the Snow Avalanche Section controls avalanches along approximately twelve hundred kilometres of provincial roads. Most of the avalanches near these roads occur in sixty hazardous areas that include Kootenay Pass, Bear Pass, the **Trans-Canada Highway** near Revelstoke, Allison Pass, the **Fraser Canyon**, the **Coquihalla Highway**, Duffey Lake Road, and Highway 16 between Terrace and **Prince Rupert**. On average there are about sixteen hundred avalanches recorded either above or on provincial highways per year.

In various avalanche-prone areas, snowsheds have been constructed to cover and shelter the highway. The Coquihalla Highway is further protected by the first two avalanche control ropeways used in North America. Similar to chairlifts, they carry explosive packages up to pre-set targets where they are placed and detonated above the snow to trigger avalanches in areas that experience repeated snow buildup sufficient to spark an avalanche.

Babine Lake

With a length of 177 kilometres, Babine Lake is British Columbia's longest natural lake. The lake's southern end is about thirty-six kilometres north of Burns Lake off Highway 16. The lake is narrow, walled on both flanks by steep mountain ridges. Creeks draining into Babine Lake are important **salmon**-spawning grounds.

Barkerville

In 1858 Cornish potter-turned-sailor William (Billy) Barker jumped ship to join the Fraser Canyon gold rush. He didn't have much success prospecting until August 21, 1862, when he struck gold on Williams Creek. Within a year a community had sprung up near Barker's claim with an estimated population of ten thousand, complete with hotels, banks, stores, and the requisite gold-mining town population of hurdy-gurdy girls, prostitutes, and show girls. Barker became rich, reportedly worth about $600,000 at the peak of his mine's short production life. But his fortune was squandered and allegedly stolen by the woman he fell in love with, and, left impoverished, he died in 1894 at an Old Men's Home in Victoria.

Barkerville street scene before the devastating September 16, 1868 fire.
(BCARS photo A-03786)

For several years Barkerville was the largest city west of Chicago and north of San Francisco. On September 16, 1868, a miner tried to embrace a hurdy-gurdy girl while she was doing her laundry; they struggled, an oil lamp was knocked over, and the entire commercial area burned, resulting in $690,000 damage to buildings and the loss of $700,000 in goods. Although the town was quickly rebuilt, the gold rush was already in decline. By 1871 all but about two thousand people had drifted away from Barkerville and the rest of the **Cariboo**. How much gold was unearthed at Barkerville is unknown. In the 1860s almost $20 million in diggings was reported, but it is believed a further $10 million was removed clandestinely overland by miners returning to the United States.

The community was largely a ghost town from 1871 until the early 1930s, when it enjoyed another brief surge in population due to the discovery of several new gold veins at nearby Wells. That strike soon fizzled, and by the early 1950s Barkerville was again deserted.

In 1958, however, the provincial government decided to restore Barkerville as part of the centennial celebrations and it is now a historic provincial park. Forty historical buildings, historic displays, theme restaurants, gold-sluicing operations, theatre performances, an old-fashioned bakery, and an 1860s-era newspaper office are highlights.

Barkerville is eighty-eight kilometres east on Highway 26 off Highway 97 at Quesnel. The park is open daily year-round, although many attractions are not open in winter months.

Bats

With sixteen different species of bats, British Columbia has more than any other Canadian province or territory. Considering that there are approximately 1,065 known bat species in the world, however, B.C.'s species diversity is relatively low compared to other areas of the world, particularly the tropics. Eight B.C. species occur nowhere else in Canada.

All of B.C.'s bat species are of the family *Vespertilionidae,* so are exclusively insect eaters. They have flight speeds ranging from seven to thirty-nine kilometres per hour, beating their wings ten to twenty times per second. (One non-*Vespertilionidae* species was found in B.C. in November 1939 at New Westminster, but this is believed to have been a stray.) All B.C. bat species are fur covered. Several are quite colourful. The western red bat is rusty-red; the spotted bat is black except for three white spots on its back; and the hoary bat and silver-haired bat both look frosted due to their hair being silver-tipped.

In summer, the **Okanagan Valley**'s dry southern region is home to fourteen of the province's species, making it the most diverse region for bat populations. Populations decrease in northern parts of the province with only one or two species occurring. At elevations above fifteen hundred metres (almost 75 percent of the province) few bat species are found.

Eight of the province's bat species currently appear on the Red and Blue lists of potentially endangered and threatened species prepared by the B.C. Ministry of Environment. (*See* **Endangered Species**.)

Some bat species occur almost exclusively within the province. The Keen's long-eared myotis, for example, is concentrated along the B.C. coastline with only small populations found on the Olympic Peninsula to the province's south and in southeastern Alaska. The largest populations of this bat are believed to exist on the **Queen Charlotte Islands**.

Other bat species are common elsewhere but rare in B.C. The pallid bat population, for example, is so small in B.C. that it is considered one of the rarest mammals in the province. Only nineteen individual pallid bats have ever been captured by researchers, all in a narrow region of the Okanagan Valley.

The largest known bat colony in B.C., comprising about fifteen hundred to two thousand adult females of the Yuma Myotis species, is located in an old church on the Little Shuswap Indian Reserve at Squilax near **Shuswap Lake**. Efforts are underway to ensure the preservation of this colony which has been listed with Bat Conservation International, a non-profit organization engaged internationally in bat conservation and programs to educate people about the importance and unique characteristics of bats.

The big brown bat, one of B.C.'s largest, has gained a certain notoriety in provincial politics due to its often turning up during the autumn and winter months inside the provincial legislative buildings in Victoria.

BC Ferry Corporation; BC Hydro; BC Place; BC Transit Authority.
See **British Columbia** headings.

Bears

Two of Canada's three species of bears inhabit British Columbia—grizzly bear and black bear. There are no polar bears in the province. Both grizzlies and black bears are omnivores, eating meat or vegetables.

Black bears are common throughout most of the province with an estimated total population of 120,000 to 160,000. With an approximate population of ten thousand, **Vancouver Island** has one of the province's highest density levels. Male black bears range in weight from 80 to 250 kilograms, with females being about 10 percent lighter.

Along the central coast of B.C. a unique colour variant of black bear—

known as the Kermode bear—is found, especially in the vicinity of Terrace. Unlike most black bears, which are usually black, brown, or cinnamon, the Kermode is a creamy colour that is almost as white as a polar bear. The Kermode bear is found nowhere else in the world. It is named after the former director of the B.C. provincial museum (now Royal British Columbia Museum), Dr. Francis Kermode, who first identified it, incorrectly, as a subspecies in 1905. Biologists believe the Kermode bears occur due to the presence of a gene variation that is a form of albinism. Although there is no estimate of how many Kermode bears there are, sightings in the Terrace area are common. Hunting of Kermode bears is prohibited.

Another pigmentation variant in black bears results in what is called the glacier bear. The fur on this bear is a blue-black colour. As the glacier bear is found only in **Tatshenshini-Alsek Wilderness Provincial Park** and neighbouring glacial mountain regions it derives its name from the glacial surroundings of its habitat.

Grizzly and black bears live within coniferous and deciduous forest, swamp, and, sometimes, tundra habitats. Estimating the number of grizzlies in the province is complicated by the fact that an adult male typically has a home range of between one thousand and fifteen hundred square kilometres, which makes accurate counting difficult. Provincial authorities believe there are approximately thirteen thousand grizzlies in B.C.—the largest population in any Canadian province or territory. This figure, however, is questioned by some environmental activists who estimate that clearcut logging of grizzly habitats, trophy hunting, and illegal poaching of grizzlies for bear parts sold to the Asian market have reduced the province's grizzly population to about three thousand—leaving the species seriously endangered.

Grizzlies have a distinctive hump on their back and a dish-shaped facial profile. Colour ranges from blond to brown to almost black. The grizzly name derives from the fact that most grizzlies have white or grey flecks on the tips of the hair on their flanks, back, and shoulders, which gives them a "grizzled" appearance. Large male grizzlies weigh from 250 to 500 kilograms; females range between 150 and 300 kilograms. Exceptionally large grizzlies have been recorded at 680 kilograms.

Grizzly bears are capable of running in short bursts at speeds of fifty kilometres per hour, especially during an aggressive charge against a perceived threat. Although they will kill and eat large animals, such as ungulates, they primarily eat plants, insects, and **salmon** (especially during the spawning season).

Grizzly bears have one of the lowest reproductive rates of North American terrestrial mammals. Females reach reproductive maturity between the fourth and seventh years, and normally produce young every two to three years after that. They have litters ranging in size from one to four cubs, but usually numbering two. The cubs remain with the female for the first two to three years, during which time she will not breed again. Grizzlies rarely live past the age of twenty-five.

Both grizzly and black bears typically avoid human contact, but are lured into densely populated areas by the presence of garbage. Most black bear attacks occur when the bears—often used to people—are trying to get at human food or garbage. These attacks seldom result in serious injury. Grizzly attacks—particularly by mother grizzlies with young—usually occur as the result of a sudden unexpected encounter. In most cases there is only about fifty metres separating the humans from the bears. More than 50 percent of all grizzly attacks result in serious injuries to the victim. Such attacks, however, remain rare with about one person in every two million visitors to Canada's national parks being injured by a grizzly.

When hiking in known bear areas, hikers are advised to make periodic noise so that the bears will be warned of the approach of humans. This should give the bears time to take evasive action to avoid a confrontation.

Beetles. *See* Invertebrates.

Bicycling

Most of British Columbia has weather temperatures and conditions that are suitable for recreational bicycling from March to October. The Lower Mainland, **Vancouver Island**, the **Gulf Islands**, and the majority of the **Sunshine Coast** can be cycled year-round.

The Gulf Islands and the Sunshine Coast are two of the province's most popular cycling areas, with the Gulf Islands combining a mix of country roads and ferry crossings to link islands together. Another favourite cycling route is known as the "Golden Triangle" and proceeds west from Golden, through **Yoho National Park** to Lake Louise in Alberta, south to **Radium Hot Springs**, with a return circuit to Golden. This is a very strenuous route with many steep uphill grades and heavy motor vehicle traffic during summer months.

A circuit of **Stanley Park** in Vancouver is considered one of the best urban-cycling routes in Canada. In **Victoria**, the Galloping Goose Regional Trail, one of Canada's first Rails-to-Trails conversions using the abandoned Canadian National Railway railbed, provides fifty-two kilometres of off-road cycling that extends from the heart of the city to the Sooke Hills. Victoria claims to have the highest bike density per capita in Canada.

Licensing of bicycles is not required by provincial law, but some municipalities require bikes to be licensed for operation within municipal boundaries. Wearing of bicycle helmets is also not required by provincial law, but is recommended by provincial health and safety authorities. Provincial law does require cyclists to equip their bikes with both a working headlight and taillight when night riding. When operating on provincial or municipal roads, bicycles fall under the jurisdiction of the B.C. Motor Vehicle Act and must obey all motor vehicle laws. Failure to do so can lead to violations being posted against the operator's driver licence and fines under provisions of the act.

Big Foot. *See* **Sasquatch.**

Biodiversity

Encompassing fourteen ecological zones and a wide range of ecosystems, from coastal temperate rainforests to dry interior grasslands to alpine tundra and northern boreal forests, British Columbia is Canada's most biologically diverse province or territory. The biodiversity of a province is determined by calculating and measuring the amount and variation of all life-forms found within it and the habitat and natural processes supporting that life.

British Columbia's rich variety of habitats, including forests, grasslands, meadows, wetlands, rivers, and inter-tidal and sub-tidal zones supports a vast array of life-forms. Within the province are found 143 mammal species, 454 birds, 20 amphibians, 19 reptiles, and 453 fish species. Individual **invertebrate** species (species lacking a backbone) are harder to identify but have been estimated at numbering between 50,000 and 70,000, including 35,000 insect species. There are approximately 2,850 species of vascular plants, 1,000 bryophytes (mosses and liverworts), 1,000 lichens, 522 species of attached algae, and more than 10,000 fungi species.

The province is home to 70 percent of Canada's native breeding bird species, 70 percent of its native mammal species, and 75 percent of the nation's bryophyte species.

Many scientists believe there is currently a global "biodiversity crisis" underway. This crisis is the result of human action, either directly through such things as pollution or forest clearing, or indirectly through the introduction of exotic species that subsequently crowd out native life-forms. Scientists believe that between 1994 and 2020, humans will destroy more species than the entire process of natural selection culled in the past 3.5 billion years.

In British Columbia, about ninety-five wildlife and freshwater fish species are on the province's **endangered species** Red List (legally designated, or being considered for legal designation, as endangered or threatened) and another ninety-six are on the Blue List (considered sensitive or vulnerable). Some

634 vascular plant species are rare, and of these, 153 are considered threatened or endangered.

Biodiversity hot spots in B.C. are found primarily in the southern interior and along the southwest coast, where the warmer climate has created a thriving diversity of life increasingly threatened by human development pressure, which is heaviest in these same areas. The increasingly rare **Garry oak ecosystems** of southern **Vancouver Island** and the grassland ecosystems of the southern interior have been singled out by scientists as particularly threatened.

In an admittedly belated effort to address the province's biodiversity crisis, the federal and provincial governments have started a process of improving environmental assessment techniques to lessen the impact of new development, reformed forest industry practices, involved the public in discussions regarding future land- and water-use decisions, and started an expansion of protected habitat areas from a mid-1990s level of 6 percent to a projected target of 12 percent of the province's land base.

Birds

The diverse habitats of British Columbia support 454 bird species that breed, stage, and winter, or are resident to the province. Including bird subspecies and exotic species introduced to the province, such as starlings, the total rises to 505. B.C. supports more species of breeding birds than any other province or territory—297 species, or 70 percent of all species known to breed in Canada. It is also rich in species that nest exclusively in a single province (although many of these species also nest in areas outside Canada). There are sixty-five single-province nesting birds in Canada and thirty-five of these are found in British Columbia. These species include the rhinoceros auklet, the tufted puffin, the glaucous-winged gull, the California quail, the spotted owl, Anna's hummingbird, the white-headed woodpecker, the pigmy nuthatch, the European skylark, and the canyon wren.

For some bird species either the majority or a large proportion of their numbers breed exclusively in British Columbia. Between 60 and 90 percent of Barrow's goldeneyes breed in B.C., for example, as do 20 to 35 percent of all bald eagles, and 74 percent of ancient murrelets.

The great blue heron is common to all of the B.C. coastal islands and mainland. (Mark Zuehlke photo)

British Columbia sits astride a major migratory corridor—the Pacific flyway—along which many bird species travel, often using the province's various habitats as staging grounds for the next portion of their journey. More than half of North America's population of "lesser" sandhill cranes, for example, pass through northeastern B.C. en route to and from Alaskan breeding grounds, and virtually the world's entire population of western sandpipers descend on southern B.C.'s mudflats twice a year.

Habitation destruction or degradation by human development has contributed to or been directly responsible for the designation of thirty-one species or subspecies of birds on the province's Red List and fifty-three on the Blue List. (*See* **Biodiversity** for list definitions.) Among the species on these lists are the sage grouse, burrowing owl, spotted owl, American white pelican, yellow-billed cuckoo, western grebe, and marbled murrelet. Wildlife specialists warn that unless the province's land development and resource exploitation practices are altered to ensure bird habitat protection, the number of species endangered or ultimately extirpated from the province will continue to grow.

Boating. *See* **Pleasure Boating.**

Border Crossings

There are twenty-two points of entry crossing the Canada-U.S. boundary within the province of B.C., as well as customs services at all airports offering commercial flights between Canada and the U.S. or other foreign destinations.

U.S. citizens coming into Canada via one of these crossings should carry identification that proves citizenship. People from other countries are required to show passports. The busiest border crossing in B.C. is the Douglas/Blaine crossing located south of Vancouver.

Non-residents entering B.C. by boat must report to marine customs ports or contact customs on entering a non-customs port to arrange an inspection. The following marine ports all have customs facilities: Victoria, Vancouver, Nanaimo, Courtenay/Comox, Campbell River, Sidney, Port Alberni, Powell River, Kitimat, Ucluelet, White Rock, Prince Rupert, Bedwell Harbour, and Stewart. Inland, there is a customs facility at Waneta on the Columbia River to process boat visitors.

(*See also* **Alaska-Canada Boundary**; **49th Parallel—U.S.-Canada Boundary**.)

Bowron Lakes

In the heart of the Cariboo Mountains, west of the Rockies, this rectangular chain of six major lakes and several smaller ones has been protected as a provincial park since 1961. Bowron Lake Provincial Park encompasses the lakes and a surrounding 121,600 hectares of terrain. A 116-kilometre canoe circuit of the lakes is one of the longest freshwater paddling trips possible in B.C. Paddlers pass glacier-streaked mountains that rise to altitudes of twenty-one hundred metres, follow blue lakes bordered by dense woods that thrive with moose, deer, caribou, mountain goats, black bears, occasional grizzly bears, and beaver. Reservations through the Bowron Lake Registration Centre at Bowron Lakes Park Headquarters are mandatory for groups of more than six and advised for smaller groups. Seven to ten days should be allowed for this rigorous canoe trip, which entails several portages.

Bridges. See **Lions Gate Bridge; Okanagan Lake Floating Bridge; Point Ellice Bridge Disaster.**

British Columbia Ferry Corporation

The British Columbia Ferry Corporation was established in 1977 to operate the province's coastal ferry operations. Measured by traffic carried and routes served, it operates one of the world's largest ferry systems. The fleet of forty-one vessels operates on twenty-five routes.

Ferries link **Vancouver Island** to the Lower Mainland with three separate routes. Many small islands in the **Strait of Georgia** are linked to either Vancouver Island or the mainland. Ferry routes also service the **Sunshine Coast**. The corporation operates services connecting **Prince Rupert** to the **Queen Charlotte Islands** and to northern Vancouver Island. The Prince Rupert-Queen Charlotte Islands service also transports unmanned commercial vehicles and drop-trailers.

About twenty-one million passengers and more than one million vehicles are carried by the BC Ferries fleet each year.

In 1994, the corporation added two new ferries—the *Spirit of British Columbia* and *Spirit of Vancouver Island*. With an overall length of 167.5 metres, these are the biggest ferries in the fleet—measuring about the length of two football fields—and can carry 470 vehicles and twenty-one hundred passengers.

The ferry corporation's annual operating budget is in excess of $300 million and is partially subsidized by the provincial government as fares seldom manage to offset expenses.

British Columbia Fruit Growers' Association

Founded in 1889, the British Columbia Fruit Growers' Association (BCFGA) was the first formal producers' organization in the province, formed to expand markets in the Prairies and to control fruit marketing. In 1913, supply of fruit in the **Okanagan Valley**—the province's major fruit-growing region—outpaced demand, leading to the BCFGA forming a cooperative marketing and distribution agency that would officially become B.C. Tree Fruits in 1939. Today, the company remains one of the province's largest locally owned enterprises, responsible for the packing, processing, and marketing of the majority of B.C. fruit production.

BC Hydro

Of commercial Crown corporations, British Columbia Hydro and Power Authority (BC Hydro) is the province's largest. It is the third largest electric utility in Canada and serves more than 1.3 million customers in an area containing more than 92 percent of B.C.'s population. Between forty-three thousand and fifty thousand gigawatt-hours of electricity are generated annually by the corporation. More than 70 percent of this is produced by four major hydroelectric generating stations on the **Columbia** and **Peace** rivers. Electricity is delivered through an interconnected system of over sixty-nine thousand kilometres of transmission and distribution lines.

BC Hydro was formed in 1962 by provincial legislation and was given the mandate to provide a secure energy future for the province after the province acquired the last major privately owned electric utility company in B.C. and merged it with an existing government-owned operation. This was the final step in an ongoing amalgamation of electric utility operations that was initiated by the government in 1945.

British Columbia Lions

On August 11, 1954, the British Columbia Lions (usually called the BC Lions) kicked off their first football game at Vancouver's Empire Stadium. It was an inauspicious start—they lost. Not until 1959 did they manage to reach the Western Conference play-offs—they were eliminated. In 1963, under coach Dave Skrien and led by quarterback Joe Kapp, the Lions played their first Canadian Football League Grey Cup title game. They lost 21–10 to the Hamilton Tiger-Cats. In 1964 they were back and this time took the CFL title 34–24 from their nemesis of the previous year. It was another nineteen years before they returned to the finals in 1983, a game they lost to the Toronto Argonauts. This was the first title game played in **BC Place**, Vancouver's new stadium. They would be back in the Grey Cup again the following year, but lose to the Winnipeg Blue Bombers. In 1985, however, before a home-town crowd, they took the title in a 13–3 victory over the Hamilton Tiger-Cats. That victory would cap their best season in club history.

The Lions again made CFL history in the 1994 season when they captured another Grey Cup with a 26–23 win over the unnamed Baltimore franchise team; the first United States-based team to enter the CFL under an expansion plan.

BC Place

Canada's first covered stadium opened June 19, 1983, after taking twenty-eight months to construct and costing $126 million. With a circumference of 760 metres, a sixty-metre height, and covering ten hectares, it is the world's largest air-supported domed stadium. Home to the **British Columbia Lions** football team, the stadium is also a popular venue for big-name concerts and trade shows. The stadium is capable of seating sixty thousand people. Its unique air-venting system that helps keep the dome stable has given rise to BC Place being locally nicknamed the "Giant Pincushion." The roof is constructed of Teflon-coated fibreglass.

British Columbia Sports Hall of Fame and Museum

Founded in 1966, and located in **Vancouver**, the British Columbia Sports Hall of Fame and Museum pays tribute to British Columbians who have excelled provincially, nationally, and internationally in sports activities. It is one of the largest multi-sport museums in North America. The displays, photos, scrapbooks, newspaper clippings, memorabilia, trophies, and film theatre trace the development of sports in B.C. from before the turn of the century. The Hall of Fame offers extensive biographical and career information on its honoured members.

BC Transit Authority

Established in 1978, BC Transit Authority is a **Crown corporation** charged with ensuring a uniform provincial policy for urban transit. As well as providing transit services in the regions of Vancouver and Victoria, the corporation operates in forty-three other communities throughout the province.

BC Transit manages a provincial fleet of 1,755 vehicles, including 130 SkyTrain cars and two SeaBus ferries (operating between Vancouver and North Vancouver). SkyTrain denotes the Light Rapid Transit system linking several Vancouver area suburban communities with the city's downtown core. BC Transit also funds transportation services for disabled persons unable to use conventional public transit. This custom transit service, known as HandyDart, serves twenty-three communities.

Broken Group Islands

The middle part of Pacific Rim National Park consists of the Broken Group Islands, which lie south of Ucluelet and north of Bamfield in **Vancouver Island**'s west-coast Barkley Sound. Covering an area of about 130 square kilometres, it is home to about one hundred islands and islets that are no larger than two kilometres across. This is one of the most concentrated groupings of islands on the Pacific coastline of North America.

In recent years these islands have become an immensely popular **diving** and **paddling** area, especially in July and August when the weather is at its warmest and storms are less common. The picturesque scenery and abundant marine life, which includes **killer** and **Pacific grey whales**, porpoises, seals, sea lions, river otters, basking sharks, nesting cormorants, and bald eagles, is the primary draw.

Camping is restricted to several designated campgrounds on specific islands and only a few of the islands have fresh water sources.

Brother Twelve. *See* **Aquarian Foundation.**

Bugaboo Glacier Provincial Park and Alpine Recreation Area

This world-class mountaineering area of 25,274 hectares, which contains the largest icefields in the Kootenay region's Purcell Mountain Range, is located southwest of Golden. Erosion over some seventy million years by wind, rain,

The granite peak of Hounds Tooth Spire in Bugaboo Glacier Provincial Park has been carved by seventy million years of erosion by ice, wind, and rain. (BCARS photo I-08392)

and glacial ice movement has removed most of the overlying rock to expose solid granite masses that have been chiselled into spectacular spires known collectively as the Bugaboos. The rugged peaks separated by alpine tundra combine to make the area a favourite international mountain-climbing destination. The famous mountaineer and guide Conrad Kain, who first visited the Bugaboos in 1910 and who ascended the South Ridge of Bugaboo Spire in 1916, said this was his most difficult Canadian ascent.

The Bugaboos are believed to have derived their name from an early Scottish prospector who declared the area a "bugaboo" because he found its isolation and stark landscape lonely and frightening. B.C. Parks authorities advise that visitors should be experienced in wilderness hiking and camping.

Buses. *See* **BC Transit Authority.**

Butterflies. *See* **Invertebrates.**

Campbell River Fire

The second largest forest fire in North American history, the Campbell River Fire, often called the Bloedel Fire because it broke out near the train-loading station of the Bloedel, Stewart & Welch logging company, started on July 5, 1938. That summer was unusually hot and arid for **Vancouver Island** and the woods were tinder dry—consequently, at its height, officials feared the massive blaze might spread throughout the island's forests. By the time the fire finally burned out in mid-August, it had consumed about thirty thousand hectares of timberland covering an area 64 kilometres by 6.4 kilometres extending in a long finger from north of Campbell River to near Courtenay.

No human lives were lost during the fire and actual damage to property other than cut timber supplies and small sawmill operations was slight, but timber sufficient to build 200,000 homes was destroyed and thousands of wild animals were killed.

The fire was officially determined to have started when sparks from the stack of a locomotive fell into a pile of timber. At first, firefighters thought they had controlled the blaze within just a few days, limiting its damage to only 323 hectares. But the fire had gone underground and was smouldering through root systems. On July 14, it broke through to the surface and within hours was running east and southeast before a strong wind. By the time firefighting crews responded, the fire was out of control. Each day it spread between 3.2 kilometres and 16 kilometres—the firefighters were reduced to forming isolated pockets of resistance around the edges of small, sometimes fire-encircled communities. The Mennonite community of Black Creek, fifteen kilometres north of Courtenay, evacuated its 210 residents. Two Canadian naval destroyers—the *St. Laurent* and *Fraser*—were stationed in Duncan Bay in case evacuation of Campbell River proved necessary.

By July 22, the provincial government closed all logging operations in southern Vancouver Island and conscription of unemployed men drawn from across the island and from **Vancouver** was ordered. Almost seventeen hundred men were finally involved in battling the fire. To stop the fire's southward movement, a 22.4-kilometre continuous firebreak was cut through old-growth forest across rough terrain.

In the end, however, it was rain and cooling temperatures that contained the fire and led to its petering out in mid-August. In the fire's wake, logging operators and farmers who had suffered property loss banded together to sue Bloedel, Stewart & Welch for damages. Six years later they were paid a total of $428,000 by the company.

Because the fire had destroyed most of the trees in its path, there was little possibility that the forest would replace itself through natural reseeding. Consequently, the provincial forestry service planted seventy-five thousand seedlings throughout the burn area in what is usually cited as the province's first active attempt at reforestation.

Campfires

Campfires are allowed on Crown land unless a campfire ban is in effect. When campfires are permitted, B.C. Forest Service regulations prohibit any fire being set within fifteen metres of flammable debris such as slash or dry grass. Grass, moss, and other debris must be cleared within one metre of the fire. Before abandonment, the fire must be extinguished so the coals are cold enough to pick up in a bare hand.

More than 50 percent of all B.C. forest fires are caused through human carelessness—usually from improperly set and supervised campfires or the discarding of cigarette and cigar butts.

Canada Day. *See* **Annual Events and Celebrations.**

Canadian Coast Guard—Western Region

Although, at thirty thousand kilometres, Canada's coastline is the world's longest, it was not until 1962 that the federal government created a national coast guard service to patrol the nation's coastal waters. The Canadian Coast Guard—Western Region has responsibility for British Columbia's coastline. It has a wide range of duties, including responsibility for placing and maintaining navigational aids; providing vessel traffic services and marine coast radio communications; carrying out search-and-rescue operations; participating in marine pollution control and cleanup; dredging navigation channels; providing support services to the Royal Canadian Mounted Police and the federal departments of Fisheries and Oceans, the Environment, and Energy, Mines, and Resources; administering public ports and harbours; and enforcing the Navigable Waters Protection Act.

The Canadian Coast Guard fleet in the Western Region is composed of sixteen vessels, six helicopters, and three hovercraft, plus about one hundred auxiliary vessels and small craft. The Coast Guard's largest operational base on the Pacific coast is in **Victoria**—a base that has been an active naval station continuously since 1872. Five of the region's major vessels and four of its helicopters are based here. Some 133 large lighted buoys, 275 minor buoys, 671 automatic shore lights, 45 minor fog alarms, and 302 day beacons, plus 30 manned and unmanned light stations are serviced by the Victoria base.

A secondary base at Prince Rupert is responsible for 581 beacons, 180 buoys, and 13 light-stations in an area reaching from Cape Caution, near northern **Vancouver Island**, north to the Canada-U.S. border at Alaska.

Each year the Coast Guard responds to about two thousand distress calls involving vessel fires, collisions, groundings, and overdue or broken-down vessels. More than 250,000 pleasure craft, 6,500 fishing vessels, and 3,000 merchant ships sail B.C.'s waters each year. On any summer weekend, 30,000 pleasure craft may be on the move. The Rescue Coordination Centre, operated by the Department of National Defence in Victoria, directs both air and sea operations, but the Coast Guard provides the majority of search-and-rescue vessels and helicopters. The Coast Guard's regular fleet is supported in search-and-rescue operations by more than twelve hundred volunteers and 530 boats that make up the Coast Guard Auxiliary.

(*See also* **Lighthouses**.)

Canadian Military Forces—British Columbia

In 1968, Canada's air, navy, and army forces were integrated into one body and redesignated as the Canadian Forces. Each arm of the force, however, maintains its own operational entity and is deployed at specialized bases. In British Columbia there are three major Canadian Forces bases.

The largest military presence in British Columbia is found in Esquimalt, immediately to the west of **Victoria**, where Canadian Forces Base Esquimalt is home to the Maritime Forces Pacific command and headquarters. Esquimalt Harbour has operated as a naval base since 1865, when the British Royal Navy established a port here.

Two naval surface operation groups, numbering about twelve ships, operate from the base, as does one maritime helicopter squadron. Scattered throughout the Victoria region, but concentrated in Esquimalt, are a number of satellite operations that include a dry dock, various barracks facilities, a heliport, and ammunition storage and firing grounds.

The 19 Wing of the air force is based at Comox on the east-central coast of **Vancouver Island**. The wing has four squadrons—maritime patrol's 407 Aurora Squadron, search-and-rescue's 442 squadron, and two combat support squadrons.

The primary Canadian Forces army presence in the province is based at Chilliwack in the Fraser Valley. Here, Canadian Forces Base Chilliwack is home of the 3rd Battalion of the Princess Patricia Canadian Light Infantry (3 PPCLI), a supporting regiment of combat engineers, and an officers' basic training school.

As part of a major federal restructuring of the Department of National Defence initiated in 1995, the Chilliwack base, including the officers' training school, is slated for closure by 1999. Most of the personnel there will be relocated to units outside of B.C. The fate of 3 PPCLI remains undetermined, pending a large-scale restructuring of regular and reserve army forces.

Two military stations in the province serve as communication facilities. The two hundred personnel at Canadian Forces Station Masset on the **Queen Charlotte Islands** provide a communications link to Canadian Forces aircraft and ships operating throughout the world. Marine Communications Station Aldergrove near **Vancouver** acts as a marine communications link.

There are slightly more than two thousand personnel distributed across the province as part of various reserve units. These units are under the direction of about seventy-eight full-time personnel at the B.C. District Headquarters for Land Forces at Jericho Beach in Vancouver. By 1997, the Jericho Beach detachment will be closed and the personnel here relocated to other stations within the province.

The economic impact of the military's presence at its three major bases is significant and in Esquimalt and Comox will remain so even after the planned reductions in staffing. Esquimalt base annually pours $306.5 million into the local economy. Comox contributes $74 million. At its operational height in 1994, Chilliwack was contributing $128.5 million to the local economy through pay and expenditures.

Canadian Pacific Railway. *See* Craigellachie; Railways.

Candlefish. *See* Oolichan.

Canoe. *See* Kutenai Canoe.

Canucks. *See* Vancouver Canucks.

Cape Scott

Cape Scott, on the extreme northwestern tip of **Vancouver Island**, is such a harsh environment—storm battered and subjected to drenching rains much of the year—that it successfully defeated all attempts to establish permanent settlements both by **First Nations peoples** and whites. Three native peoples: the Tlatlasikwala, Nakumgilisala, and Yutlinuk all tried. The Yutlinuk died out in the early 1800s. The Tlatlasikwala and Nakumgilisala amalgamated and moved to the far more sheltered Hope Island at the northern entrance to Queen Charlotte Strait on Vancouver Island's northeastern side in the mid-1850s.

In 1897, the first white settlement attempt began when a colony of about one hundred Danes, mostly first-generation immigrants to Minnesota, Iowa, Nebraska, and North Dakota, sought to establish an ethnically pure community here. They were lured to this inhospitable location by a provincial government promise of a road linking them to the outside world via the community of Holberg about twenty kilometres to the east. Until the road was built, they hoped to subsist on fishing. With completion of the road they planned to raise cattle and market beef and dairy products to the outside world. The road never materialized and by 1907 most of the colonists, admitting failure, abandoned the settlement. Only about sixty people lived in the cape's area by 1909, when yet another influx of hopeful settlers arrived. By 1913, the area's population peaked at about one thousand. Its decline started almost immediately, however, as the settlers found the environment as harsh as had the Danes and native people before them. With conscription of men for military service in 1917, the majority of these settlers left. No further attempts were made to establish permanent settlements and, in 1973, a total of 15,070 hectares encompassing the cape were turned into a rugged, wilderness provincial park.

The park's interior and the cape itself are accessible by land only to backpack hikers outfitted for coping with conditions of extreme mud, heavy rain (375 to 500 centimetres annually), strong winds, and dense fog. Within the park's boundaries are twenty-three kilometres of sandy beaches, many abandoned implements from the various settlement attempts, dense forests, and stunning coastal scenery. Also included in the park is the Cape Scott Sand Neck, a peculiar bridge of sand that actually joins the cape to the Vancouver Island mainland. This is the only place where both sides of Vancouver Island can be seen at once. Beyond the sand neck is Cape Scott Lighthouse, built in 1960 on the extreme tip of the cape.

Not surprisingly, given its harsh environment, Cape Scott was also a hazard for ships. No fewer than ten ships are known to have either gone down in storms or been wrecked on the area's rocks between 1860 and 1938, including the presciently named *Cape Scott,* which went down in 1910 just south of the cape off Lowrie Bay.

Cariboo-Chilcotin Region

The Cariboo-Chilcotin region extends over a vast area from Lillooet in the south to **Prince George** in the north; west through **Tweedsmuir Provincial Park** all the way to the coast at Bella Bella and east to the Alberta border. The Cariboo portion is the plateau and mountain country east of the line extending between Cache Creek in the south and Prince George to the north; the Chilcotin is the country to the west of this line.

Forestry, mining, and cattle ranching provide the region's major economic base. The population is centred on Highway 97 north, which runs from Cache Creek to Prince George across the **Interior Plateau**.

Cariboo Cross-Country Ski Marathon. *See* Annual Events and Celebrations.

Cariboo Gold Rush

In 1860, placer miners exploring outward from the played-out Fraser River gold fields found rich deposits on the shores of Horsefly River near Lac La Hache—B.C.'s largest gold rush soon began. Between 1860 and 1862, discoveries were made on the shores of numerous Cariboo rivers and creeks, including Quesnel River, Antler Creek, Keithley Creek, Lightning Creek, Lowhee Creek, and the richest creek of them all—Williams Creek east of present-day Quesnel. As word spread throughout the world of the strikes being made in the Cariboo, thousands of hopeful adventurers descended on British Columbia and made their way inland over rough tracks. In the spring of 1862, five thousand people travelled north by foot and packhorse trails to Williams Creek.

As new gold claims were established, incoming miners had to press farther east along the creek's shores to find unclaimed land. In the sum-

The Calvares Gold Mining Claim on Lower Creek, circa 1868.
(BCARS photo D-04118)

mer of 1862, this process brought William Barker to a small stretch of creek where he made a major strike. Within weeks, the community of **Barkerville** sprang up.

The rush led to the creation of three supply and service communities—Richfield, Camerontown, and Barkerville. Only Barkerville would survive the end of the mining boom.

Placer gold production in the Cariboo from 1858 to the mid-1930s, when the last major working of Williams Creek ended, approximated $50 million—about half of all placer gold found in B.C. since 1858. The Cariboo rush's lasting legacy, however, was not so much the gold discovered but the development of the **Cariboo Road**, which led to the opening of much of the interior to settlement and development.

Cariboo Road

Extending 650 kilometres from Yale in the Fraser Canyon to Barkerville in the Cariboo, construction on the Cariboo Road began in 1862. It was the grand design of Governor James Douglas, who was convinced that a better system of communications than the existing packhorse- and foot-trails was necessary for the exploitation of the resources being discovered in the Cariboo. For the times, the road was an ambitious and costly project.

A freight wagon travelling the Cariboo Road with supplies for the Cariboo Gold Rush mines. (BCARS photo F-02645)

The road was to be eighteen feet (5.48 metres) wide to accommodate wagon traffic. Total construction cost was £112,780 and the project was completed by 1864.

Two sections—ten kilometres from Yale to Boston Bar and fifteen kilometres from Cook's Ferry (Spence's Bridge) along the Thompson River were constructed by the Royal Engineers. A contingent of fifty-three sappers had to blast these stretches out of solid rock walls. The rest was completed by private contractors rewarded for their efforts either in cash and bonds or with the right to collect tolls from those using their road section.

As the road was developed, roadhouses cropped up alongside it, some of which remain settled communities today. They took their names from their distance north of **Lillooet**, a major terminus during the gold rush for travel into the Cariboo region. Some of these communities are 70 Mile House, 100 Mile House, and 108 Mile House. A few underwent name changes after the Cariboo Gold Rush ended. Clinton, for example, was 47 Mile House, but was renamed upon completion of the road in honour of Henry Pelham Clinton, who was Colonial Secretary from 1859 to 1864.

Much of today's **Trans-Canada Highway** section from Yale to Cache Creek follows the route of the original Cariboo Road. Highway 97 running north into the Cariboo from Cache Creek to Quesnel also follows the historic roadway.

Carmanah Giant

At a towering height of ninety-five metres, this ancient Sitka spruce found in Vancouver Island's **Carmanah Pacific Provincial Park** is believed to be Canada's tallest tree. Currently the park trail leading to Carmanah Giant is closed to the public. Visitors to the park can, however, hike to eighty-one-metre Heaven Tree, about 2.5 kilometres from the park entrance.

Carmanah Pacific Provincial Park

The majority of the ancient **rainforests** found in the sixty-seven-hundred-hectare Carmanah Valley watershed are protected by this park. The park was created in 1990 by the provincial government in response to intense pressure from environmental groups and concerned citizens and expanded to include the upper half of the Carmanah Valley in 1994.

Carmanah is about a four-hour drive from **Victoria**. Follow Highway 1 to Highway 18 and then take logging access roads from Honeymoon Bay on the south side of Cowichan Lake for eighty-one kilometres. The park has no visitor services beyond limited camping sites, water, and outhouses. An extensive trail system provides some of the best hiking accesses to ancient temperate rainforests found in British Columbia.

Carr, Emily. *See* Cultural History.

Cascade Mountains

An enormous mountain range that dominates the northwestern United States from northern California through Oregon and Washington, the Cascade Mountains extend a wide salient northward into British Columbia. The mountains stretch along the **49th parallel** from **Cultus Lake** in the west to the Similkameen River valley in the east. Their maximum northward penetration in B.C. is 137 kilometres to Lytton. Their western flank is bordered by the **Fraser River** and **Fraser River Lowland**. The **Skagit River Valley**, Manning Provincial Park, and the Pacific Crest Trail trailhead are all found in the B.C. section of the Cascades. Intensely glaciated in the Pleistocene era, the B.C. Cascades are now home to few glaciers; only a small number remain in the Skagit area.

Unlike the U.S. portion of the Cascades, there are no clearly distinct volcanic cones in the B.C. Cascades, although many of the peaks are the product of volcanic activity. The nearest of the U.S. volcanoes, Mt. Baker, is, however, visible from most of the Georgia Basin region—the province's most populated area—and serves as a reminder of this range's fiery origins.

Castlegar

The community of Castlegar was first settled by **Doukhobors**, a Russian emigrant pacifist group, in 1908. It remains today a small community, heavily influenced by its Doukhobor roots.

Standing on a benchland on the **Columbia River**'s west bank, opposite its confluence with Kootenay River, Castlegar is a vital Kootenay-region crossroads. Highway 3 enters from the west, Highway 22 to the south, and Highway 3A from the north.

The **Hugh Keenleyside Dam** is located eight kilometres west of Castlegar.

Cathedral Provincial Park

Situated within the transition belt between the dense, wet forests of the **Cascade Mountains** and the arid, desert-like **Okanagan Valley**, Cathedral Park is one of the most beautiful parklands in British Columbia. It derives its name from the twenty-eight-hundred-metre peak of Cathedral Mountain, so carved and eroded that it is often described as resembling a ruined European abbey. The thirty-three-thousand-hectare wilderness of the park is accessible by thirty-two kilometres of trails. Prime hiking season is July to October.

Found within the park is Stone City, a huge quartzite formation eroded by wind and glaciers into flat rounded shapes. Symmetrical columns known as Devil's Woodpile were formed by quick-cooling lava.

In summer, more than two hundred species of wildflowers bloom in the park, including alpine larch—found only in a small area of the Rockies and in Cathedral and Manning parks—which blooms in mid-September.

The park is accessible from Highway 3 at Keremeos by a twenty-five-kilometre gravel road.

Caving

Explorable caves and cave systems in British Columbia are mostly carved out of limestone beds dating back some 600 million years. The province's best caving area is **Vancouver Island**, where there are more than one thousand caves and several provincial parks that contain caves which are open to public spelunking. The other significant caving area in B.C. is Cody Caves Provincial Park in the Kootenays, on the eastern slopes of the Selkirk Mountains north of Ainsworth. The caves here are actually a series of explorable passages that stretch more than eight hundred metres through one vast limestone cave. About 100 million years ago this limestone bed was thrust upward during the mountain-building process and cracked open in many places to allow water erosion. The resulting caves feature many stalagmites and other limestone cave formations.

Northern Vancouver Island, especially in the vicinity of Gold River, is riddled with caves that account for most of the island's 1,050 known caves. There are two easily accessible major cave systems here—Little Hustan Lake Caves Park and Upana Caves. Little Hustan's Thanksgiving Cave is the longest, running for 5.5 kilometres. There are several other island caves exceeding two kilometres. Within the vast subterranean world of Little Hustan is found a maze of lakes, rapids, and stadium-sized halls and chambers full of stalagmites and stalactites. Farther south on the island's east coast, Horne Lake Caves Provincial Park, north of Qualicum Beach, has seven caves. Three of these are large and open to the public. Euclataws Cave is an **ecological reserve** that is closed to spelunking.

Living within Vancouver Island's caves are white frogs, salamanders, spiders, crickets, and depigmented trout.

Charlie Lake Cave Site. *See* Archaeology.

Chemainus

Located seventy-eight kilometres north of Victoria, just two kilometres east of Highway 1, Chemainus is home to the largest permanent outdoor art gallery in Canada. Chemainus stands as a symbol for community resilience in the face of hardship. In the early 1980s the town's sawmill, on which most of the population depended, closed. Instead of picking up stakes and abandoning

Many of the murals on the buildings of Chemainus are incredibly lifelike. (BCARS photo I-07546)

the community, the citizens decided to transform it from a mill town to a vital tourist attraction. They commissioned talented artists to paint murals depicting the region's history on downtown walls. About 250,000 visitors come annually to see these larger-than-life murals and the community continues to grow as a major Canadian art centre. The revitalization effort earned Chemainus a national reputation as "The Little Town That Did."

Chilcotin War

In April 1864, a small group of Chilcotin natives launched a series of raids against road-building crews pushing a route through their lands lying between Bute Inlet on the coast and Quesnel in the interior.

The limited rising was sparked by a fear of the rapid gold-rush-driven invasion of whites into the region and the spread of smallpox that was devastating local native populations. The attacks resulted in the deaths of nineteen whites and disruption of the road construction. Fearing a general native insurrection throughout the interior, two volunteer forces were dispatched into the region on May 15 to quell the uprising. With the help of Chief Alexis, one of the most important local native leaders, the natives involved in the killings were soon tracked down and their leaders taken into custody. In September, five natives alleged to have been the ringleaders were tried in Quesnel, found guilty, and hanged.

Further conflict between the Chilcotin people and whites was averted primarily by the fact that the planned road project was abandoned in favour of the **Cariboo Road** route. Ironically, the promoter who had initiated construction of the failed road project, Victoria entrepreneur Alfred Waddington, succumbed to smallpox in 1872.

Chilkoot Trail

Often referred to by Klondike gold stampeders as the "cussedest trail this side of hell," the fifty-three-kilometre trail remains one of the ruggedest and most demanding long-distance trails in Canada. Between 1897 and 1898 about thirty thousand adventurers braved the Chilkoot Pass as their route to the Klondike gold fields around Dawson City in Yukon Territory. The trail starts at Dyea Road, thirteen kilometres east of Skagway and ends at Bennett, B.C., the Canadian gateway to the Klondike **gold rush**. Between the two communities lies a torturous route through wild terrain that crosses the Coastal Mountain Range at a maximum elevation of 1,067 metres and is subject to frequent severe weather changes.

Today, Chilkoot Trail is an international hiking trail and wilderness preserve jointly managed by the Canadian Parks Service and the U.S. National

Parks Service. The trail has been somewhat improved from its 1890s condition but is still strewn with well-preserved debris cast away by weary stampeders hoping to lighten their load and improve their chances of crossing the pass alive. About two thousand backpackers make the challenging four- to five-day hike annually.

Chilkoot Pass derives its name from the Chilkat Indians, a tribe of the Tlingit, who used the route to reach the Nahanni tribes along the Yukon River for trading purposes. The international border between B.C. and Alaska is at the summit, about 26.5 kilometres from the trailhead.

China Bar Tunnel

With a length of 610 metres, this tunnel just west of **Hell's Gate** in the **Fraser Canyon** is one of the longest highway tunnels in North America.

Chinatowns

Chinese immigrants first arrived in Canada from San Francisco in 1858, at the beginning of the **Fraser River** gold rush. When the rush for gold moved north to **Barkerville** four years later, the boomtown became the home of Canada's first true Chinatown. By 1860, the Chinese population of **Vancouver Island** and British Columbia numbered about seven thousand. Chinese immigration to British Columbia increased dramatically throughout the period of 1858 to 1923 and, due to a series of unique circumstances surrounding this immigration, the creation of racial enclaves known as Chinatowns developed.

Canada's immigration policies, largely due to lobbying by British Columbian politicians, were strictly racist against immigration by Asians—especially Chinese, Japanese, and East Indians. Most immigration of Asian peoples was organ-

Fan Tan Alley in Victoria's Chinatown was once home to several opium dens. Today, the spaces that held the dens are occupied by small specialty shops and the alley is promoted as being the narrowest commercial street in North America. (BCARS photo I-03386)

ized by contractors seeking cheap labour to work in mines, or as road and railroad builders. Fifteen thousand, for example, were encouraged to immigrate to Canada to labour on the construction of the Canadian Pacific Railroad's B.C. sections. The work was dangerous and poor paying, and living conditions were usually squalid.

From 1885, Chinese migrants were required to pay an entry or head tax. As a consequence of this tax, which made the cost of bringing a wife or aged parents to Canada prohibitive, men came alone and lived as bachelors. Most hoped to save sufficient funds to return eventually to China or to bring their wives and families to Canada. But increasing pressure to ensure the head tax worked to prevent an influx of Chinese to British Columbia led to its being steadily increased. In 1900 it was raised to $100 and to $500 in 1903. On July 1, 1923, Chinese immigration was virtually suspended under the Chinese Immigration Act. The act remained in effect until 1947 when it was repealed and Chinese and East Indian Canadians were granted the right to vote in federal and provincial elections.

The imbalance of male to female Chinese in Canada fostered by the head tax was so extreme that in 1931, out of a total Canadian population of 46,519 (about 80 percent of whom lived in B.C.), only 3,648 were women.

By 1900, most Chinese coming to British Columbia were settling in the urban areas rather than scattering into rural regions to work in the mines or on construction crews. Facing intense prejudice, the Chinese communities in **Vancouver** and **Victoria** concentrated in specific areas both out of choice and because of legislative restrictions on Chinese property ownership. Until the 1930s, for example, restrictive covenants prevented Vancouver Chinese from buying property outside the area designated officially as Chinatown. This ghettoization of the province's Chinese led to creation of an insular economic and social system within the Chinatowns. Because of the high number of men, associations developed to provide services to single men who lived primarily in formally organized households of bachelors. The association structure was extended throughout Chinese society, providing personal and community welfare services, social contact, and a base for political activity. Some of these associations survive today and remain a vital part of the urban Chinese community.

While the concentration of B.C.'s Chinese community within the confines of Chinatowns has greatly decreased in modern times, the areas remain as vital commercial and social hubs. Victoria's Chinatown, for example, is primarily a shopping district that retains a strong Chinese character. Vancouver's Chinatown remains the continent's second-largest Chinese community but also is a major tourist attraction and commercial district.

Clayoquot 800

On April 13, 1993, the B.C. government announced its land-use plan for **Clayoquot Sound**. The plan included approval for logging of about one thousand hectares annually over an 80- to 120-year period and permitted forest companies to begin some logging operations in the area immediately. About 70 percent of Clayoquot Sound was slated for strictly controlled logging of commercially viable timber. No sooner was the plan announced than it was attacked by virtually every environmental group in the province, as well as numerous organizations around the world. One environmental spokesperson warned, "It's going to be a long, hot summer in Clayoquot."

On July 5, after a series of demonstrations in the preceding four days outside Canadian embassies in England, Australia, Germany, Austria, the United States, and Japan, one hundred protesters blocked logging roads leading into Clayoquot. A three-month campaign of road-blocking had begun.

The year previously, the forest company giant MacMillan Bloedel had attained a court injunction barring road blockades. Those blocking the roads were legally in contempt of court because of the injunction's existence. Over the next three months, several thousand protesters conducted demonstrations alongside the logging road access points and more than fifteen hundred people physically blocked the roads to stop logging traffic into Clayoquot Sound.

Within days of the start of the blockades the provincial government responded by ordering the arrests of blockaders. On one day alone, 216 people were arrested. In all, 932 protesters were arrested and 857 charged with contempt of court. Those charged ranged from children to the elderly, and included the unemployed, clergy, professionals, and foresters. The arrests and charges constituted the largest mass arrest in Canadian history, displacing the Lower Canada Rebellion of 1838, which had an arrest record of 106 people for treason.

The province's court system proved incapable of granting each arrested protester an individual trial, so they were tried in large groups numbering up to forty or more. Sentences varied from suspended sentences, to fines, to combinations of jail and fines. The most severe sentence handed down was sixty days imprisonment and a $3,000 fine to a Tofino doctor. Charges brought against one of the major organizers of the blockades and demonstrations were dismissed by the court. Although the blockades seriously hampered logging operations throughout the summer of 1993, they failed to stop the forest company from continuing to log the area and failed to convince the government to change its logging plans for Clayoquot Sound.

Clayoquot Sound

One of the largest contiguous tracts of ancient temperate **rainforest** left on the planet is found in Clayoquot Sound on the west coast of **Vancouver Island**. This 350,000-hectare region extending from Estevan Point southeast to include Flores, Vargas, and Meares islands, and encompassing **Pacific Rim National Park**, has become a symbol of the **environmental conflict** that has raged throughout British Columbia over land-use since the mid-1980s. In 1993, attempts by environmental protesters to block logging companies from gaining access to the area resulted in the largest mass arrest in Canadian history. The provincial government's proposals to allow controlled logging in the region, while promising to sustain the environmental sensitivity and uniqueness of the area have been condemned by all sides of the debate—by environmentalists as ensuring the loss of the sound's biodiversity and habitat, by the forest industry as being too restrictive of timber harvests, and by native people as an attempt to downplay or ignore their claim to the area and right to guide its preservation or development.

Contained within the Clayoquot Sound region are nineteen major watersheds, including virtually all of Vancouver Island's watersheds that have not yet been encroached by logging. Clayoquot is a major wildlife habitat, salmon-spawning ground, and each year is a migratory stopover point for about 250,000 birds. It has been heralded by international conservationists and outdoor recreationalists as one of the most spectacular remaining wilderness areas in the world.

Under the agreement reached between the provincial government and the forest industry, 600,000 cubic metres of wood—fifteen thousand logging trucks' worth—can be logged in Clayoquot Sound annually.

On March 19, 1994, the First Nations of the Central Region of the Nuu-chah-nulth Tribal Council and the province of B.C. signed a historic two-year Interim Measures Agreement that set in place a First Nations-veto authority over resource management and land-use planning within Clayoquot Sound. This interim agreement was implemented with the intention that upon its expiry a formal long-term agreement would replace it. The agreement between the Nuu-chah-nulth and the B.C. government was the first of its kind in Canada and may pave the way for other similar agreements regarding land use of areas that fall within territory subject to an aboriginal land claim.

Climate

B.C.'s climate is a contradiction of extremes and averages directly linked to its remarkably diverse **physiography**. Generally, B.C. can be divided into wet and dry climatic zones—the coast is wet, the interior east of the **Coast Moun-**

tains is dry. There is a small third zone in the northeastern Peace River region that is part of the Great Plains of the Canadian prairie and has weather influenced by this geographic link. The **Gulf Islands**, **Victoria**, Saanich Peninsula, and Qualicum are home to localized anomalies that result in their climate mirroring the warm, dry regions of the Mediterranean.

Any attempt to divide the province into tidy climatic packages fails. The primary reason for this is that the landscape is riven with valleys, mountains, plateaus, highland benches, coastal inlets, and other geographical features that all work to impose unique localized weather patterns upon the province's major climatic influences.

About 75 percent of B.C. is mountainous and the air masses rolling in from the North Pacific to cross the province have to hurdle these mountains or slip up the valleys and through mountain passes. This air off the ocean is moist when it hits the coast and is blocked from easy passage inland by the **Coast** and **Cascade** mountain ranges. To get inland the air has to climb the steep mountain slopes and in doing so it cools, condensing its moisture into clouds that drape the mountains' western flank in fog and rain.

When these air masses cross the summits and descend eastward they warm, the little remaining moisture not shed on the western slopes is burned off and the winds actually suck up the moisture from the land below. This effect is known as a rainshadow. As the air mass reaches the next of six major mountain ranges running north to south through British Columbia it again cools and generates precipitation; then, once over the summits, it dries and warms. Finally it slips across the Rockies into the Canadian prairies and is no longer hindered by mountains.

The effect of the province's mountain ranges, including several lesser ones such as the **Vancouver Island** mountains, creates a condition of weather anarchy giving birth to hundreds of microclimates. The Gulf Islands and Victoria region, for example, have unusually dry weather for a coastal region because they lie in a rainshadow cast by the Olympic Mountains in Washington State. Victoria's annual precipitation is only 619 millimetres. Yet just ninety-five kilometres west of Victoria, where the Pacific air masses have to clamber over the higher summits of Vancouver Island mountains, residents of Port Renfrew splash through 3,943 millimetres of precipitation annually. A little over 150 kilometres east of **Vancouver**, Canada's wettest city, is **Lillooet**, the hottest, driest community in the nation.

Such compact diversity in a province as vast as British Columbia results in it laying claim to most Canadian weather records for wettest, driest, coldest, hottest, and the like. What follows is a list of some of the records racked up by the province.

- Nowhere else in Canada has as many frost-free days as parts of the West Coast, which get up to 220.
- All of the B.C. coastline is ice-free year-round.
- Sumas Canal, sixty kilometres east of Vancouver, with an annual temperature of 10.7° Celsius, is the most consistently warm place in Canada.
- Ocean Falls is the nation's wettest populated place.
- Longest wet spell of any major Canadian city—Victoria with thirty-three days of rain, beginning April 19, 1986.
- Canada's wettest known place is Henderson Lake on the west coast of Vancouver Island on Barkley Sound. In 1931 its single resident and weather station volunteer collected 8,122.4 millimetres of precipitation. Understandably, he abandoned the gloomy place in 1936 and it has since remained uninhabited.
- **Prince Rupert** has the lowest average number of days of sunshine.
- B.C. holds all Canadian snowfall records. Greatest average annual: 1,433 centimetres at Glacier. Most in one season: 2,447 centimetres at Mount Copeland, near Revelstoke. Most in one month: 535.9 centimetres on Highway 3 in the **St. Elias Mountains** in December 1959. Most in one day: 118.1 centimetres at Lakelse Lake, near Terrace, on January 17, 1974.
- For twenty-four days in 1958, **Kamloops** had temperatures exceeding 35° Celsius, making it the hottest city in Canada.

Following are British Columbia weather records that are not Canadian records.
- Neighbouring Lytton and Lillooet shared the highest recorded temperature, 44.4° Celsius on July 16, 1941.
- Oliver in the south Okanagan Valley and Hedley in adjacent Similkameen Valley experienced the most consecutive days with temperatures exceeding 32° Celsius: thirty-one days, beginning July 14, 1971.
- The lowest temperature recorded in B.C. was -58.9° Celsius at Smith River in the province's northwest corner on January 31, 1947.
- Smith River also claims the most cold days below -18° Celsius: eighty-five days, starting November 30, 1968.
- On October 6, 1967, Ucluelet received 489.2 millimetres of precipitation, setting a twenty-four-hour precipitation record.
- The most wet days ever recorded was at Langara, on the **Queen Charlotte Islands'** southernmost tip: three hundred days in 1939.
- The longest frost-free period was 685 days in Victoria during 1925 and 1926.
- Victoria also claims the highest recorded annual rate of sunshine: 2,426 hours in 1970.

- Cranbrook is the province's sunniest community, averaging 2,244 hours per year.
- On average, Stewart is the least sunny place with only 949 hours per year.

A common, totally fictitious, myth believed by many is that B.C.'s west-coast climate is moderated by the presence of a warm Japan Current, visualized as a "ribbon of warm water" stretching from the Orient to the shores of the province and gracing it with a gentle warmth. There is a North Pacific Current that flows eastward to North America from near Japan but it reaches the continent well to the south of B.C. The flow that does reach B.C. takes two to five years to complete its journey and is self-defined by its name—the Subarctic Current. What determines the coast's temperate climate is the flow of marine air whose temperatures are moderated by heat exchange with the warmer upper ocean surface. In simple terms, the ocean retains heat better than air does, resulting in little surface temperature change—winter or summer variations ranging only about ten degrees Celsius, as opposed to radical fluctuations of air temperatures over interior landmass areas of about twenty-five degrees Celsius. As a consequence, in summer the ocean contributes to cooling the air mass passing over it en route to the inland; in winter it warms the air causing a net effect of a moderation of climate.

Why is the Atlantic coast of Canada not similarly blessed? Weather moves west to east around the globe. The Atlantic's dominant weather influences consequently roll out of the North American interior. These continental air masses— land and air being less capable of exchanging heat than ocean water—vary much more in both seasonal temperatures and precipitation. B.C., then, owes its moderate climate to the ocean waters lying at its western doorstep.

Cloverdale Rodeo. *See* **Annual Events and Celebrations.**

Coastal Trough

Extending northwestward through British Columbia from Puget Sound and the San Juan Islands in Washington State to Dixon Entrance north of Graham Island in the **Queen Charlotte Islands**, the Coastal Trough is about 805 kilometres long. Entering Alaska, the trough continues to its termination at Chatham Strait, site of a major north-south faultline.

The majority of the Coastal Trough serves as an essential waterway for ships to move up and down the rugged provincial coast along a corridor sheltered by the heights of the **Insular Mountains** of the Queen Charlotte Islands and Vancouver Island.

Within B.C. the trough has a maximum width of about 160 kilometres where it extends inland up the Fraser River Valley to Hope. Its narrowest constriction is sixteen kilometres in Johnstone Strait at Sayward; this choke-point is known as the Seymour Arch and divides the trough into a northern section, the Hecate Depression, and a southern section, the Georgia Depression.

Most of the Hecate Depression is below sea level, containing Queen Charlotte Strait, Queen Charlotte Sound, Hecate Strait, and Dixon Entrance. The northeastern part of Graham Island, known as the Queen Charlotte Lowland, the northern tip of **Vancouver Island**, and a strip of low-lying country including both mainland coast and adjacent islands running from Prince Rupert south to **Vancouver** are the only above-sea-level portions of the trough in the Hecate Depression.

The Georgia Depression is partly submerged beneath the Strait of Georgia and Puget Sound. Eastern lowlands on Vancouver Island, the **Gulf Islands**, and the Georgia Basin area of the mainland from Vancouver to Hope are part of the trough.

The lowlands from Nanaimo on Vancouver Island to **Victoria** and east on the mainland from Vancouver up the **Fraser River** Valley constitute the Georgia Basin region, where the majority of the province's human population is tightly clustered.

Coastline

British Columbia's coast is flanked by the continental shelf of North America. This gently dropping edge of the platform on which rests the continent runs from Dixon Entrance north of the **Queen Charlotte Islands**, along the Charlotte's west coast, and then widens out slightly to an average of forty-five to ninety kilometres off **Vancouver Island**'s west coast. The water above the shelf is the most productive fishery area on the West Coast and most of the province's fisheries operate here rather than in deeper offshore waters. Along the west coast of the Queen Charlottes the shelf is almost nonexistent, with water depths plummeting more than twenty-five hundred metres to the ocean floor.

Landward of the shelf, B.C.'s coast is a complex network of inlets, straits, passes, sounds, and narrows. Measured linearly from north to south along the mainland it is 7,022 kilometres, but that figure fails to measure accurately the true contour length of the province's coastline. Including island circumferences, if the coastline were stretched out in a long line it would measure 27,300 kilometres from the border of Washington State to the Alaska Panhandle. Numerous rivers empty into the ocean through glacier-formed valleys. The larger rivers, especially **Skeena**, Nass, and **Fraser**, profoundly affect the structure and circulation of coastal waters through the influx of large outflows of freshwater into the ocean stream. The Fraser River, with an average maximum daily flow of 15,178 cubic metres, influences the currents of the entire inside passage from the entrance of **Juan de Fuca Strait** to the entrance of Queen Charlotte Sound, north of Vancouver Island. It may even cause variations in surface water on Vancouver Island's outer coast. Water depths close to the coast vary from about 400 metres in the basins of **Strait of Georgia**, Puget Sound, and Juan de Fuca Strait, to 650 metres or more in Bute and Jervis inlets, so closeness to shore in no way means shallower water.

The rugged headlands of East Sooke Regional Park west of Victoria are typical of the B.C. coastline. (Mark Zuehlke photo)

For humans, water temperatures in much of B.C.'s coastal waters can be dangerously cold, so that submersion for more than twenty minutes may prove life threatening. In winter, average temperatures off Vancouver Island hover around 8° Celsius; near the Alaska Panhandle it's a couple of degrees colder. From spring to late August, temperatures rise slowly to an average high of 18° Celsius and occasionally exceed 20° Celsius. With fall, temperatures drop dramatically. Burrard Inlet's Spanish Banks and English Bay experience a warming anomaly because of the heating effect of their sandy beaches and the outflow of warm, silty water from the Fraser River. In summer, **Saanich Inlet**, due to its weak tidal currents and resulting sluggish turnover, can often warm to well over 20° Celsius.

The B.C. coastline only emerged from glacial ice about eleven thousand years ago, so erosion by ocean forces has had little time to soften the landscape. Such erosive forces face a tough battle as the shoreline is mostly bedrock that is so hard it greatly resists erosion. When it does give, the shoreline rock tends to shatter or simply wear away under the polishing effect of the waves in such a gradual process that the headlands are not visibly altered. As a consequence of this rugged shoreline's resistance to erosive forces, beaches are scarce. The only extensive beaches are on the west coast of Vancouver Island between Ucluelet and Tofino (*See* **Pacific Rim National Park**), along the north and east coasts of Graham Island, and on Vancouver Island's east coast. These have resulted from glacial deposits on gently sloping land that allowed the creation of sand by wave action. Elsewhere the shoreline was too steep for such deposits to be left by glaciation.

Intense glaciation of the mountains pressing in hard against the coastal shoreline led to the creation of B.C.'s most distinctive oceanographic feature, its numerous fjords and fjord-like inlets. The province's coastline is riddled by seventy-nine inlets—long, narrow channels bounded by steep mountainous sides that make them reminiscent of Norway's fjords. With **Mount Waddington** looming over its head and an icefield extending down to the water's edge, Knight Inlet is usually considered B.C.'s most spectacular inlet. Some of these inlets push a remarkable distance inland. Burke Channel extends ninety kilometres from the coast into the very heart of the **Coast Mountains**, Dean Channel is ninety-six kilometres long, and the head of Gardner Canal is about 193 kilometres from the outer coast of this inlet maze that also provides ocean-going shipping access to **Kitimat**, which, were it not for the inlets, would be well inland and incapable of supporting one of the province's deep-water ports. The inlets all share several common features: a deep U-shaped basin with glacial mud bottom, a river at the head, and an underwater ridge (sill) across the mouth. When run-off in the river is at its highest, salinity of the inlet is often reduced because of the salt being pushed into deeper waters. So narrow is the mouth of Vancouver Island's only true west-coast inlet, **Nitinat**, that at some times in the late winter and early spring the water here is fresh enough to drink because more freshwater is entering the inlet out of the rivers than salt water being pulled in by the negligible tidal flow.

The other primary feature of B.C.'s coastline is estuaries, of which the Fraser River estuary-delta is the largest and most important. Smaller estuarine areas are also found at the head of most inlets and sounds. Estuaries are the most productive habitats for marine life in the province. Because of the isolation of many of the province's inlets these estuary regions are relatively safe from environmental endangerment deriving from human habitation or exploitation of estuary resources. The same, however, is untrue of the Fraser River Delta, which is considered by many researchers as doomed to eventual destruction because of adjacent human overcrowding, pollution, and damming and infilling of waterways. While in recent years attempts have been made to slow or stop this degradation, there is little indication that the estuary will not continue to decline as a habitat for marine and other wildlife.

Coast Mountains

The Coast Mountains extend as an unbroken chain along the mainland coast of British Columbia from their southern end at the **Fraser River** northward for about 1,530 kilometres to the province's northern boundary and into the Yukon for a further eighty kilometres. Their width ranges from 56 kilometres to a maximum of 160 kilometres. To the west they are flanked by the **Coastal Trough**, and to the east by the **Interior System** (*See also* **Physiography**) section of the Canadian Cordillera.

For most of their length the Coast Mountains rise abruptly above a narrow coastal strip, facing the Pacific Ocean with rugged slopes and extreme variations in terrain due to many fjords and inlets. The mountains were intensely glaciated, leading to the creation of many of the fjords. Remnants of these glaciers can still be found, especially north of the **Skeena River** and in the vicinity of **Mount Waddington**. About the time of the glacial retreat ten thousand to fifteen thousand years ago, the mountains were also subject to volcanic action. The eastern slopes of the Coast Mountains are less severe, descending gradually toward the **Interior Plateau** country.

The Coast Mountains dramatically influence much of British Columbia's climate. Their steep western slopes force Pacific air mass flows to cool and drop most of their moisture, creating dense wet forests. On some western slopes, precipitation reaches 440 centimetres annually. The eastern slopes are drier, resulting in forests composed of dryland pine and fir growth.

Colleges. *See* Post-Secondary Education.

Columbia Mountains

A block of mountains 608 kilometres long and 256 kilometres wide, the Columbia Mountains lie between the **Interior Plateau** to the west and the **Rocky Mountain Trench** to the east. On the eastern slopes of the mountains the clean-cut walls of the trench clearly define the boundary between itself and the mountains. On the western side, highlands rise up from the Interior Plateau and the dividing line is somewhat obscured, being arbitrarily determined by physiographers as running from the trench's northern tip at Slim Creek east of Prince George to the **49th parallel**.

The Columbia Mountains are broken into four subdivisions—the Cariboo, Monashee, Selkirk, and Purcell ranges. Each is somewhat divided from the other by steep-walled valleys through which the Columbia River basin drains to the **Columbia River**. All four ranges contain massive and profuse peaks, shrouded by glaciers, to produce some of the most scenic country in British Columbia.

The mountains enclose a harsh landscape that experiences heavy snowfalls in winter, is densely forested, home to only the hardiest of wildlife, and little populated by humanity even within the long, narrow valleys that run between mountain ranges. Glaciers of the most recent ice age scoured the valleys and sheared mountain summits to the hard stone cores to produce spectacular peaks.

Columbia River

Of Columbia River's vast two-thousand-kilometre length, 748 kilometres lie within British Columbia, where the river has its headwaters in the southeast corner of the province. The river flows north-northwest around the Selkirk range of the **Columbia Mountains**, turning abruptly south past Revelstoke, through the **Arrow Lakes**, and then south into the United States. From here it cuts a broad swath through central Washington State before entering the spectacular Columbia Gorge and exiting into the Pacific Ocean on the Washington-Oregon border at Astoria, Oregon.

The river has one of the largest drainage basins in North America, totalling 155,000 square kilometres, of which 103,200 square kilometres lie in British Columbia.

During the last ice age the Columbia River's original course was interrupted by the edge of glacial ice forcing it southward into a great curve known as the "Big Bend." This diversion was a precursor of things to come for the mighty river. Starting in the 1930s, U.S. government-sponsored hydroelectric and irrigation projects both diverted the stream from its new course and siphoned off large quantities of its flow into reservoirs to provide irrigation water for a major transformation of the eastern and central Washington drylands into grain and fruit farms.

In 1961, the British Columbia government, headed by W.A.C. Bennett's Social Credit Party, agreed to build three massive storage dams in the province for downstream flood control purposes and as a source of hydroelectricity for primarily U.S. consumption. The **Columbia River Treaty**, as this agreement was called, resulted in the construction of the Duncan Dam (completed in 1967) north of Kootenay Lake, the **Hugh Keenleyside Dam** (completed in 1968) on the Columbia near Castlegar, and **Mica Dam** (completed in 1973) north of Revelstoke. Massive reservoirs were created behind each of these dams resulting in the flooding of thousands of hectares of land, destruction or relocation of several small communities, and the disruption and diversion of Columbia River's natural flow.

South of the border a chain of dams was constructed and more reservoirs created. The huge Grand Coulee Dam (built in the 1930s well before the treaty) denied millions of salmon access to their traditional spawning grounds in the Canadian section of the river and its tributaries. Despite these massive transformations of the natural flow and course of the Columbia, the river remains a major waterway in British Columbia. The reservoir lakes created by the dams are also becoming increasingly popular for recreational use.

Columbia River Treaty

For many British Columbians the Columbia River Treaty stands as one of the most controversial and blatant sell-outs of Canadian interests to those of the United States to occur in recent history. For fifteen years—from 1946 to 1961— Canadian and American negotiators struggled to hammer out a deal to implement a program designed to tame and exploit the powerful **Columbia River**. South of the border the river was famed for its destructive flooding of vast tracts of lowlands that could be prime farmland if only the river could be controlled and its flow tapped for irrigation purposes. Even more important was the increasing demand from rapidly growing Pacific Northwest cities for power, which could be supplied by hydroelectric dams situated on the Columbia on both sides of the border.

An initial agreement was finally reached on January 17, 1961, under which the two federal governments agreed to a cooperative plan of developing the Columbia as a natural resource. Implementation of the agreement, however, was stalled as the provincial and federal governments wrangled over jurisdiction and control of the massive dam-building projects planned. The B.C. premier at the time, W.A.C. Bennett, envisioned mega-dam-building projects on the **Peace** and Columbia River as a ticket to financial wealth for the province and was determined to retain control, and the benefits realized, for British Columbians. Acting virtually independent of the federal government, provincial authorities entered into a tentative agreement in 1961 with the United States that guaranteed half the power produced would be for American consumption. Although the federal government initially tried to block the agreement it finally demurred and, in 1964, Bennett signed a historic thirty-year agreement that obligated B.C. to supply power to the U.S. until 1994. Thirsty for cash to fuel his grand dam-building schemes that would provide much employment and possibly a secure future for the province, Bennett met then-U.S. President Lyndon B. Johnson on September 16, 1964, at the Peace Arch on the border at Blaine, Washington, and received a cheque from the president for $273,291,661.25 for the first thirty years of power. Cash in hand, Bennett was able to start contracting out the work on the three dams that had to be built to honour the agreement.

The price paid by the U.S. for the thirty-year supply of power has been repeatedly criticized as far too low and that, further, most of the money was eaten up by the dam construction costs. Additionally, critics say, the environmental damage from the project far outweighed the gain for British Columbia.

During the life of the agreement, B.C. also sold extra power from the Mica, Hugh Keenleyside, and Duncan dams to the U.S. under a complex formula that required the U.S. to repatriate the estimated downstream benefits accrued from provision of this power to the province beginning in 1998. These benefits are estimated at $1 billion and negotiations continue over the various options for its repayment. Negotiations also continue for moving the Columbia River Treaty into its new stage now that its original term has expired. Meantime, the changes wrought on the Columbia River and the many regions of southeastern B.C. that were forever affected by the creation of the dam reservoirs have been described by the provincial governments of the 1990s as "a real tragedy."

Continental Divide

Often called the Great Divide, the Continental Divide is a line running north to south through North America down the centre spine of the main **Rocky Mountain** ranges creating a barrier that forces water on its western slope to drain to the Pacific, water on its eastern slopes to run toward the Arctic or Atlantic oceans. The divide's presence is a major reason that B.C. has so many rivers draining through its rugged mountainous interior to the Pacific Ocean. Only the **Peace River** flows east from British Columbia to eventually drain into the Arctic. There is a second Continental Divide that runs east to west across the breadth of Canada and determines whether drainage basins flow north to the Arctic Ocean or east to the Atlantic Ocean, but this divide has no influence on British Columbia except in the 10 percent of the province in the extreme northeast that lies east of the Rocky Mountains Continental Divide.

Coquihalla Highway (Highway 5)

This is the largest, newest, and fastest route connecting the Lower Mainland with B.C.'s interior. Completed in just over two years, this four- and six-lane two-hundred-kilometre highway is seventy-three kilometres shorter than the **Trans-Canada Highway**, but an average 110-kilometre speed limit and the multiple lanes reduce driving time by approximately ninety minutes. Construction cost about $415 million—money the provincial government is hoping to recover through B.C.'s only highway toll ($10 for cars and recreation vehicles). The toll gate is near the 1,240-metre summit of Coquihalla Pass, fifty-five kilometres northeast of the western starting point at Hope.

The section from Hope to Merritt is 115 kilometres, from Merritt to Kamloops is 95 kilometres. Although the first section is relatively scenic, passing beneath some impressive peaks of the **Cascade Mountains** and moving from coastal forests to the semi-arid grasslands of the Fraser Plateau, this is a route designed more to offer speed and convenience than sightseeing opportunities. Travellers will find the **Fraser Canyon** section of the **Trans-Canada Highway** and the Hope-Princeton Highway (Highway 3) routes to interior destinations more scenic and less frenetic.

In winter, driving conditions on the Coquihalla can be treacherous. The area is subject to **avalanches** (there are numerous snow sheds, including one that is three hundred metres long, and avalanche-stop dams on the Hope to Merritt section), extreme iciness, and heavy fog. Long uphill grades can cause engines to overheat in summer.

(*See also* **Okanagan Connector.**)

CORE (Commission on Resources and Environment)

The use of British Columbia's land and resources has been the subject of heated debate since the mid-1980s, as the province's **economy**, built on a foundation of **forestry** and **mining**, moved into a transition away from being centred almost exclusively on natural resource extraction. Lands targeted for logging and mining development were also being identified as prime natural habitats and a primary draw for tourists. New resource industries, such as **aquaculture**, and the recognition of the need to preserve watershed and **salmon**-spawning grounds often conflicted with logging use of these lands. Additionally, large tracts of B.C. were subject to **First Nations land claims**.

Early in 1992, the provincial government sought to develop a rational land-use plan that would offer an acceptable compromise to all the various interest groups and ensure the preservation of the province's natural resources for future generations. The Commission on Resources and Environment (CORE) was given the mandate to develop a comprehensive land-use strategy. The CORE commissioner was in charge of developing regional and local planning processes, designing a dispute resolution system, coordinating government planning initiatives, and ensuring First Nations participation in the entire process.

In 1994, four regions of the province—**Vancouver Island**, **Cariboo-Chilcotin**, East Kootenay, and West Kootenay-Boundary—were subject to development of CORE land-use plans. Involvement of all interested parties in the process leading up to the plan's development was designed to reduce conflict and to bring about community consensus for land-use in each region. The plans, however, were generally condemned by environmentalists as allowing too much logging and mining, and decried by logging and mining advocate groups and industry for protecting too much land from intensive development.

Highly controversial, it soon became evident that the CORE regional land-use plans would require much fine tuning and that, whatever the final result, most parties would feel they were on the losing side of the agreement.

Cougars

Cougars are the largest wild cat native to British Columbia. They are found only in the Western Hemisphere, with a range from northern British Columbia to Patagonia in southern Argentina. In Canada, cougars have been recorded from British Columbia east to New Brunswick. Distribution in mainland B.C. ranges from the **49th parallel** to the Big Muddy River on the **Alaska Highway**. South of about 54° north latitude, cougars are generally found from the B.C.-Alberta border west to, and including, most coastal islands. Cougars have not reached the **Queen Charlotte Islands**, but are plentiful on **Vancouver Island**.

Because cougars range over such a large land area, humans in different geographical areas have assigned the species different names. These include cougar, puma, mountain lion, deer tiger, Indian devil, and Mexican lion.

Adult cougars are large. In B.C. they have been recorded at weights between eighty-six and ninety-five kilograms, but the average adult male weighs about fifty-seven kilograms and the female about forty-five kilograms. A large adult male may measure 2.7 metres in length, including a seventy-six-centimetre-long tail.

The fur is short and, in B.C., ranges in colour from reddish brown to a grey-brown, with lighter underparts. Very young kittens are spotted, with ringed tails; this coloration is gradually lost as the young cougar reaches adulthood. Black cougars have been reported from South America and one was sighted in recent years in the north **Okanagan Valley**.

Cougars are solitary creatures, seeking each other out only for breeding purposes. Biologists believe the female cougar emits a screaming sound, described as a trilling wail, to draw a male cougar to her. Only the female tends the young. Usual litter size is one to four kittens.

Cougar distribution in the province is governed by the distribution of its major prey species—deer. While cougars will follow deer populations into virtually any habitat, they prefer rough, rocky, semi-open areas. Cougars stalk their prey, attacking with two or three powerful jumps that will carry them a distance of fifteen metres in an instant. If the prey escapes the initial attack, cougars will seldom pursue the animal further, preferring instead to begin stalking another animal. To make a kill, the cougar will leap from the ground onto the shoulders and neck of the prey. The most effective kills are made when the cougar holds the head with a forepaw and bites down through the back of the neck, near the base of the skull. Cougars usually eat about

70 percent of a big-game animal kill. An adult cougar will consume approximately fourteen to twenty average-sized mule deer each year. This number is lessened if the cougar is successful in making smaller animal kills.

In addition to deer, another favourite prey for B.C. cougars is wild sheep. Due to their opportunistic hunting practices, they will also eat mice, porcupine, beaver, hares, moose, elk, mountain goats, bear cubs, grouse, coyotes, other cougars, domestic stock, and household pets.

The B.C. population of cougars is estimated at about three thousand. Although these cats have been largely extirpated from other parts of Canada, the population in B.C. is considered healthy and stable. **Vancouver Island**, because of the presence of a large deer population, has the largest concentration of cougars—about six hundred or one-fifth of the province's total population.

Cougars rarely attack humans. Their normal behaviour is to avoid people, although they are often curious about human activities. Cougars have been observed sitting at a vantage point and watching, sometimes for hours, humans either working or playing out-of-doors. People in the woods have reported discovering cougar tracks that clearly indicated the animal was following their own tracks. Infrequent attacks on humans are usually attributed to old, starving cougars, or to cougars defending their young.

Courts. *See* **Judiciary.**

Craigellachie

On November 7, 1885, Donald Smith, a financial backer of the Canadian Pacific Railway project, drove the symbolic "last spike" here in a ceremony that marked the linking of the western and eastern sections of the national railroad. Craigellachie is named for a rocky crag in Morayshire, Scotland, where Smith and fellow financier and cousin George Stephen grew up. The rock was the historical rallying point for Clan Grant and their battle cry was "Stand fast, Craigellachie!" In 1884, when the railway project was foundering for lack of cash, Stephen sent a cable from London to Smith in Montreal that read "Stand fast, Craigellachie"—an agreed-upon code that signalled Stephen's success in securing a desperately needed loan.

A cairn, plaque, and small park mark the site of the ceremony and are found just off Highway 1 to the east of the tiny community.

Crown Corporations

Crown corporations and agencies are entities established or acquired by the provincial or federal government. There are three types of provincial Crown corporations. Commercial Crown corporations generate revenue from the sale of services at commercial rates and pay their own operating expenses, including debt service charges. Economic development Crown corporations generate revenue from the sale of services to the public. These corporations, while undertaking projects deemed by the government as providing economic benefits to the province, may operate at a loss. The remaining Crown corporations and agencies receive government financial assistance to administer social and government services and to assist in financing other public bodies.

BC Hydro is the province's largest Crown corporation. Another provincial commercial Crown corporation is the British Columbia Railway Company. This is the third largest railway in Canada, operating on 2,202 kilometres of mainland track from North Vancouver to northeastern British Columbia. It maintains port facilities in North Vancouver and Squamish, has a rolling stock fleet of about 110 locomotives, 9,650 freight cars, 12 passenger cars, and 400 work cars. In addition, the railway holds about 21,100 hectares of land. Other major commercial Crown corporations are the **Insurance Corporation of British Columbia**, the British Columbia Petroleum Corporation, and the Liquor Distribution Branch.

Economic development Crown corporations include **British Columbia Ferry Corporation**, **BC Transit Authority**, British Columbia Trade Development Corporation, and British Columbia Pavilion Corporation.

Crown corporations providing social and government services include British Columbia Buildings Corporation which provides and maintains facilities housing government operations, the Provincial Rental Housing Corporation, and several other operations generally involved in serving as the borrowing agencies for financing specific social service operations such as the funding of regional hospitals and schools.

Crowsnest Pass

With a maximum elevation of 1,357 metres this pass through the **Rocky Mountains** runs from Sparwood, B.C. to Coleman, Alberta. Only forty kilometres north of the U.S. border, the pass is traversed by Highway 3—the southernmost highway route transiting British Columbia and linking with Alberta. This highway is noted for spectacular scenery and less traffic than other west to east routes crossing the province.

Historically the Crowsnest Pass served for centuries as an easy travel route for native tribes. The Kutenai used the pass to journey east to join in buffalo hunts with the Crow people.

White explorers, including geologist George Mercer Dawson, found evidence of major coal deposits here. In 1898, the Canadian Pacific Railway pushed a line through the pass to provide access to the mining operations developing in the region. The railway was built partly as a way of raising the national flag over the area, which was beginning to be encroached by American mining interests.

To raise funds for the rail construction the CPR negotiated an agreement with the federal government known as the Crow's Nest Pass Agreement. Under the agreement, the CPR was given a cash subsidy of $3.3 million and title to pass into B.C. in exchange for reducing, in perpetuity, eastbound shipping rates on grain and flour and westbound rates on specified products. Although the agreement was fiddled with constantly since the 1920s as the federal government and the CPR tried to return rates to their real costs, Prairie farmers continued to lobby effectively for the preservation of the ideal behind the lower rates, which enabled Canadian grain to reach world markets at competitive rates. Consequently, "Preserve the Crow" was an oft-rung battle cry heard in Prairie grain-farming communities far removed from, and little concerned about, the pass itself. In 1995, however, the agreement was finally scrapped by the federal government despite protests by Prairie farmers.

Cultural History

Until 1900 most of the province's non-native population were recent or second-generation British immigrants who drew their cultural affiliations from Britain and the Empire of which the province and, after joining Canadian confederation in 1871, Canada were a part. In the early twentieth century, these British influences were diversified moderately by the movement into the province of eastern Canadians who had second- or third-generation British origins. Following World War II, this eastern influence became more dominant when internal migration from the eastern provinces to B.C. increased rapidly. With this migration came development of institutions, societies, and cultural events found across the rest of Canada.

B.C.'s culture was also diversified in a way not felt in the rest of Canada by the mixture of its immigration patterns. People from India, Pakistan, Malaysia, the Philippines, Hong Kong, Japan, and China constitute the largest share of the province's non-European immigrant population and have, despite the province's historical racism against Asiatic immigrants, left an indelible impression on the fabric of B.C. society. The development and continued existence of ethnic enclaves in the major cities—especially **Vancouver** and, to a lesser extent, **Victoria**—largely occurred in response to the racist policies and attitudes of the majority British population that persisted until after World War II.

The other major cultural group is the **First Nations peoples**. The highly developed culture existing before the arrival of Europeans was sustained in many significant ways despite assimilationist government policies. Today, the revival of native art, theatre, language, and spiritual beliefs is felt throughout B.C. society. Many non-native artists have been profoundly influenced by native culture. Emily Carr, probably the province's most famous artist, is a case in point.

Since 1967, the B.C. government has offered financial assistance to cultural and ethnic groups, publishers, the film industry, and community organizations through a variety of public funding initiatives. Additional activities are also aided by grants from provincial lotteries. The federal government, through such bodies as the Canada Council, also supports cultural activities throughout the province, as do some municipal and regional governments. About $550 million is expended annually by all levels of government on culture in B.C.—a percentage participation that has been declining yearly since 1990 due to government restraint programs.

Major museums, archives, and art galleries are located in Vancouver and Victoria, with local museums of some size maintained in several smaller cities in the interior. Across the province there are approximately two hundred museums, thirty-five archives, forty historic sites, and seventy-five public libraries or library systems. The Centennial Museum and H.R. MacMillan Planetarium, located on the waterfront in the western part of Vancouver, adjoin the City Archives and the distinctive Maritime Museum. The University of British Columbia Museum of Anthropology holds an impressive collection of Northwest Coast native artefacts in a facility designed by famous Vancouver architect Arthur Erickson.

The Royal British Columbia Museum houses a collection of more than ten million objects and artefacts. It is the only institution in B.C. containing detailed information on all of the province's natural and human history. The biological and human history collections contain unique historical information and the museum is a renowned research, education, and tourist centre. It also serves a leadership role for B.C.'s museum community, offering technical advice and assistance to other provincial museums, providing annual speaking tours, and circulating travelling exhibits. More than one million people use the services of the Royal British Columbia Museum annually, many of them school children.

Numerous theatrical, symphonic, and operatic companies perform in Victoria and Vancouver, occasionally taking productions on tour to coastal and interior cities. Some interior cities sustain professional and semi-professional theatrical and symphonic groups. Kelowna, for example, has a professional seasonally operating theatrical group and is home to the Okanagan Symphony, which performs throughout the **Okanagan Valley**. Despite strong grassroots cultural communities throughout the province, cultural facilities, groups, and services remain centred in Vancouver and Victoria due to the concentration of population in these areas. In all, there are about fifty professional performing groups in the province.

The cultural sector is defined by the provincial government as comprising all those individuals and organizations working in the arts (performing, literary, and visual arts), cultural industries (film and video, publishing and sound recording), archaeology, heritage, and human and natural history. This entire sector constitutes a labour force of about forty-three thousand—an increase of 55 percent over 1981 levels.

Sports is an important part of the province's cultural life. The **Vancouver Canucks** hockey team opened its first season with the National Hockey League in 1971. The **British Columbia Lions** have been competing in the Canadian Football League since 1954 and now play in **BC Place**—Canada's first covered stadium. In 1954, as well, Vancouver was host to the Empire Games (now called the Commonwealth Games). Victoria hosted the 1994 Commonwealth Games. Each year thousands of athletes from across the province gather in a host community for the B.C. Games.

All major cities in B.C. have daily newspapers and the smaller coastal and interior cities publish weekly newspapers. Most areas are serviced by AM and FM radio stations and the larger communities have local television stations that are usually affiliated with one of Canada's major networks.

There are about twenty major book-publishing firms producing over two hundred new titles annually. Yearly revenues in the book publishing sector are more than $26 million. About 150 periodicals are printed by the province's magazine publishing firms.

Since the 1970s, the province has been increasingly attractive as a location for film and television production. About seventy-five feature film and television productions are shot annually, primarily in the vicinity of Vancouver. About $286 million is contributed each year to the province's economy by this growing industry. In 1994, Vancouver emerged as the third-largest film production centre in North America, behind Los Angeles and New York.

The province's cultural heritage is also preserved and promoted through a large network of registered tourist attractions. More than 65 percent of all registered tourist attractions in B.C. have a cultural or heritage component.

Cultus Lake

The local Coast Salishan Indians had little good to say about this lake, located thirteen kilometres from Chilliwack. Cultus is derived from the Salishan-language word *kul,* meaning "bad" or "worthless." The Salishan believed a

Slellucum or supernatural being taking the form of a great bear inhabited the lake area, causing terrible storms on the lake. They declared the lake taboo and seldom went there.

Today, Cultus Lake is home to a provincial park that is one of the province's most popular, as visitors come to boat, swim, fish, hike, and ride horses.

Dams. *See* **Columbia River Treaty; Hugh Keenleyside Dam; Mica Dam; Peace River; Revelstoke Dam; Water.**

Deserts. *See* **Okanagan Pocket Desert.**

Desolation Sound

This sound is one of the province's most popular salt-water boating regions and is home to Desolation Sound Provincial Marine Park. The sound joins Lewis Channel between Cortes and West Redonda islands, just northwest of Lund, terminus of Highway 101, known as the **Sunshine Coast** Highway.

The sound got its dreary name from Captain George Vancouver, who visited here in 1792. He described the sound in his log as "truly forlorn; an awful silence pervaded the gloomy forests . . . the steep rocky shores prevented the use of the seine, and not a fish at the bottom could be tempted to take the hook." Vancouver went on to bemoan the absence of fresh berries in the forests.

Today, the park, which is B.C.'s largest marine park, covers 8,256 hectares of the north shore of Gifford Peninsula and has more than sixty kilometres of shoreline. There is no road access.

Dinosaurs. *See* **Elasmosaur; Fossils.**

Disasters. *See* **Air Disasters; Avalanches; Campbell River Fire; Earthquakes; Hope Slide; Landslides; Nanaimo Mine Disaster; Point Ellice Bridge Disaster; Rogers Pass; Shipwrecks; Tsunamis;** *Valencia* **Sinking.**

Diving

At least 450 fish species, 600 plant species, and over 4,000 invertebrate species live along the coastline of British Columbia. This prolific marine life, the rugged underwater landscape, and the presence of many accessible shipwrecks make the province's ocean coast excellent for diving. *National Geographic* magazine has hailed B.C.'s diving waters as "the finest in the world second to the Red Sea."

Popular diving spots include **Powell River** and **Vancouver Island's** west coast, particularly around the **Broken Group Islands**. Also found off the west coast of Vancouver Island is an area called "The Graveyard of the Pacific," where divers can explore underwater wrecks. Many of these ships, as well as those on the periphery of **Pacific Rim National Park**, are designated historic sites and the removal of artefacts is prohibited.

Saltery Bay, just south of Powell River, has the first underwater statue to be erected in Canada—a mermaid. Whitecliff, Copper, and Telegraph coves in West Vancouver are also popular dive points. There is an underwater park in **Saanich Inlet**. Most coastal areas of B.C. have good diving areas and local sites can be found by consulting with dive shops.

Dogwood. *See* Symbols.

Douglas Lake Cattle Company

Established in 1884, the Douglas Lake Cattle Company is Canada's largest cattle ranch. Situated southeast off Highway 5A, about 47.5 kilometres from Merritt, the ranch runs some nineteen thousand head of cattle on 200,000 hectares of grazing land.

As an economic sideline the ranch offers guided day-tours of ranch operations.

Douglas Treaties. *See* First Nations Land Claims.

Doukhobors

In 1785, Archbishop Ambrosius of the Russian Orthodox Church declared a group of dissident Russian peasants as religious heretics by calling them "Doukho-bortsi"—meaning Spirit Wrestlers. To his surprise the dissidents adopted the intended debasement, claiming to indeed be Spirit Wrestlers because they wrestled with and for the spirit of God.

A fundamental religious sect, the Doukhobors rejected Russian Orthodox Church ritual, and espoused pacifism, vegetarianism, and abstinence from alcohol and tobacco. Their pacifist philosophy caused them to reject militarism and to refuse military conscription. The Czarist regime in Russia, backed by the Russian Orthodox Church, harshly oppressed the movement's followers. Doukhobors were stripped of normal freedoms and privileges of citizenship and were subject to arrest, torture, and exile to detention camps. The persecution of the Doukhobor community attracted international attention in the late 1800s, and between 1898 and 1899, seventy-five hundred Doukhobors were allowed to emigrate from Russia to Canada. This was the largest single group ever to migrate to Canada at one time.

They initially moved to Saskatchewan, where they set up communal settlements. In 1905, however, the federal government denied homestead titles when the Doukhobors refused to swear an oath of allegiance—believing their only allegiance could be to God.

In 1908, spiritual leader Peter Verigin led most of the Canadian Doukhobor population to settle in the Kootenays, initially in the **Castlegar** region. By 1910, about six thousand Doukhobors had resettled, establishing communities near Nelson, in the Slocan Valley, and at Grand Forks.

Their communities were developed separately from existing non-Doukhobor settlements and were operated communally until 1938. Of the six thousand original settlers, all but about one thousand participated in the communal-living experiment that remains one of the largest such enterprises undertaken in North American history.

Although the communal lifestyle enabled the Doukhobors to weather the Great Depression better than most Canadian farmers, they were unable to pay back the large mortgages they had acquired to establish the communities initially. The federal government's policy that protected individual farmers from foreclosure was deemed as not applying to the Christian Community of Universal Brotherhood, Ltd.—the title under which their community was registered—and foreclosure proceedings were initiated against their land holdings. Eventually the B.C. government took over the Doukhobor lands and sold them back to the Doukhobors on an individual basis.

Despite the termination of the communal settlements, the Doukhobors retained strong group ties and preserved their cultural and religious traditions. From the Christian Community of Universal Brotherhood evolved the Union of Spiritual Communities of Christ (USCC). This organization still binds together most of the province's Doukhobors. The majority of this group lives in the West Kootenay and Grand Forks areas of southeastern B.C. Most Doukhobors living outside these areas are known as independents, but also retain some group affiliations through an organization called the Society of Doukhobors of Canada.

The smallest group is known as the Christian Community and Brotherhood of Reformed Doukhobors, or the Sons of Freedom. This group was founded in 1902 and has attracted much public attention because of its radical responses to perceived and real persecution by government. Sons of Freedom extremists have also attacked other Doukhobors, using bombings and burnings of property as their main weapons. At various times schools have also been burned when provincial authorities were perceived to be trying to educate Doukhobor children to beliefs that ran counter to the group's philosophies. During trials of Sons of Freedom members, supporters and defendants have used public nudity and hunger strikes as a form of passive protest.

The USCC operates a number of independent Russian-language schools in the Kootenays. It also maintains cultural centres in most Doukhobor communities, has several cooperative retail stores and a milling cooperative. The continuation of the Doukhobor communal cultural heritage has enabled this small group to sustain its unique identity.

Dragon Boat Festival. *See* **Annual Events and Celebrations.**

Drug Laws

Use of various drugs in British Columbia is regulated by federal laws enforced throughout Canada. Most non-pharmaceutical drugs are controlled by the Narcotic Control Act, while other drugs are regulated by parts three and four of the Food and Drugs Act. Possession of restricted drugs in contravention of either of these acts is a criminal offence.

Most commonly used illegal drugs in Canada are controlled by the Narcotic Control Act. Cannabis (in all its forms), PCP (phencyclidine), opium, heroin, morphine, all narcotic analgesics, and cocaine fall under the jurisdiction of the Narcotic Control Act. For Narcotic Control Act violations, a summary conviction for a first offence can result in a maximum fine of up to $1,000 and/or six months' imprisonment. Subsequent offences carry a maximum fine of $2,000 and/or one year's incarceration. Conviction by indictment, rather than summary conviction, can result in imprisonment for up to seven years. Trafficking and possession for the purpose of trafficking are automatically indictable offences and are punishable by a maximum sentence of life imprisonment. Importing and exporting of illegal drugs are punishable by imprisonment up to life, but not less than seven years; cultivation of opium poppy is punishable by up to seven years' imprisonment.

Part 3 of the Food and Drugs Act regulates the use and distribution of controlled drugs, legally available only by prescription. Anyone convicted of trafficking in these drugs or possessing them for the purpose of trafficking can be sentenced to a maximum of eighteen months'·imprisonment upon sum-

mary conviction or up to ten years' imprisonment upon conviction by indictment. Barbiturates and many tranquilizers fall under the jurisdiction of Part 3
of the Food and Drugs Act.

The Food and Drugs Act Part 4 controls such drugs as LSD (lysergic acid
diethylamide), mescaline, and psilocybin (magic mushrooms). Summary conviction for a first offence possession charge under Part 4 of the Food and
Drugs Act carries a maximum fine of $1,000 and/or up to six months' incar-
ceration. Subsequent offences have a fine up to $2,000 and/or one year's im-
prisonment. An indictable conviction has a maximum fine of $5,000 and/or
three years' imprisonment. Trafficking and possession for the purpose of trafficking are punishable upon summary conviction by up to eighteen months'
imprisonment and upon indictable conviction up to ten years.

In Canada, possession or use of tobacco products in a public place by
anyone under sixteen years of age is an offence under the Tobacco Restraint
Act, intended to reduce tobacco consumption by young people. In B.C., it is
illegal for anyone under nineteen to purchase tobacco. Provincial law also
makes it a punishable offence to sell tobacco products to anyone under nineteen. Local government regulations in many communities throughout B.C.
restrict the use of tobacco products in public places, including restaurants and
drinking establishments.

(*See also* **Liquor Laws and Regulations**.)

Duncan

This city, sixty-two kilometres north of **Victoria** on Highway 1, is home to
twenty-two hundred Cowichan **First Nations people**—B.C.'s largest band.
The band's heritage is celebrated by forty-one **totem poles** that have been
erected throughout the city's downtown core and alongside the highway.

Earthquakes

It could happen tomorrow or not for several hundred more years, but Canadian earthquake experts are confident that in terms of a geological time frame
the Lower Mainland and **Vancouver Island** will inevitably be struck by a
devastating earthquake exceeding Richter scale magnitude of 8.0. There is a
5 to 10 percent probability of such an earthquake occurring before 2050.

Each year, as many as one thousand earthquakes occur in B.C. or off the coast, but most of these are barely felt and cause no damage.

If an earthquake exceeding 8.0 Richter happens near urbanized areas of the Lower Mainland or Vancouver Island there will be severe damage, many casualties, and loss of services over a wide area from a combination of ground shaking, landslides, flooding, tsunamis (long, high sea waves caused by underwater earthquakes), and fires. The principal cause of deaths and injuries will be from the collapse of buildings and other manmade structures, especially older, multi-storey, and unreinforced masonry buildings. Schools and hospitals, most falling into the most vulnerable category, are expected to suffer at least 50 percent damage or complete collapse.

For the Lower Mainland, a federal government response plan predicts that in the event of a major earthquake 10 to 30 percent of single-family housing, 50 to 100 percent of unreinforced masonry buildings, 10 to 20 percent of highrises, and up to 60 percent of older schools and hospitals that have not been earthquake-strengthened will be destroyed or rendered uninhabitable.

The southwest coastal regions of the province are the most likely to see earthquake activity because three large tectonic plates—the Pacific, Juan de Fuca, and North America—come together here. These constitute the Cascadia Subduction Zone (comparable to the famed San Andreas Fault), which stretches from north of the **Queen Charlotte Islands** south to the Oregon coast. The continental North America Plate creeps westward, overriding Juan de Fuca plate, which subducts (slides under) in an easterly direction of 4.3 centimetres per year. There is also a small fourth plate, the Explorer Plate, which moves independently. Offshore, the Pacific Plate moves west from the Juan de Fuca Ridge found about 150 kilometres west of Vancouver Island. Here, molten new plate material wells up from deep in the earth's crust, feeding volcanic mountains such as Mount Garibaldi and the Cascade Range, as well as causing the sea floor to spread and lift.

Scientists are uncertain whether the absence of major earthquakes at this critical juncture of plates results from a subduction process that is smooth (known as aseismic creep) or whether they are actually caught in a form of gridlock that is preventing further movement but creating an increasing strain that is literally causing the earth's crust to bulge upward. Those supporting the upward bulge theory see it as concentrated in a north-south corridor extending from Washington State's Olympic Peninsula to Campbell River on Vancouver Island.

Three types of earthquakes threaten British Columbia—strike-slip, interplate, and subduction. The first results from sideways motion along breaks or faults in the earth's crust, the second from movement along the edges of two adjoining plates, and the latter from locked tectonic plates jolting loose. All can cause major damage. Scientists predict, however, the most likely is an interplate earthquake of a magnitude range between 6.0 and 7.0 Richter. If such an earthquake occurs in a populated area there will be extensive damage.

The West Coast of B.C. has experienced one great earthquake (exceeding 8.0 Richter) and five major earthquakes (7.0 to 7.9) since the earliest known seismic event recorded in 1841. Earthquakes of lesser magnitudes are commonplace with about forty a year recorded that are in excess of 4.0. These earthquakes are not confined to southwestern B.C. They extend throughout all of the western portion of the province. Although potential damage from earthquakes is high, actual losses to date have been small.

Only three major earthquakes have caused notable damage in British Columbia since 1841. In 1872, an earthquake believed to exceed 7.0 Richter magnitude had an epicentre in northern Washington State. The area that would today be downtown Vancouver was badly shaken although there was little real damage, as the few buildings were of flexible wood-frame or plank construction. There were no casualties.

On June 23, 1946, a 7.3 magnitude subduction earthquake, with an epicentre near Mount Washington on Vancouver Island, caused one death due to a **tsunami** wave and widespread damage to property throughout the island. In Campbell River, Port Alberni, **Powell River**, Courtenay, and Cumberland, houses suffered crumbled plaster, cracked walls, shattered windows, and collapsed chimney and brick facings. Comox-area farm fields and the main street of Cumberland rippled. Again, damage was restricted due to the fact that most buildings close to the epicentre were of wood construction. In Courtenay, however, a two-storey wood and masonry elementary school suffered extensive damage when its chimneys crashed through the roof into the classrooms. Luckily, the earthquake occurred on a Sunday, so the classrooms were empty of students at the time. Farther to the south in Victoria, many chimneys broke and windows shattered. The greatest damage was to the British Columbia Packers plant at Kildonan on Vancouver Island's west coast. Here pilings settled beneath the plant and the repair bill totalled $100,000.

On March 27, 1964, an 8.5 Richter earthquake centred 102 kilometres east of Anchorage, Alaska, produced a tsunami that caused extensive damage to communities on the west coast of Vancouver Island (*see* **Tsunamis** for more detail).

Since 1973, when earthquake-proofing specifications were included in the National Building Code and enacted in B.C. through the Municipal Act, new buildings have been increasingly constructed to withstand earthquake motion. There remains, however, a serious problem with thousands of older buildings, especially commercial and institutional structures in the southwest coastal region, that are particularly vulnerable to earthquake damage. In most communities, because the cost of reinforcing these structures to add earthquake protection is extremely high, earthquake proofing proceeds slowly. The upgrading of only four Vancouver heritage office buildings by reinforcing with steel columns and beams, strengthening the walls, and construction of new elevator shafts, for example, cost in excess of $8 million.

Earth Voice Festival. *See* **Annual Events and Celebrations.**

Ecological Reserves

In 1968, after several years of intense lobbying by provincial biologists—especially Dr. Vladimir J. Krajina of the Department of Botany at the University of British Columbia—a committee was formed to develop legislation whereby the provincial government could identify and set aside areas of ecological significance as protected reserves. On April 2, 1971, The Ecological Reserves Act was passed by the B.C. legislature. The act allows setting aside areas of Crown land either for research and educational purposes or to protect representative examples of natural ecosystems, rare or endangered native species, or unique natural phenomena.

To meet its goal of preserving representative examples of natural ecosystems, Dr. Krajina envisioned one percent of the province's total land base ultimately coming under protection. Since 1971, about 160,000 hectares—one-third of which are marine subtidal areas and so not part of the province's land base—have been preserved as ecological reserves. This totals only one-tenth of one percent.

There are about 130 reserves scattered across the province that have been set aside under the Ecological Reserves Act. The reserves tend to be individually quite small, sometimes little more than tiny ocean islets that are vital nesting colonies for sea birds.

The reserves are subject to different public usage restrictions that apply to provincial parks, recreational areas, or wildlife management areas. In some, only scientific or outdoor classroom use is permitted. Other reserves, especially many of the seabird islands, are completely closed to public access.

Economy

Since the arrival of Europeans in British Columbia the economy has been fuelled by natural resource exploitation. Forestry, mining, fishing, and agriculture have been the dominant economic forces in the province and, except for the rise in the importance of tourism, remain so.

The province's small population is unable to support local production of a full range of consumer goods or to provide a major market for its natural resource products. The province's economy grows primarily through the development of extensive trading relations within Canada and internationally. Most of the province's exports are resource-based.

Dependency on a natural resource economy reliant on exportation of products means the province's economic health is particularly vulnerable to developments in world markets and fluctuations in internationally determined commodity prices. Swings in world commodity prices subject the provincial economy to periods of rapid growth followed by slowdowns, recessions, and occasional depressions.

B.C.'s recent economic history has revolved around the province's industries and government seeking to diversify market bases to lessen some of this dependence on economic performance in traditional markets, such as the United States and European nations. An export-based economy is less likely to undergo significant upward or downward shifts in economic fortune if it has many widely distributed markets to supply. Market diversification by B.C. industry and government has focused primarily on gaining entry to the Pacific Rim marketplace. Exports to the Pacific Rim nations, until the 1980s virtually insignificant, now account for about 36 percent of all exports. While the province's ability to build significant export trade with the Pacific Rim looks favourable, its overall significance is lessened by the fact that about 25 percent of this trade is with one nation—Japan—rather than being spread across the region. As half—53 percent in 1993—of the province's exports go to the United States, B.C. is especially vulnerable to economic developments within these two nations.

The **forest industry** is unrivalled in its influence on the province's economic character—accounting for more than 16 percent of the Gross Domestic Product and about 44 percent of the value of all shipments from manufacturers in the province. Most statistical measurement scales place **mining** as the next most significant economic force in the province, followed by **tourism**, **agriculture**, and the **fishing industry**.

There is some argument among statisticians that tourism may have already supplanted mining for second-most-important sector status. It is generally accepted that declining world mineral, coal, and energy markets combined with the depletion of numerous mineral supplies will continue to reduce mining's contribution to the province's economic health. At the same time, the province's rapidly increasing popularity as a tourist destination will inevitably lead to this sector claiming second spot in the near future—if it has not already done so.

Although B.C.'s service sector employs well over one-third of the province's **labour force**, much of this employment is largely dependent on the overall health of the natural resource sector for its sustainment. A depression in any sector of the natural resource industries will yield an immediate decrease in service-sector jobs. The bulk of the province's manufacturing jobs also are related to processing or transforming natural resource products into various goods or products.

(*See also* **Agriculture**; **Aquaculture**; **Fishing Industry**; **Forest Industry**; **Labour Force**; **Mining Industry**; **Tourism**.)

Education System

In an average year B.C.'s government spends approximately $3.4 billion (about 20 percent of its total budget) on providing educational services to the more than 500,000 children attending kindergarten to grade twelve. About 68 percent of all children entering the province's educational system will ultimately graduate from grade twelve.

The province has an extensive infrastructure of schools and services that ensures every child, regardless of location, race, or creed, has access to the B.C. educational system. There are about 1,600 public schools in the province and 285 independent schools. Independent schools are required under the B.C. Education Act to ensure their students attain the same basic level of education and curriculum exposure as is available to children in the public schools.

Delivering education to the province's children is complicated by the unequal distribution of B.C.'s **population**. Thirty percent of all students live in the Lower Mainland's five largest school districts. These districts face unique pressures associated with rapid urban growth and poverty, unknown to many districts outside this metropolitan centre. The province's five most northern districts, covering about half of the geographical area of B.C., account for only 3 percent of total student enrollment. For these and other remote districts, providing services, programs, and learning resources that match the more populated school districts is extremely difficult.

More than fifty thousand students—almost 10 percent of the student population—receive English as a Second Language instruction. This number rises significantly each year. Nine percent of all B.C. children under fifteen are of First Nations origin.

The importance of acquiring secondary level education in preparation for **post-secondary education** or training is self-evident from labour market educational demands. Almost three-quarters of all new jobs being created in the province require some post-secondary education or training. Only 13 percent of new jobs are open to people lacking secondary school graduation.

Elasmosaur

In 1988 the fossilized remains of an elasmosaur were discovered on the bank of Puntledge River near Courtenay. Believed to be eighty million years old, this marine reptile fossil is the largest ever discovered in British Columbia, and the first significant fossil discovery in B.C. west of the Rockies. The area of Puntledge River in which the discovery was made has been designated a provincial heritage site.

Elasmosaurs were marine reptiles which lived during the Jurassic and Cretaceous ages. They had a streamlined body, a short tail, two pairs of paddle-like limbs, a long flexible neck, and a tiny head with long interlocking teeth that they used to capture fish.

Among the eighty-two bones excavated from the first elasmosaur discovery site was one that had an elasmosaur tooth deeply lodged in the pad between two vertebrae located high on the neck of the fossil. This has led palaeontologists to speculate that the elasmosaur died during a fight with another of its kind.

Since the first elasmosaur find on Puntledge River, palaeontologists have made two other elasmosaur discoveries on the nearby Trent and Browns rivers.

Endangered Species—B.C. Wildlife Act Designation

Four of the estimated 1,086 vertebrate animal species in B.C. are listed by provincial authorities as endangered. These are the burrowing owl, the American white pelican, the **Vancouver Island** marmot, and the sea otter.

The American robin-sized burrowing owl historically maintained small nesting colonies in the southern **Okanagan Valley**, Similkameen valley, and in the vicinity of **Kamloops**, preferring dry valley-bottom grasslands that constitute only about one percent of the province. These areas have also been heavily encroached by urban and agricultural development, so that very little of the grassland remains in its natural state. By 1980, grassland encroachment and deaths from human interference led biologists to believe the owl was extirpated as a breeding species from B.C. In 1983, an ambitious plan was undertaken to re-establish burrowing owls into the southern Okanagan from Washington State. Wildlife officials transplanted 82 adults and 348 juveniles into recovery areas near Vaseux and Osoyoos lakes over a seven-year period. The owls near Osoyoos Lake were located within the boundaries of the **Okanagan Pocket Desert** Federal Ecological Reserve, 7.5 kilometres north of Osoyoos. A recovery team worked in the reserve to improve the chances of the owl population's survival. Between 1986 and 1992, eighty-seven of the introduced owls returned as adults and produced a total of about ninety offspring. But the population is only tenuously established and return figures vary erratically from year to year. In 1994, for example, only one burrowing owl was believed to have returned in the summer to the south Okanagan, raising serious doubts that the recovery program can succeed.

Approximately three hundred Vancouver Island marmots remain, mostly concentrated in alpine areas of the south island. Resembling a woodchuck, these chocolate-coloured animals are also the focus of a recovery team, which is using radio-tagging methods to track the animals and help improve their propagation levels.

Before 1900, ruthless hunting of sea otters for their valuable pelts had eliminated all but a few found in Alaska and California. Formerly the otters had thrived throughout the shallow seas of the north Pacific Ocean, ranging from Japan to California. In the late 1960s and early 1970s a small number of these survivors were re-introduced to B.C. waters from Alaska. Now there are about eight hundred in B.C. Most live in the waters of Checleset Bay, an ecological reserve off northwest Vancouver Island, near Fair Harbour, thirty-five kilometres northwest of Zeballos. A smaller colony inhabits Bajo Reef, near Vancouver Island's Nootka Sound.

B.C.'s only nesting colony of American white pelicans is located at Stum Lake in the Chilcotin region, seventy kilometres west of Williams Lake. Approximately four hundred nests are established annually on various small islands in the lake. The lake is protected as White Pelican Provincial Park.

(*See also* **Biodiversity**.)

Environmental Conflict

With an economy founded on natural resource extraction, especially by the **forest** and **mining** industries, British Columbians and the provincial government—as was true throughout most of Canada and the world—paid scant attention to environmental preservation until the 1960s when environmental and conservation movements developed. These movements were primarily a result of growing public concern that the massive industrialization between 1945 and the early 1960s was generating previously unknown levels of environmental pollution and causing the destruction of the province's habitat.

Prior to the early 1960s the only concerted environmental movements in British Columbia were found among naturalists, often scientists engaged in natural science research or avid outdoor recreationalists, who witnessed the destruction of wildlife habitats by logging and mining operations. Their response was usually to try and work within the political and economic system to win recognition for the need to consider environmental protection in resource exploitation planning. This strategy was only somewhat effective, although a number of provincial and national parks did result from such efforts.

In the 1960s environmentalism became a popular movement—drawing on a broad base of British Columbians for participants and financial support. **Greenpeace**, the Sierra Club of Canada, and other such groups emerged during the late 1960s and early 1970s. Throughout the 1970s the province's environmental movements grew and broadened their popular support base.

By the 1980s, government and industry could no longer afford to disregard the concerns of the public that resource exploitation operations and planning be undertaken in concert with environmental protection. Within government and industry there was also a growing recognition that past natural resource extraction methods had resulted in long-term environmental damage and that new practices were necessary. Many plans, such as major diversions of waterways for irrigation and power generating purposes, died while still in the early planning phase because such undertakings were no longer acceptable to the public. It was, for example, recognized by the provincial government that a major dam construction program such as the **Columbia River Treaty**, which raised the levels of lakes in the Kootenays and submerged large tracts of land, would be politically unacceptable in the new environmentally conscious climate.

In the mid- to late-1980s the ongoing period of intense conflict between environmental advocates and organizations on one side and industry, business, and government on the other emerged. The provincial government's role in this struggle is somewhat nebulous. In most cases it has tended to align with business and industry in refuting environmentalist claims and blocking their demands for improved resource exploitation regulations, practices, and management, but at the same time has introduced extensive legislation that has served to protect the environment and led to the creation of protected tracts of land. Often these environmentally friendly steps on the part of government have come following intense lobbying by the environmental movement, backed by extensive public support.

By the early- to mid-1990s, the level of environmental conflict intensified and today shows no sign of lessening. Industry and business increasingly complain that environmental protection legislation and practices threaten their ability to continue resource-extraction operations. The environmental movement argues that sustainability of the province's environmental diversity is imperilled unless major resource extraction practices are either curtailed or strictly regulated.

Industry and environmentalists regularly square off over the fate of specific regions of the province, which are often referred to as environmental hot spots. The number and size of these areas are increasing rapidly as the forest and mining industries, in particular, seek to exploit new—often more remote and untouched—areas of B.C. When such an area is targeted for either mining or forest extraction, the environmental movements work locally, provincially, nationally, and sometimes internationally to pressure government into preventing or greatly limiting the harvesting of forests in that area or the opening of large-scale mining operations.

Ancient temperate **rainforests** and other old-growth forest regions of the province are major flashpoints for conflict. In every region of the province there are areas that have been targeted by industry for resource extraction that environmental movements are trying to prevent by having the government grant the area some form of protected status. On **Vancouver Island** such areas include **Clayoquot Sound**, the Kyuquot area, Tahsish River, Robson Bight, and Tsitika River south of Telegraph Cove. On the mainland, environmentalists are seeking protection for such areas as: the **Stein River Valley** west of Lytton; the Chilko Lake/Taseko River/Big Creek area and the Blue Lead Creek Watershed; the **Stikine River** and **Kitlope** watershed between Fiordlord Recreation Area and **Tweedsmuir Provincial Park**; and, in the **Rocky Mountains**, Elk Valley.

For its part, the provincial government has tried to cool off the conflict by bringing industry, business, and the environmental movement together to negotiate future land-use strategies for the entire province and specific environmental hot spots. In 1992, the government initiated a protected-areas strategy with the intention of doubling parks and wilderness areas from 6 percent to 12 percent of the province's total area by the year 2000. It also implemented the Commission on Resources and Environment **(CORE)** to develop a comprehensive land-use strategy which attempted to gain overall consensus from all parties on how the province's natural resources and lands should be used. To date, the government's strategies remain highly controversial, with neither industry, business, the environmental movement, nor a more recent player in the disputes—the **First Nations peoples**—agreeing on what the province's future land-use practices should be. In the meantime, the conflicts, including demonstrations and road-blocking efforts at various hot spots, continue with little sign of abating.

Ethnicity

About 40 percent of the province's population is of British extraction. A further 30 percent is drawn from other European groups, with Germanic people making up almost 8 percent of this number.

British Columbia's largest non-European ethnic group is Chinese, who constitute 9 percent of the population. The other two major ethnic groups in

B.C. are East Indians (4.4 percent) and **First Nations peoples** (3.7 percent). Other Asian groups as a whole represent 5.5 percent of the population.

Eulachon. *See* **Oolichan.**

Eurasian Watermilfoil

In 1970, Eurasian watermilfoil was first discovered growing in Okanagan Lake. Various theories exist as to how it got established, ranging from the most likely that it was carried into the lake's waters on the bottom of a boat from out-of-province to someone dumping the contents of a tropical aquarium into the lake. Whatever the source, Eurasian watermilfoil firmly established itself on the lake's shallow, silty bottom and has since clogged most beaches.

This aquatic weed has also spread to many other lakes throughout the province. It is established in **Shuswap** and Mara lakes to the **Okanagan Valley**'s north, in Christina and Campion lakes in the Kootenays, and in lakes throughout the Lower Mainland. In 1985, isolated pockets were discovered in several lakes on **Vancouver Island**, and in the interior's Nicola Lake in 1991. Many other B.C. lakes remain susceptible to Eurasian watermilfoil's introduction.

The aquatic plant grows and spreads rapidly. During the primary spring- and summer-growth season, it can reach the water surface from depths exceeding five metres. Floating plant fragments produced by waves and boaters spread on currents, making the plant difficult to contain. New plants develop when the fragments sink and take root, most often in protected locations such as inlets and sheltered beach areas. The plant is usually spread from one lake to another by recreational boaters carrying plant fragments attached to the boat's hull or entangled in the engine props.

Eurasian watermilfoil can have devastating effects on the natural ecosystem of a lake because it invades and replaces native-plant communities. The aquatic plant also obstructs swimming, boating, water skiing, and fishing.

Boaters can help control the spread of the weed by ensuring all plant materials are cleared from hulls, motors, trailers, wet wells, and anchors before launching, and that any weeds found are disposed of well away from water bodies.

Exploration. *See* **Historical Overview.**

Expo 86

The international exposition, Expo 86, which opened in **Vancouver** on May 2, 1986, and closed October 1, 1986, was attended by more than twenty million people, and was the largest single-theme exposition ever held. The theme statement "World in Motion—World in Touch" was symbolized by a logo of three concentric circles using the figures eight and six intersecting to represent transportation by land, sea, and air. The statement reflected the fair's theme of transportation and communications.

Expo 86 was held on two downtown Vancouver sites. The main exhibition grounds were located on a sixty-seven-hectare site running for 4.5 kilometres along the north and east shores of False Creek. The Canada Pavilion was located off the main site on a three-hectare plot of land adjacent to Burrard Inlet. Using the land site as an anchoring point, the 10,800-square-metre Canada Pavilion was extended 3.5 city blocks into the inlet. A dramatic white building, with the mountains, water, and city serving as a backdrop, was constructed to resemble a ship with five large "sails" of suspended fabric. The pavilion, which cost $145 million, now serves as a convention centre and cruise ship terminal.

In all, there were sixty-five pavilions at Expo 86, composed of forty-one international, seven provincial, two from Canada's territories, three from American states, nine from corporations, as well as two theme pavilions and a special pavilion containing treasures from the life of the Egyptian pharaoh Ramses II.

Expenditures for the fair were $802 million and revenues generated were $491 million. The final deficit was $311 million. It has been calculated, however, that the Canadian economy, especially that of Vancouver, received an extra $3.1 billion boost as a result of Expo 86. Further, Vancouver's SkyTrain light-rail transit system was partly funded through the Expo 86 initiative, the waterfront of False Creek was greatly revitalized by the fair, and Canada Pavilion remains an important factor in fuelling the city's growing convention and trade show industry.

For many British Columbians another side benefit of the fair was the loosening of the province's **liquor laws**. Worried that international tourists would be offended or inconvenienced by laws requiring closure of all drinking establishments on Sundays, the provincial government allowed Sunday openings. Initially, this was planned only for the duration of Expo 86, but following the fair's closure the Sunday openings were allowed to continue without a murmur of public protest.

Exports. *See* **Economy.**

Fairweather Mountain

With an elevation of 4,663 metres, Fairweather Mountain in the province's extreme northwest corner is B.C.'s highest peak. Part of the **St. Elias Mountains**, Fairweather's western and southern flanks lie in Alaska. The fact that Fairweather is not wholly within B.C. often leads to the province's second-highest mountain, **Mount Waddington** (elevation 4,016 metres), being reported as the highest peak.

Ferries. *See* British Columbia Ferry Corporation.

Film Industry. *See* Cultural History.

First Nations Art

Throughout British Columbia, designs that varied greatly both in subject and style adorned the houses, graves, weapons, domestic utensils, and occasionally the bodies of **First Nations peoples**. The traditions, designs, styles, and many of the methods of artwork practised before the arrival of Europeans to the province are still used by many native artists.

Most coastal art depicted realistic animals that were part of the natural environment as well as the symbolic or spiritual essence associated with the animal.

Interior native art was less clearly realistic, often containing geometrical designs with no apparent purpose beyond adornment of an object. In most cases, however, these designs were intended to represent reality. Many basket designs of the Interior and Coast Salishan and the Dene peoples, for example, which often appear to be simple geometrical patterns, have such names as "flying geese," "arrowhead," and "snake track."

Native art traditionally involved creation of objects designed to lines of symmetry and balance that allowed easy handling and efficient usage. The designs, then, were selected to conform to the shape and function of the object. A bowl, as with most other artistic creations, was designed firstly to serve its function as a container and secondly was adorned with imagery to transform it into artwork.

Although coastal art was more realistic in its imagery of the natural world than was true of the art of Interior peoples, the images were highly complex and somewhat abstracted because of the challenge of portraying a three-

This Kwakwaka'wakw wolf mask made in 1893 is part of the Royal BC Museum's collection. (Royal BC Museum Artifact No. 18)

dimensional subject on a two-dimensional plane. To achieve this, coastal natives commonly resorted to dissecting the image of an animal into its various parts laid out on one plane and arranged to conform to principles of balance and harmony rather than trying to depict the animal's body accurately in both scale and form. Often, other images were interlaced within the body parts of the subject animal to symbolize the mythological or spiritual relationship of the animal to the native people.

Most B.C. native peoples, as was true of the majority of First Nations peoples, did not have a tradition of art unrelated to practical application of the work created. Even those B.C. peoples that created personal ornaments, such as the Nuu-chah-nulth and Haida, did so primarily as an illustration of the wearer's status in the community. The ornate and highly complex masks carved from wood by the peoples of the coast and to a lesser extent in the interior were created to serve religious and performing-arts purposes.

First Nations Basketry and Weaving

Baskets filled an important place in the domestic life of most British Columbian **First Nations peoples**, except for those in the northwest portion of the province who tended to use wooden cedar boxes. Two major basket-making techniques prevailed—woven basketry and coiled-sewn basketry. There were five types of weaves used: chequer-work, twilled work, wickerwork, wrapped weft, and twined work. Chequer-work involved using materials of the same width, thickness, and pliability for both warp and weft. Twilled work entailed using two or more weft strands to pass over a matching number of warp strands. In wickerwork, a thin flexible weft was woven on stiff warp strands. Wrapped weft involved wrapping the weft strand around each warp strand. Twined work was produced by making a weft strand composed of several pieces of material twisted together.

Coiled basketry used either wide splints of pliable wood or inner bark, or else bundles of split cedar or spruce root. Both materials yielded baskets of great symmetry and beauty. Those made from split cedar or spruce root also could hold water for cooking purposes.

Patterns on the woven baskets were made by the use of dyed grasses worked in with the weft strands. A method called imbrication—using strips of material, such as bark or dyed rushes, to overlap and double under the overcast stitching—was also used. Patterning through the imbrication method was unique to First Nations peoples west of the **Rocky Mountains** and north of the **Columbia River**.

In B.C., the art of weaving reached its highest peak of perfection in the coastal areas, where the populations were settled and non-nomadic. The nomadic Interior peoples relied more on hides for clothing and bark for container material. Their weaving techniques were consequently simpler in form and design.

A wide variety of materials was used for weaving by the coastal peoples. Among the poorer classes, shredded bark was used for capes and aprons. Wealthy upper-class natives wore blankets and robes woven from goat wool and dog hair. Bark, rushes, and roots were used for making mats, bags, and hats. Duck down and the cotton from fireweed and other plants were woven into fabric to produce a finer texture in the woollen articles. Weavers utilized forms of both the spindle and loom.

First Nations Land Claims

Throughout Canada, **First Nations peoples** are engaged in a complex series of negotiations with federal and provincial governments over land claims that individual aboriginal nations have to vast tracts of both urban and rural territory. The validity of these claims is rooted in the historical development of the native peoples' legal relationships initially with the government of Britain and eventually, after Confederation in 1867, with the Canadian federal government.

In 1763, Britain issued a Royal Proclamation recognizing First Nations rights in Canada. The proclamation reserved traditional hunting grounds for the exclusive use of native people, and stated that native lands could only be purchased by the Crown through government-to-government negotiations.

At the time of the proclamation British Columbia was administered by the Hudson's Bay Company, but was not part of the Hudson's Bay Company's vast territory known as Rupert's Land, which included most of Canada, and to which the proclamation was generally considered to apply. For this reason, until 1991 when the provincial government recognized the proclamation's entitlement ruling applied to land within B.C., successive provincial governments argued that B.C. natives did not have the same entitlement to land claims as did native peoples in the rest of Canada.

Despite this long-term provincial government position there was precedent in B.C. history for recognition of the proclamation's applicability to British Columbia's First Nations peoples. From the time that James Douglas became chief factor in 1839 of all of the Hudson's Bay Company's territory in what would become British Columbia, Douglas systematically entered into formal relationships with the native peoples. He continued this practice after becoming the province's first governor in 1858, and before that as the governor of **Vancouver Island** from 1851 to 1858.

It was primarily in his role as governor of Vancouver Island that Douglas formally recognized First Nations rights and sought to purchase land from the original inhabitants. Between 1851 and 1860, Douglas ratified fourteen treaties, known as the Douglas Treaties, on Vancouver Island.

In 1860, Douglas was blocked from entering into further treaties by the British Colonial Office's refusal to supply any further funds for such purchases. To both protect the native land claim rights and enable unhindered European movement outside designated lands, Douglas ordered existing native village sites and other lands throughout the Colony set aside for exclusive use of native people in the province. These land allocations were, however, even further reduced by later administrations without consulting the native people living there.

With Confederation in 1867, Canada's federal government was given, under the Constitution Act, sole jurisdiction and "responsibility for Indians and lands belonging to Indians." In 1871, when B.C. joined Confederation, the federal government assumed control of all First Nations lands. In 1876, the federal government formalized its relationship with native peoples by invoking the Indian Act. Under the terms of this act, special privileges and protections were granted to on-reserve natives throughout Canada and its territories, including an exemption from taxation. The federal government assumed control over status designation, as well as band structure, activities, property rights, band assets, and education. In effect, the federal government controlled virtually all aspects of on-reserve native government and social organization. Although the act would be revised four times over the next 118 years, it would remain a punitive and discriminatory legislative instrument that effectively stripped native people of fundamental control over their destiny and the right to exert their rights to property.

The Indian Act effectively scuttled the framework established by James Douglas for reaching treaty settlements, as various committees established after 1876 to oversee the issue of land entitlement were denied a mandate to negotiate official treaties between the federal government and native peoples. As European settlers flooded into British Columbia, the question of whether First Nations peoples were entitled to any claims to their traditional lands became increasingly controversial. For the next century only one formal treaty agreement between the federal and provincial governments and native peoples would be entered into. This was Treaty Eight, signed by five native bands from the **Peace River** area between 1900 and 1914.

Meanwhile, in 1912, the Nisga'a (then known as Nishga) tribal council initiated the first legally constituted native land claim action over ownership of their traditional lands along the Nass River in northwestern B.C. For sixty-seven years the Nisga'a continued to advance their claim until finally they launched direct legal action in 1969. The Nisga'a tribal council declared in its suit against the federal and provincial governments that its aboriginal title to lands in the Nass Valley had never been extinguished because of the Nisga'a's continuous occupation of those lands, including non-reserve land the Indian Act had forced them to abandon in order to live on prescribed reserve land.

Initially dismissed in B.C. courts, the Nisga'a took their claim to the Supreme Court of Canada and in 1973 the court recognized that aboriginal title could exist in common law. The court, however, split three to three over the validity of the Nisga'a claim and Chief Justice Pigeon tipped the balance against the Nisga'a on a procedural point—that permission to sue the B.C. government had first to be obtained from the province's attorney general before a lawsuit could be launched. Although Nisga'a Chief Frank Arthur Calder lost his case, the recognition by the court that native people could claim title to their lands under common law had a landmark effect as it provided a legal context under which the federal government considered itself legally obligated to resume comprehensive treaty negotiations with native peoples. The Supreme Court of Canada decision is now known as the Calder Decision.

Since 1973, treaty negotiations between the federal government and the province's native peoples have continued based on acceptance of the principle that First Nations peoples have status as the province's first inhabitants.

For seventeen years the provincial government refused to participate in these treaty negotiations, but in 1990 agreed to participate in talks with the Nisga'a Tribal Council which led to establishment of a Treaty Framework Agreement. It also established the British Columbia Claims Task Force to make recommendations to government on how to negotiate treaties. In 1991, the provincial government recognized the concept of aboriginal rights and self-government. It also expressed willingness to end decades of indifference and share the costs of treaty settlements in British Columbia.

On May 18, 1993, the provincial government passed the Treaty Commission Legislation, establishing the B.C. Treaty Commission. The commission is an independent body of five representatives appointed by the federal and provincial governments and the First Nations people. It serves as an umbrella organization overseeing the resolution of treaties in B.C.

Modern-day treaty negotiations between federal and provincial governments, and First Nations tribal councils are lengthy and complex, most treaties taking years to settle. There are a number of steps in the process, which begins when a First Nations tribal council files a Statement of Intent to negotiate with the B.C. Treaty Commission. A timetable and the substance and objective of each specific claim must be agreed upon by all parties. After further negotiations, agreements in principle are struck and, only when all details have been ironed out to the satisfaction of all parties involved, final agreements are signed and implemented. It is recognized by the governments involved that the process of redressing a century of indifference to and violation of First Nations land claims will require decades of negotiation to resolve all outstanding and still-to-be-declared land claims.

First Nations Peoples

Archaeologists generally agree that human habitation of the Western Hemisphere occurred in most regions no more than ten to fifteen thousand years ago and first occurring no earlier than thirty thousand years ago. Habitation is believed to have begun with the recession of the glacial age when peoples from other continents started to enter the Western Hemisphere. There is no evidence of humankind having evolved independently anywhere in the hemisphere.

Although there are several theories regarding where and when the migration of humans into the Western Hemisphere took place, the generally agreed upon theory is that of Asiatic migrations out of what is present-day Siberia via a land bridge crossing the Bering Sea into Alaska. These migratory populations were the ancestors of the First Nations peoples that eventually established a presence throughout North and South America—including British Columbia.

These migrant populations did not enter North America in a steady stream or even a constant trickle; rather it appears they came in a series of pulses to the narrow Bering Strait entranceway to the continent. Having entered North America, they drifted east and south along ice-free corridors, especially, at first, by an ice-free route that stretched through several Alaska and Yukon valleys to a gap between the two great glacial ice masses that existed to the east of the **Rocky Mountains**. It was this gap that is believed to have encouraged the oldest migrating groups to continue moving southward deeper into North America and even South America.

At this time, glacial ice thickly covered most of British Columbia and it would not be until the retreat of the ice between eight thousand and fifteen thousand years ago that the First Nations peoples started entering the province. Some undoubtedly migrated south down newly exposed ice-free corridors between the major north-south running mountain ranges. Others are believed to have circled into the province's southern portions from the larger eastern corridor.

The First Nations' ancestors were nomadic peoples—living by hunting and gathering. There is little evidence to support their having any significant knowledge of agriculture. They knew how to trap animals, how to make fire, and how to build crude boats or rafts. They relied solely on gathering wild vegetation and berries to supplement their meat-based diet. Later groups brought with them the bow and arrow and other innovations, such as improved stonework and basketry.

The First Nations peoples involved in the migratory phase were not of one racial or ethnic grouping. They did not share a common language or customs. It is believed that their linguistic groups were as varied as those of Europe. At the time of the European discoveries, for example, it is believed there were some eleven languages and forty dialects in Canada alone. Of these languages, at least six were represented by the peoples living in British Columbia.

Migration from Asia to North America is believed to have ceased abruptly six to eight thousand years ago. The cause of this cessation is unknown. Geological evidence indicates that land fold changes may have broken the Bering Strait passageway, making it hazardous for non-seagoing peoples to risk the crossing. There is also evidence that many glacial types of animals in parts of Alaska suddenly perished in some kind of mass destruction. Perhaps this unknown natural cataclysm made conditions in the region untenable or unattractive to human passage as well.

About fifteen thousand years ago the first native peoples started to drift into parts of British Columbia. The first human habitation appears to have occurred in the **Peace River** region. Eventually two major linguistic groups established the largest presence within the province—the Athapaskan (or Dene), and the Salishan. Both tongues contain many dialects or sublanguages, some of which are not mutually understood.

These two peoples are divided roughly by a line running southwest from the Alberta-British Columbia border in the vicinity of the **Fraser River** headwaters to the head of Bute Inlet.

The northern native people were the Dene, subdivided into six groups: Dene-thah, Dunne-za, Sekani, Tahltan, Kaska, and Inland Tlingit. The Salishan, inhabiting much of the southern portion of the province, were subdivided into two major groups—the Coast Salishan and Interior Salishan, which further broke down into several dialect groups. Although the Salishan peoples were related by language, the way of life between the two groups and, in some cases, within their subgroups was widely divergent and the languages developed in isolation, leading to the emergence of various dialects.

These two peoples are believed to have migrated into the province from the east and are related by language to the plains First Nations peoples. The Ktunaxa (formerly Kutenai or Kootenay) are believed to have entered B.C. from the south and their language is distinct.

On the western half of **Vancouver Island**, the Nuu-chah-nulth and Ditidaht cultures (formerly known jointly as Nootka) extend from Port Renfrew in the south to Quatsino Sound in the north. These two groups are part of the same linguistic group as the Kwakwaka'wakw (formerly known as Kwakiutl), whose lands incorporate northern Vancouver Island and two large regions of the coastal mainland extending north to the **Skeena River** but broken by an intrusion of Salishan known by Europeans as the Bella Coola, and now called the Nuxalk. The Nuxalk took on many aspects of their more numerous and powerful Kwakwaka'wakw neighbours, while retaining their own unique language.

To the north of the Nuxalk is found a great diversity of native peoples who used to be grouped by Europeans under the umbrella of the Tsimshian, despite variations in language and culture. These are the Heiltsuk and Nuxalk (who both spoke dialects of Kwakwaka'wakw), and the Haisla, Tsimshian, Gitksan, and Nisga'a. These groups of First Nations peoples inhabit the mainland and coastal archipelago in the vicinity of the Nass and Skeena rivers. Inland from these are the Wet'suwet'en (who speak a dialect of Dakelhne or Carrier) and the Dakelhne (formerly Carrier) who have a territory extending east all the way to the Alberta border.

The last major native group is the Haida of the **Queen Charlotte Islands** and the southern portion of Prince of Wales Island.

First Nations Religion

Before the coming of Europeans the **First Nations peoples** of British Columbia believed primarily in animism. Under this belief, every object, animate or
inanimate, such as trees, mountains, fish, animals, tools, weapons, and domestic utensils possesses a spirit which, if properly approached, can be in-
duced to respond to a human's needs or desires. If improperly approached,
especially through insufficient demonstration of respect, the spirit will likely
refuse to cooperate. As a consequence of this belief a great deal of ceremony,
use of incantations, and spells was common in day-to-day activity. Incantations were directed at mountains in hopes of bringing rain, to trees to bear
fruit, and to animals and fish to allow themselves to be caught.

Achieving ceremonial purity through fasting, use of spell-casting medita-
tion, and other ceremonies was perceived as enabling the practitioners to influence the spirit world favourably.

The name of an object or person was viewed as an intricate part of that
being and carried its own powerful value. To know someone's name, then, was
to have a certain degree of power over that person. For this reason, names
were usually kept secret from all except those close to the holder.

Animistic beliefs were also the basis of the guardian-spirit theory, prevalent throughout North American First Nations peoples. Through puberty trials
youths experienced a revelation in the form of a dream or trance that revealed
a spirit that would be intimately related, and a source of strength and wisdom,
to them in their adult existence.

The guardian-spirit theory had many variations among the people of the
province. Northern coastal natives sought to be accepted by ancestral guardian spirits so they could participate in secret societies and be eligible to use
the songs and dances, and enjoy the privileges of the family group. Puberty
trials, here, were a sort of "coming out" ceremony. Among interior peoples
the guardian spirit was an individual spirit guide and did not influence a person's relationship within the family. Many guardian-spirit powers were believed to be directly related to a specific ability. A Coast Salishan believed to
have "wolf power," for example, would be perceived as a great hunter. The
spirit with which the person was associated was never perceived to have entered the person; only the specific power or attribute of the spirit became a
part of the person. Shamans, however, were believed to lose their identity and
become the incarnation of the spirit itself when visited by a guardian spirit.
Both men and women possessed guardian spirits, although it was usually the
spirits of various pieces of domestic equipment that provided powers to women.

There were many taboos existent in native religious beliefs. Some objects
and places were considered to have spirits that were antagonistic to humans.

Also, certain actions might turn a guardian spirit against the individual. If a person's guardian spirit was believed to reside in a living creature, for example, it was taboo to kill or eat the flesh of that creature. Certain types of behaviour, either at all times or during specific activities, was also taboo. When the Haida departed on raids and wars their behaviour became highly ritualized to avoid violating a taboo. This extended to the order in which war canoes were manned and the position that the wives of warriors assumed for sleep while their men were away on a raid. To break the taboo in any way was believed to lead to misfortune befalling the community. At puberty, children of both sexes were subject to many taboos on their eating habits and general behaviour. If a taboo was violated only a long and involved ceremony could pacify the spirits and avert dire consequences.

Due to the profusion of spirits and forces at work in the native peoples' spiritual view, anything reflective of a hierarchical religion did not exist prior to the imposition of such beliefs by European influence. Any concept of a supreme being was only given scant attention. It was generally accepted that some spirit had created the world or given birth to their peoples and this spirit was acknowledged in ceremonies, but the various spirits of the everyday world were given far more attention because they were of immediate and ongoing relevance.

The closest the native peoples had to a priesthood was the presence in most communities of a shaman. The shaman was believed to have the power to control a human's soul and so was more potent in appealing to spirits, especially in exorcising evil influence and mischievous spirits. The influence shamans exerted on their group was more powerful in the loosely integrated interior nomadic groups. The settled village communities of the coast gave greater authority to chiefs and wealthy upper-class members and relegated the shaman to a combination of community doctor and spiritual adviser or intermediary. Within some communities there were several shamans, who competed for trade or specialized in treating specific ailments and afflictions. The various spells, incantations, dances, and procedures used by shamans differed in detail from group to group and from one practitioner to another. Fire and water usually played a large part in all magic. Not all shamans would participate in the placing of evil spells on a supplicant's enemies, and in some native groups such activity was illegal or viewed as unethical, especially if applied against a member of the local community. Such offences were often punishable by death or banishment.

Shamanism was not restricted to men, but women shamans were generally perceived to be less powerful. Their activities were usually restricted to treatment of women's ailments and assisting with childbirth.

Knowledge of their complex spirit world was passed on by all native peoples through an extensive tradition of folklore based on legends and myths that were related through oral tales, dramatic performances, dance ceremonies, and some forms of artwork. This folklore can be divided roughly into three classes: those dealing with supernatural beings and their world before the coming of the native peoples or transpiring during the earliest period of a peoples' existence; those of humans engaged in activities with other humans or the mystical forces of nature; and those dealing with the adventures of legendary ancestors of a specific family.

The stories of ancient mythology were of religious importance. These included the stories of the Transformers, such as Coyote and Raven, who changed the material world in specific ways and dealt with other supernatural beings. They also included tales of a Supreme Being who created the universe and, in past times, wandered the earth altering things which the Transformers had done badly, or sometimes in disguised form competing with them in contests of magic power. During this time, animals and humans were believed to have shared a common language and animals were capable of assuming human form.

Prior to European contact these tales contained little in the way of moral overtones and whatever benefits fell to humans were usually a chance by-product of the spirit's self-serving actions. Later, perhaps due to the influence of European Christian beliefs, the Transformers emerged more as supernatural mediators between the spirit world and unfortunate humans. There were also legends that spoke of a golden age of peace and plenty from which humans were cast out because of greed, covetousness, uncleanliness, and spite, which were seen as undesirable qualities by the spirit world. Instead, possession of the qualities of kindliness, hospitality, and purity of mind and body were the best means of gaining cooperation from the supernatural world.

Fish. See Aquaculture; Salmon; Salmonid Enhancement.

Fish Farms. See Aquaculture.

Fishing—Recreational

British Columbia has a reputation as one of the continent's best locations for both salt and freshwater recreational fishing. Given the province's long **coastlines** and multitude of inland waterways this is hardly surprising.

The best saltwater fishing is found on various parts of **Vancouver Island**, especially around Campbell River (where chinook **salmon** often top twenty-two kilograms) at Alberni Inlet, Rivers Inlet, and off Tofino and Ucluelet.

Saltwater recreational fishing is generally for chinook, coho, and spring salmon, as well as lingcod and halibut.

Freshwater fishing is good throughout the province. Primary fish are steelhead (sea-run rainbow trout), rainbow trout, cut-throat trout, Dolly Varden, and kokanee (land-locked sockeye).

Licences are required for anyone fishing in tidal waters. All freshwater anglers over sixteen years old require an angling licence. Licences are sold in many sporting good stores, department stores, and marinas. They are also available from various government agencies.

Tidal waters in Canada fall under the administrative jurisdiction of the federal Department of Fisheries and Oceans, and freshwater areas of the province are administered and regulated by the provincial government's fish and wildlife branch.

Fishing Industry

With an approximate annual value of about $1 billion in wholesale seafood production, the B.C. fishing industry is a major contributor to the provincial economy. The number one food export, seafood generates about $750 million with shipments going to more than fifty nations.

The industry provides full- and part-time employment for about twenty-five thousand people on boats, at fish farms, and in processing plants. There are approximately six thousand fishing boats in the Canadian Pacific coast fishing fleet and about 670 farms practising **aquaculture**.

Although the province's fishing industry is heavily concentrated on the harvesting and processing of wild and farmed **salmon**, a total of eighty-three aquatic species are harvested in B.C. Salmon, however, accounts for nearly 60 percent of the industry's annual wholesale value—approximately $530 mil-

A fishing boat operates in the rich fishery of Dixon Entrance in the Queen Charlotte Islands. (BCARS photo I-15467)

lion. In landed tonnage, about one-third of all fish harvested in the province are salmon, with about 50 percent of these being sockeye salmon.

In terms of wholesale values—after salmon—the most valuable fish in B.C. is herring, especially the harvest of roe herring (about $162 million of the total herring value of

$176 million), followed by groundfish catches, of which the most valuable are rockfish, sole, sablefish, Pacific cod, and shellfish—primarily geoduck, sea urchins, and crabs.

Very little of B.C. fishing industry activity is centred on the province's fresh waterways. There is a small trout-farming sector that maintains pen farms in mostly interior area lakes and rivers. Its total wholesale value, however, is only about $600,000.

The rest of the industry is focused on the province's Pacific coastal waters. Tidal waters fall under the jurisdiction of the federal government in Canada, so the fishing industry's primary operations are regulated and controlled by the federal Department of Fisheries and Oceans, which enforces the Fisheries Act. The act extends federal jurisdiction into the province's freshwater areas for management and protection of fish stocks and spawning grounds.

On January 1, 1977, Canada extended its jurisdiction over ocean coastlines to 370 kilometres offshore, commonly known as the two-hundred-mile limit. Any fishing vessels operating inside this boundary, regardless of the flag under which they sail, are regulated and subject to the laws of the Canadian Fisheries Act. Since the two-hundred-mile designation, there have been various legal skirmishes between Canadian enforcement authorities and non-Canadian fishers over their operations in Canada's waters.

A major decline in salmon stocks along the Pacific coast of North America has led to increases in violations of Canada's territorial waters by fishers from other countries—chiefly the United States. Serious conflicts between Canada and the U.S. over fishing issues on the Pacific coast are, however, mostly averted as a result of the terms of the 1985 Pacific Salmon Treaty, which provides initiatives for joint-national fishery management, a coordinated fish stock restoration program, and harvest sharing.

The primary reason for Canada enforcing the two-hundred-mile limit was the fact that the bulk of the fish stocks hug coastal shorelines to remain in the shallower waters of the Continental Shelf. In the late 1960s, and intensively in the early 1970s, Japanese, Russian, Polish, and other foreign fishing operations began overfishing off Canada's coast through the use of large factory freezer-trawler fleets that could remain on station for weeks at a time without returning to home ports to unload their catches. Extending its territorial limit allowed Canada to restrict and regulate the operations of these fleets. Canada's fishing fleet, especially on the Pacific coast, is primarily composed of smaller vessels—under twenty-five gross tonnes.

There are about 210 fish processing and packing plants in B.C., mostly located in the Lower Mainland or on **Vancouver Island**, or centred around **Prince Rupert**'s large fishing fleet. For some of the small coastal communities the fishing industry is a major part of their economic infrastructure. Tofino, on Vancouver Island's west coast, is a good case in point. Fully 25 percent of the community's adult workforce is employed year-round by the community's fish processing plants and numerous fish farm operations.

Flag. *See* Symbols.

Football. *See* British Columbia Lions.

Forest Fires

As most of British Columbia is heavily forested the province is especially prone to forest fires, also known as wildfires. On average, B.C. suffers 34 percent of the total wildfires in Canada—about twenty-nine hundred annually. Forty-eight percent of these fires are caused by lightning, the other 52 percent by people. The average area burned each year is about 34,800 hectares.

In terms of area burned, the worst fire year on record in B.C. was 1958, when 835,876 hectares were burned by 3,058 fires. The damage to **forests** during these blazes reflected the relative inadequacy of fire-fighting techniques at the time. By comparison, in 1994—the worst fire season in B.C. history as far as numbers of fires—only 28,380 hectares were burned by 4,068 fires. The 1994 year was not only a record in numbers of fires, but an unusually large number of the fires resulted from lightning strikes. A single lightning storm sweeping across the province from August 3 to August 5 delivered an unprecedented fifty-one thousand lightning strikes and triggered more than twelve hundred fires. Nationally in 1994, B.C. had 43 percent of the country's wildfires, but lost less than one percent of its forest to fire damage.

B.C.'s fire-fighting forces have undergone a major advance in technology and tactics since the early 1970s. Each fire season, squadrons of air tankers equipped with turbine engines deploy across the province. When a fire is detected the planes attack the blaze by dropping large amounts of chemical fire retardant both on and around the fire to contain its spread.

Fire detection technology was extensively upgraded and computerized during the 1980s, including development of a sophisticated lightning detection system. Also developed in the 1980s was the rapattack program, which uses helicopters to airlift trained fire-fighting crews into isolated fire sites within hours of a fire being detected so it can be swiftly brought under control.

The 1994 fire season, given its extremely favourable fire conditions of low humidity, high temperatures, prevailing winds, and severe lightning storms, was a major test of the efficiency of the province's fire-fighting program. The program operated by the Forest Protection Branch of the B.C. Ministry of Forests proved successful in limiting forest fire damage, but the cost in controlling these fires was about $79 million.

Forest Industry

Forty-six percent of British Columbia (43.3 million hectares) is covered by **forests**. This massive land base supports more than eight billion cubic metres of mature timber. About 96 percent of this timber is coniferous, giving the province approximately half of the national softwood. Western hemlock is the predominant coast forest species, while spruce and pine are the major interior species.

Since the beginning of European settlement, the forest lands have been a dominant factor in the province's **economy**. Major development of forest resources, however, did not start until after completion of the Canadian Pacific Railway in 1886. Development then expanded rapidly as transportation systems within the province, as well as nationally and internationally, improved. Pulp production began in Western Canada in 1909 at a mill in **Powell River**, while Fraser Mills, near **New Westminster**, began producing plywood in 1913. In the early 1900s, coastal sawmills prospered by exporting lumber to world markets. Until World War I, interior sawmills depended on local markets but at war's end underwent a boom, providing lumber to house settlers moving into the prairie provinces.

From 1918 the growth of the forest industry in B.C. was rapid. Pulp and paper mills, producing sulphite pulp and newsprint, were built at sites throughout the province, but were especially concentrated on the West Coast, where many rivers and dense forests offered abundant water, energy, and wood supplies. Following World War II, the rapidly rising demand for paper products shifted the emphasis to kraft or sulphate pulp.

Until the end of World War II, B.C.'s forest industry was largely unregulated. In some areas close to population centres, sawmills, and ports for exportation of forest products, the forest land was intensively logged well before the outbreak of World War II. **Vancouver Island**'s east coast, for example, was stripped of 40 percent of its old-growth forest between 1918 and 1937, while the island's more isolated west coast saw only 8 percent of its ancient temperate **rainforest** logged.

Concern that the rate of logging was surpassing the ability of the forest to replenish itself naturally first arose in 1945, when the Sloan Royal Commission recommended that a policy of sustained yield forestry be implemented. The forest service subsequently sought to regulate the allocation of timber on

Crown lands to logging operators and forest companies. It also turned over large tracts of Crown forests to major corporations in the form of forest management licences, known as tree farm licences (TFLs). In return for exclusive logging rights to an area of forest, the companies were to manage Crown forests on a sustained yield basis.

This policy led to a rapid expansion from 1950 to the mid-1970s that saw the forest industry, increasingly controlled by large corporations, extending operations throughout the province. Supported by a buoyant world economy, the industry and government acted as if virtually inexhaustible and expanding markets would always be available, along with an equally inexhaustible timber supply. Although the TFLs required sustainable logging to be practised there was little real attempt to balance trees cut with natural tree regeneration rates; reforestation through silvicultural methods was also little utilized during this period.

In the 1970s it became evident that future timber supplies—especially on the coast where many remaining old-growth stands were of lower quality than those that had been previously harvested—were limited and also geographically and economically more difficult to access. By the early 1980s, although about 55 percent of available timber was still unlogged and mature, the forest ministry was recognizing that existing harvestable stocks, combined with inadequate reforestation, had left the industry incapable of supporting its existing size unless major steps were taken to sustain the forests. By 1983 the provincial government was even starting to refer to the forest industry as a "sunset industry" and a potential future financial liability. Since 1983 the government, industry, and an increasingly involved populace expressing itself through either pro-logging groups or anti-logging environmental groups have been debating the future of forest land management and of forest industry access and practices.

The forest industry's prevailing dominance of the province's economy makes any attempt to slow harvesting rates to ensure sustainability a process that threatens B.C.'s immediate, and possibly long-term, economic health. B.C.'s economy is wed inextricably to the forest industry and has been since the end of World War II. No other economic sector comes close to rivalling the industry's percentage contribution. In a typical year, for example, the forest industry's total manufacturing shipments to markets averages about $11.2 billion or 46 percent of all such shipments. Forest product exports average $9.5 billion or about 59 percent of all provincial exports. Direct forest sector employment averages about eighty-six thousand jobs, more than all other primary industries combined.

B.C.'s forest industry provides lumber, plywood, and pulp and paper products to markets around the world. Lumber is the most important export product, with about $5.7 billion shipped annually from the province. Over 80 percent of lumber exported from B.C. goes to other countries, with the U.S. being the major market, followed by Japan. About 80 percent of the province's plywood products are consumed by the North American housing industry. Most of the province's pulp and paper products, produced at some twenty-seven mills distributed throughout the province, are exported to the United States.

To fuel the forest industry's production, about seventy-four million cubic metres of timber are harvested annually, with coast forests (containing only about 15 percent of gross forest land) providing about 32 percent of the harvest and interior forests about 68 percent.

Since 1987, B.C. law has required all timber harvested on Crown land to be reforested within three to five years. In recent years, reforestation has been roughly equal to the amount of land from which timber is harvested—approximately two thousand square kilometres. Forest companies, policed by a Forest Practices Code enacted in 1994, must pay for this initial reforestation as well as all tree tending and management costs necessary to ensure the reforested area develops into a healthy young free-growing forest within eight to twenty years.

If the attempts to restore the province's forest lands are successful it is probable that this industry will continue to sustain its historical role in the province's economy, but that future will depend entirely on the development of a true sustainable forest renewal strategy.

(*See also* **Clayoquot 800; Clayoquot Sound; CORE; Environmental Conflicts; Greenpeace.**)

Forests

British Columbia's forests are incredibly diverse, covering most of the province's landscape. Most originated approximately fourteen thousand years ago when the glacial ice retreated. New forests sprouted out of the bared earth, maturing into twelve distinct forests that responded to the unique biogeoclimatic zones they fell within.

The boundaries between these zones are subtly drawn, usually intermingled in a gradual blending together so that clear lines of juncture between one and another are difficult to establish. Because of the domination of the province by forest land most of the zones are named for the dominant tree species found there.

B.C.'s most spectacular stands of timber are found in the Coastal Western Hemlock Zone. Here the trees grow tall and massive. It is usually the trees of this zone that are referred to as the coastal rainforest or ancient temperate

rainforest. Most of this zone lies west of the **Coast Mountains** on low and middle elevations, especially hugging the steep valley walls. It extends inland along major valleys, such as the **Fraser** and **Skeena**, that have rivers empty-ing into the Pacific. Most of **Vancouver Island** and the **Queen Charlotte Islands** are also blanketed by Coastal Western Hemlock forest. Western hem-lock dominates, mingling with western red cedar, amabilis fir, and yellow cedar in wetter areas; stately Sitka spruce along coastlines; and lodgepole pine and Douglas-fir in drier regions. Red alder grows throughout. Grand fir, western white pine, and bigleaf maple grow in the drier southern regions. Undergrowth is dense, composed primarily of ferns and berry-bearing vines and bushes, as well as mosses. The forest supports large populations of wild-life. This is the most productive forest region in Canada in terms of bio-mass (the literal weight of life forms) and some areas have a greater bio-mass (**Carmanah** Valley, for example) than even the tropical rainforests of the Amazon.

Blending with the Coastal Western Hemlock Zone in such a way that the two are difficult to demarcate is the Coastal Douglas-fir Zone that occupies the eastern shore of Vancouver Island and the southern side of the western reaches of the Fraser Valley. This temperate zone is dominated by Douglas-fir and grand fir. Lodgepole pine, western yew, red alder, bigleaf maple, and Pacific dogwood are also common. The majority of **arbutus** and **Garry oak** stands are also found within this zone, especially on the southern part of Van-couver Island and the **Gulf Islands**.

Inland, in the central Fraser, lower **Thompson**, Nicola, Similkameen, and **Okanagan** valleys the forest starkly contrasts with that of the coast. The Ponderosa Pine/Bunchgrass Zone is sparsely spaced, occupying the semi-arid valley slopes and ridges. Ponderosa pine dominates, but shares space with Douglas-fir, trembling aspen, western larch, western birch, and paper birch. Grasslands between small stands of timber dominate the landscape.

Wrapping around the Ponderosa Pine/Bunchgrass Zone is the larger Inte-rior Douglas-fir Zone, which occupies the dry, middle elevations of the inte-rior plateau of south-central B.C. and extends to the East Kootenays. Doug-las-fir is dominant, mingling with trembling aspen, paper birch, lodgepole pine, and ponderosa pine. In wetter areas, Engelmann and white spruce, and western red cedar grow; in southern areas grand fir is found. Undergrowth is usually pinegrass.

To the east and north of the Interior Douglas-fir Zone and occupying a small section of the northwest coast is the Interior Cedar/Hemlock Zone. This is Canada's second-most productive forest zone. This is rainforest country, mostly far from the Pacific Ocean—the majority lining the lower slopes of the

Columbia Mountains and the western side of the **continental divide** along the **Rocky Mountains**. Western hemlock and western red cedar dominate here, merging with a vast array of other timber species. The specific species mix of an area is primarily determined by the varying degree of soil moisture and prevailing local precipitation trends that range from dryland, where lodgepole pine thrives, to bogs that support spruce stands. No fewer than fifty-seven varieties of tree species are found in this zone. Vegetation beneath the trees is extremely diverse, ranging from skunk cabbage to dryland grasses.

The central interior is dominated by the Sub-Boreal Spruce Zone, a curious blend of northern and southern forests. The dominant tree here has been identified as a hybrid white/Engelmann spruce, called interior spruce by many foresters. It is believed that when the ice withdrew, white spruce migrated south and Engelmann spruce north to mix together here for about ten thousand years, resulting in a hybrid species. This zone is further complicated by the fact that it adjoins the Douglas-fir forest zones to the south, the boreal forests to the north, and the subalpine forests at neighbouring higher elevations. Ground cover is usually scrubby brush and berry bushes.

Dominating the northeastern corner of the province is the Boreal White and Black Spruce Zone, which also has scatterings throughout the rest of the province's northern regions. Forest growth here is completely dominated by a struggle to survive within a frigid, subarctic environment. The trees that survive are tough, often scrubby compared to those of the southern forests. White and black spruce, adapted lodgepole pines, tamarack, subalpine fir, balsam poplar, and Alaskan paper birch all grow here. Old-growth trees are few and far between, due to the fact that the entire area is subject to massive and regular **forest fires**. Undergrowth is extremely varied; bogs are common.

The northwestern region of the province falls mostly within the Spruce/Willow/Birch Zone. Winters are long and severely cold and the forest found here reflects that influence. White spruce dominates, mixing with subalpine fir and lodgepole pine. Black spruce and trembling aspen also occur. Scrub birch and willows form thickets beneath and around the larger trees.

Lining the mountains of B.C.'s West Coast from the start of the Coast Mountains to the southern border is the Mountain Hemlock Zone. This forest also dominates the **Insular Mountains** of Vancouver Island and the Queen Charlotte Islands. A lush coastal forest that extends up the mountains to the 850-metre level, this forest is dominated by mountain hemlock, amabilis fir, and yellow cedar. At the higher elevations the trees grow in clumps separated by heaths and meadows.

Inland mountain ranges are dominated by the Engelmann Spruce/Subalpine Fir Zone, which occupies nearly two-thirds of the interior region, especially the Kootenays. The terrain here is usually steep, rugged, and mountainous. Lower levels are heavily forested, higher elevations are of a subalpine nature with clumps of timber interspersed by stretches of meadows and grasslands. Avalanches are common throughout, leaving broad swaths bordered by timber stands. Dominant timber is the Engelmann spruce, subalpine fir, and lodgepole pine. Whitebark pine and alpine larch are found in drier regions.

A small zone found in pockets of the southern interior plateau and along the southern part of the **Rocky Mountain Trench** is known as the Montane Spruce Zone. Lodgepole pine dominates, mingling with white/Engelmann spruce and subalpine fir. The presence of lodgepole pine results from wildfires burning out spruce forests, which are then encroached by the pine forest.

On the highest parts of the province's extensive mountain ranges is the Alpine Tundra Zone. The area should be treeless because of the harsh weather and rocky soil, but where elevations dip or a shelter presents itself, stunted subalpine fir, Engelmann spruce, mountain hemlock, and white pine can often be found. These trees are almost bush-like, appearing as dwarfed versions of their species.

Fort Langley National Historic Park

On the southern bank of the **Fraser River** adjacent to present-day Fort Langley, Fort Langley National Historic Park is a re-creation of the first European community in the Fraser Valley. The re-created fort is situated on the site of the third fort established by the Hudson's Bay Company to serve as a provisioning and administrative centre for its Pacific Northwest operations. Two earlier forts were abandoned: the first, built in 1827, because of poor location; the second, built in 1838, was razed by a fire in 1840. The third fort was constructed the same year.

Between 1827 and 1886 the fort played a key role in the province's development. For many years it was the hub of the region's fur trade, serving as a collection point for interior trade operations, especially for traders using the Brigade Trail. **Salmon** processing, using mainly fish traded to the company by natives, and **agriculture** in the area were also supported by the fort. With the beginning of the Fraser River gold rush in 1858, the fort became a major equipping and provisioning centre for prospectors heading for the gold fields.

On November 19, 1858, the first colonial government of British Columbia's mainland was officially proclaimed at Fort Langley, but a year later the capital was moved from Fort Langley to nearby **New Westminster**. The colony did not include **Vancouver Island**, which had been established as its own colony at **Victoria** on August 12, 1856—the first House of Assembly to meet on British soil west of the Great Lakes.

Fort Langley was finally abandoned in 1886 and the site left to deteriorate. In 1923 a plaque was erected commemorating the fort's existence. In May 1955 the fort was declared a national historic park. By that time only a log storehouse remained. Careful restoration work has been done to re-create the palisades, buildings, furnishings, and lives of those who lived here during the fort's fifty-nine-year operation.

In summer months appropriately costumed staff display barrel making, blacksmithing, pioneer cooking, and other nineteenth-century arts.

Fort St. John

The **Peace River** community of Fort St. John is the oldest non-native settlement in the province and one of the oldest native settlements. At nearby Charlie Lake (seven kilometres north) archaeologists have uncovered artefacts that indicate a Paleo Indian settlement was located here more than 10,500 years ago.

Ten kilometres upstream on the Peace River from present-day Fort St. John, the North West Company established a fur-trading fort, named Rocky Mountain House, in 1794. Five years later the Hudson's Bay Company established a fort with the same name on the North Saskatchewan River in what is now Alberta. By 1821, when the HBC and NWC merged, the Peace River fort had been renamed Fort St. John.

When the company decided to close the fort in 1823, local natives, now dependent on the fur trade for provisions and supplies, killed the lone clerk running the fort and four traders who were intercepted near the fort. Dubbed the Fort St. John Massacre by HBC officials, the company retaliated by closing all forts in the region. Four years later, a white adventurer passing through the area reported back to then Governor George Simpson that hundreds of the local natives had perished from starvation. The governor was reportedly satisfied with this outcome; gradually trade was re-established into the area.

Fort St. John's location has changed four times since 1794. It is now known as the "Energy Capital of B.C." because of the local oil and gas industry that, combined with agriculture and forestry, are the community's economic mainstays.

Fort Steele

One of the most popular historic sites in the province, Fort Steele is a provincially operated heritage town. In summer months, this turn-of-the-century gold-mining town thrives with costumed re-enactors who display methods of wheel making, horseshoeing, quilting, baking, and other pioneer activities. There are more than fifty buildings, some of which are original town structures or date back to 1887 when the North West Mounted Police (NWMP) established an outpost here. Fort Steele is famous for its Clydesdale horses, as well as the excellent opportunity the town provides for visitors to experience B.C.'s historic past.

The first non-native settlement occurred here in 1863 when a cable ferry station was established to move prospectors across the Kootenay River to a gold strike at nearby Wild Horse Creek. Friction between miners and local natives raised fears of bloodshed and resulted in Major Sam Steele and a contingent of NWMP being dispatched to the scene to maintain peace. Intent on avoiding armed confrontation with the natives, Steele constructed an unwalled fort and proceeded to negotiate an amiable peace agreement with the local band's Chief Isadore. Within a year, when it was apparent the peace would last, Steele and his troop abandoned the fort. Locals, however, were so struck by Steele's handling of this and other problems they renamed their community from Galbraith to Fort Steele in his honour.

Fort Steele was never entirely deserted prior to its becoming a heritage town, although it went through major economic declines. Even in the 1950s a couple of stores still operated here. Although many of the old buildings were lost a good number remained rundown but escaped vandalism or destruction. In 1961, the provincial government began reconstruction of the community. The present-day heritage townsite covers 150 hectares and is located eight kilometres north of the junction of Highway 3 and Highway 93 east of Cranbrook.

49th Parallel—U.S.-Canada Boundary

The 49th parallel was agreed upon at the Convention of 1818 between Britain and the United States as the line of latitude that would form the boundary between the United States and Canada, then a collection of British colonies. The boundary was defined as stretching from Lake of the Woods in the east to the summit of the **Rocky Mountains** in the west, thus failing to address the boundary between what would become British Columbia and the U.S.'s Washington State. That border was finalized in the Oregon Treaty of 1846 when it was agreed that the latitude would hold as the boundary from the Rockies to the **Strait of Georgia**, but from there would dogleg south to enable all of **Vancouver Island** to remain a British possession.

Fossils

British Columbia is composed of rock, some of which holds within it samples of almost the entire three-billion-year history of life on Earth. In every region of the province fossils spanning fossiliferous time are to be found. Every year new fossil beds are discovered.

Many of the fossils found in B.C. are of subtropical fauna or flora—the majority being a very small size that ranges down to that of a single cell. Large fossilized creatures, such as dinosaurs, are rarely found in the province although there have been discoveries of dinosaur bones and footprints in the **Peace River** valley and near Fernie, both regions linked geologically to Alberta, which, lying on the eastern side of the **Rocky Mountains**, has been part of the North American continent for a longer time than the rest of the province's land mass.

Five hundred million years ago trilobites dominated the seas of the Cambrian Period. Large numbers of trilobite fossils can be found at Walcott Quarry on Mount Field in Yoho National Park. (Frances Backhouse photo)

Palaeontologists have discovered that the fossilized subtropical fauna found in B.C., much of it marine life, never lived in the vicinity of the province. Rather it drifted here as fossilized rock. B.C.'s rock surface is composed literally of large pieces of the earth's crust up to thirty kilometres thick that floated in from more southern regions, much as would a raft. The "rafts" piled up along the shoreline of what was then North America. Between twenty to thirty of these separate floating mini-continents, called terranes, crushed up against the shoreline and ultimately against each other at a rate of about four centimetres a year. With the process continuing for one hundred million years, however, the terranes added five hundred kilometres of tropical rock to the continent's northwest coast.

The first of these terranes eventually rose to virtually the top of what is today the Rocky Mountains. The last terrane, carrying an incredibly abundant load of subtropical fossils inside its stone, is today **Vancouver Island**. It is in the stone of Vancouver Island, on the shores of Puntledge River near Courtenay, that the first dinosaur-like reptile found west of the Rockies was discovered in 1991. This eighty-million-year-old fossil was the partial remains of an **elasmosaur**.

A significant number of dinosaur bones and tracks have been discovered in the **Peace River** area east of the Rockies. At Peace Canyon near the community of **Fort St. John**, fossils and tracks of dinosaurs were uncovered when excavation work for the construction of the W.A.C. Bennett Dam was started in the 1960s. The Peace Canyon Visitor Centre exhibits these findings.

On both sides of Williston Lake to the west of nearby Hudson's Hope is a fossil bed containing, among other fossil remains, a mass death assemblage of huge Triassic Age (about 230 million years ago) ichthyosaurs. The ichthyosaurs were aquatic dinosaurs that were porpoise-like in appearance and habits.

Dinosaur bones are relatively rare in the province, but they are merely a fragment of the majority of the planet's fossilized record of life. At Wapiti Lake, south of Tumbler Ridge, some of the world's best fish fossils are embedded in three-hundred-metre-high cliffs three kilometres above the lake's shores. Here, twenty 240-million-year-old fish species have been found and protected within a Crown land reserve that prohibits the collection of fossils without a permit.

Near Princeton, in the Similkameen Valley, is one of the best plant fossil sites on Earth. Eocene fossils (dating back forty million years) of blackberry, metasequoia, spruce, ginkgo, and apple trees, as well as early **salmon** and insects trapped in volcanic ash are found in this area. Good leaf fossils are also common.

Eleven kilometres northeast of Cranbrook on Highway 3, five-hundred-million-year-old trilobites are regularly found in the red shale. Trilobites are easily recognized by their distinctive three-lobed, three-segmented external skeleton form. They were exclusively marine animals that dominated the seas during the Cambrian Period. Trilobites grew to a maximum size of about forty-five centimetres and could weigh up to 4.5 kilograms. They were predators, but also are believed to have fed on plankton.

In Top of the World Provincial Park, twenty kilometres southeast of Skookumchuck in the Kootenays, a fossil site was located in the mid-1990s that contains 440-million-year-old spongelike stromatoporoids—tree-trunk-shaped marine creatures that were two metres tall and twenty-five centimetres wide. They lived in warm, shallow seas. The stromatoporoids were found in grey limestone above Sparkle Lake on Mount Dingley's steep slopes. Parks legislation prohibits collection without a permit.

At Field, guided summer hikes are possible to the two major Burgess Shale fossil beds in **Yoho National Park**. The Mount Stephen trilobite bed contains thousands of samples. The twenty-seven-hundred-metre-high Walcott Quarry on nearby Mount Field has more than 120 different species of Cambrian marine fossils. Unguided visits to the quarry are prohibited.

Removal of fossils from protected fossil sites in B.C. is illegal. A few deposits, like the beds around Princeton, permit surface collection.

Fraser Canyon

The Fraser Canyon is a 270-kilometre-long channel, deeply cut by the waters of the **Fraser River**. The canyon extends from Yale at the western end to Alexandra Bridge in the **Interior Plateau**. Formed during the Miocene period that ended some 5.3 million years ago, the canyon was cut by the river finding its way to the sea through an uplifting section of the Interior Plateau.

The most dramatic feature of the canyon is at **Hell's Gate**, twenty-seven kilometres north of Yale. Canyon walls here rise to about thirty-four metres above the narrow torrent of water—narrowing in places to thirty-three metres and so funnelling the water that it passes through at speeds of forty-seven kilometres per hour.

Two transcontinental railways and the **Trans-Canada Highway** have been carved into the canyon's rocky flanks.

Fraser River

With headwaters in the **Rocky Mountains** at **Mount Robson** and draining into the sea at **Vancouver**, the 1,368-kilometre Fraser River is British Columbia's longest river (Canada's fifth longest). The river's drainage basin extends over 233,000 square kilometres, nearly 25 percent of the province. From its headwaters, the Fraser flows slowly northwest along a meandering route that follows the **Rocky Mountain Trench**'s valley floor to **Prince George**. From here it bends southward, its gravel banks rising to between fifty and one hundred metres as it chews a path through the glacial deposits of the central **Interior Plateau** and its velocity increases as other streams meld with it. The largest of these is the **Nechako River**, coming in from the northwest.

South of Quesnel the Fraser enters the **Fraser Canyon** and rushes through walls of bedrock rising to heights ranging from three hundred to six hundred metres. Along this stretch, large tributaries, such as the Quesnel, **Thompson**, and Chilcotin rivers, swell its levels. Exiting the canyon near Hope, the river enters the **Fraser River Lowland** at an altitude of only about five metres above sea level. Volumes of flow in this section vary radically according to season. The Fraser's average flow is 269,000 cubic metres with a minimum flow of 70,800 cubic metres in March and a maximum of 850,000 cubic metres in June. The lowland delta at the river mouth is fifty kilometres wide and the extreme southwestern portion lies in Washington State, so not all of the Fraser River is contained inside British Columbia's borders.

The first European to discover the Fraser River was Alexander Mackenzie in 1793. The river was, however, not substantially explored until 1808 when North West Company adventurer Simon Fraser, accompanied by twenty-three others, travelled the river from what is today Prince George to its mouth.

Throughout the gruelling thirty-five-day downriver odyssey Fraser believed
he was on the **Columbia River**. During the trip he grew to loathe the river. "I
have never seen anything equal to this country. . . . I cannot find words to
describe our situation at times. We had to pass where no human being should
venture," Fraser wrote. Fraser was astonished to note a regular footpath running along the shores of the river's passage through the canyon—sure sign of
regular use of this hard land by natives. Fraser's fellow-explorer and mapmaker
David Thompson, who successfully followed the real Columbia River to its
mouth in 1811, later named the river Fraser had travelled in the other explorer's honour. Fraser's sentiments on this were not recorded.

Fraser River Lowland

The Fraser River Lowland is a triangular area at the mouth of the **Fraser
River**. Its eastern apex is at Hope, about 160 kilometres inland from the **Strait
of Georgia**. On the immediate coast the triangle broadens to about fifty kilometres. The **Coast Mountains** form the northern boundary of this delta-low-
land area; the Canadian-United States border crosses the southwestern part.

This area is known locally as the Lower Fraser Valley or the Lower Mainland. It is home to more than half of B.C.'s population, including on its northwest edge the city of **Vancouver**. Vancouver's growth has resulted in much of
the western section of the area being overwhelmed by residential, commercial, and industrial development. The **Agricultural Land Reserve** has proven
less than successful in protecting this rich arable landscape from development
since its inception in 1973.

Formed from glacial and alluvial deposits more than ten thousand years
ago and the ongoing deposits of sediment dropped by the Fraser River's channels, the combination of waterways and rich soil make this one of the most
productive fish and birdlife habitats in Canada, possibly the world. More win-
tering waterbirds, shorebirds, and raptors gather here than anywhere else in
Canada. More than one million waterfowl and shorebirds follow the Pacific
Flyway through here each fall and spring. Up to 200,000 ducks migrate into
the lowlands each November.

The waters of the Fraser River are host to one of the world's largest **salmon**
runs. Chinook spawning starts in late spring and peaks in early autumn. Coho
begin a spawning run in late summer that peaks in September. Pink salmon
run every two years with about six million entering the river between mid-
August and mid-October. Some ten million sockeye enter the river between
June and September, many making the 485-kilometre run to the **Adams River**
spawning beds. Chum salmon and sea-run cutthroat trout also spawn in
the river.

To control the Fraser's chronic flooding and to allow agricultural usage, a major dyking system has been constructed to drain much of the wetlands. This has put pressure on the migrating bird population and also destroyed much native vegetation. Peat bogs remain the only significant example of native flora. These thick mats of sphagnum keep the water table high through capillary action and produce organic acids that sustain high water acidity, which in turn reduces the rate of peat decomposition and encourages the generation of bogs in surrounding terrain.

(*See also* **Reifel Bird Sanctuary**.)

Frogs. *See* **Amphibians.**

Fruit Farming

Strawberries, raspberries, loganberries, blueberries, cranberries, grapes, and a limited number of tree fruits are grown in B.C.'s Lower Mainland and on southern **Vancouver Island**. The tree fruit- and grape-growing heartland is the **Okanagan Valley**, with a small number of tree fruit orchards found in the Kootenays.

B.C.'s berry and grape farms annually sell about $84 million worth of product. The majority of this is marketed for processing, rather than for fresh sale. The most dramatic example of this is the province's cranberry crop. Of the approximately eighteen million kilograms of cranberries harvested annually, 95 percent is pre-sold under a long-term contract to the cranberry-corporation giant, Ocean Spray Inc.

Only about 15 percent of the province's berry, grape, and small nut crop totalling about fifty-nine million kilograms of yield is sold as fresh in-season product. Of this, about three-quarters is sold directly to retail customers at the farm gate or through roadside farmer-owned outlets. All Vancouver Island's small fresh berry crop, for example, is sold directly to consumers by the farmers, as is the island's small tree fruit crop (more than 90 percent apples).

The combination of warm, sunny summers and cloudy winters that produce mild temperatures enable Okanagan Valley farmers to grow tree fruits at a northern latitude usually too prone to severe frost and harsh winter temperatures to support tree fruit growth. Since the end of the nineteenth century this valley has been one of Canada's major tree-fruit growing regions. More than 90 percent of all tree fruits harvested in B.C. are grown in the Okanagan.

Although pears, peaches, apricots, cherries, prune plums, plums, and nectarines are grown in B.C., the province's primary tree fruit crop is apples— accounting for about 150 million kilograms of the province's 168 million kilogram total tree fruit harvest. Four apple varieties account for almost all apple production—red and common delicious, McIntosh, spartan, and golden delicious. The province's tree fruit industry produces annual harvest sales averaging between $55 and $60 million annually. Unlike the province's berry and grape crops, most B.C. tree fruit is sold as fresh wholesale product—about 128 million kilograms of the annual average harvest.

The tree fruit industry's dependence on apples has increasingly jeopardized its ability to survive financially. With the advent of the North American Free Trade Agreement, Okanagan farmers have been faced with rapidly declining prices as cheaper fruit from the United States competes for Canadian retail space at supermarkets. The value of processed fruit sales, for example, has fallen off so dramatically that since the early 1990s the fruit processing industry has been operating at a loss or break-even level. Combining with the depressed prices is increased urban pressure on the small amount of arable land in the Okanagan Valley, leading to increasing losses of fruit farm land to development for non-agricultural purposes.

(*See also* **Agricultural Land Reserve**; **Agriculture**; **British Columbia Fruit Growers' Association**.)

Fur Trade. *See* Historical Overview.

Gang Ranch

Located about forty-six kilometres north of Clinton in the Cariboo, the historic Gang Ranch covers approximately 400,000 hectares (one million acres). The Gang, as it is often called, has at various times since its founding in the 1860s been the largest ranch in North America. The ranch was started by Jerome and Thaddeus Harper and is said to derive its name from the fact that the Harpers utilized the multi-bladed gang plough for the first time in the B.C. interior. Jerome died in 1874 and Thaddeus sold the Gang in 1888 as part of a desperate, futile attempt to avoid personal bankruptcy.

Although the ranch continues today to use the Harpers' famous "J lazy-T" brand on its cattle stock, the Gang has gone through an array of owners with no relation to the founders. Being among the world's largest ranches has not translated into good fortune for the ranch. It has undergone a turbulent, troubled history; with owners often following in Thaddeus Harper's footsteps of struggling to avoid bankruptcy. To bolster its economic strength it has been operated at various times as a working ranch cum guest ranch, shares in individual steers have been sold to urban folk as a more tangible stock investment than could be had on the Vancouver Stock Exchange, and other innovative cash-raising schemes have been employed.

The Gang has managed to keep going despite all its historic problems. Most of the ranch buildings are painted the same historic red that the Harpers used on all the first structures. Its vast land stretches south to the Chilcotin Mountains, where cattle are put out to summer grazing. Within the Gang's land holding is found almost every type of **Interior Plateau** terrain.

Garry Oak Ecosystem

In 1838, when Captain W. H. McNeill first sailed into what is today **Victoria** Harbour on **Vancouver Island**'s southern tip, he was awed by a vast sweep of grasslands interspersed with stands of Garry oak—a low-standing tree species distinguished by a gnarled, primarily branchless, bark trunk and a top canopy of twisted branches. Before the arrival of Europeans, Garry oak extended from the southern tip of Vancouver Island up the southeastern coastline to about Courtenay, covered much of the **Gulf Islands**, and was found in pockets of the Lower Mainland. A part of the Coastal Douglas-fir biogeoclimatic zone (*see* **Forests**), the Garry oak ecosystem favoured lowland sites, monadnock hills, and coastal locations that were sheltered from storms off the open ocean. The Garry oak forest was always a mere fragment of the Coastal Douglas-fir Zone which itself constitutes only 0.3 percent of the province's land area.

The natural Garry oak ecosystem of British Columbia occurred because of the presence of a near-Mediterranean climate created by a rainshadow of the mountains to the southwest. The climate was moderate and characterized by dry summers.

In British Columbia, the Garry oak landscape includes a mosaic of woodlands, meadows, grasslands, scattered Douglas-fir stands, and open rocky areas. Irregularly wooded landscapes are called "parklands." The term meadows, which is used commonly to describe the open areas, is particularly appropriate in spring and summer when they are lush with bright wildflowers, blue camas, white Easter lily, and yellow western buttercup. Other species found in Garry oak ecosystems are satin flower, chocolate lily, and little monkey flower. Parts of the landscape also feature shrub stands of snowberry and ocean spray. Rock outcrops support scattered scrubby oaks, along with licorice fern, rock mosses, and grasses such as Idaho fescue and California oatgrass. These grasses evoke an image of the southern origin of the Garry oak ecosystems, which spread up the southwestern Pacific coast to British Columbia from California.

Human habitation and development, combined with the introduction of exotic plant and insect species, have placed the delicate Garry oak ecosystem in danger of extinction. The "Prairie land savannah" that Captain McNeill described seeing in the Victoria area has been almost fully lost to urban development. Only small outcroppings on hilltops and a few other isolated pockets remain.

Much of the Garry oak on the southeastern coast of Vancouver Island and on the Gulf Islands has similarly been lost to urban development pressure. Remaining Garry oak landscapes near **Duncan**, Nanaimo, Comox, and on **Hornby Island** and Saltspring Island are threatened by development.

Overgrazing by domestic and feral livestock, including pigs, sheep, goats, cattle, and horses, as well as introduced eastern cottontail rabbits, has caused non-native plant species to become dominant. These introduced plants spread widely after European settlement. Exotics, such as orchardgrass and sweet vernalgrass, may constitute over 30 percent of the total species in Garry oak ecosystems. Rapid spread of Scotch broom has also replaced native plants, changed soil nutrients, and dramatically altered the Garry oak meadows.

A new peril to Garry oak is posed by the spread of two introduced insect pests—the jumping gall wasp and the oak-leaf phylloxeran. The scorching of oaks by these insects results in potential threat to the ecosystem. Scorched oaks may be mistakenly cut down on the assumption they are dead, which is not the case.

Garry oak ecosystems may have a special role to play in B.C.'s adjustment to global warming. It is predicted that the province's climate will become increasingly like that of California. The Douglas-fir ecosystem is currently retreating from its traditional range in the face of this warming trend. Garry oak could provide the important biological material necessary to repopulate the void that is being created because of its inherent ability to thrive in warmer climatic conditions than other B.C. ecosystems.

Recent recognition by provincial, regional, and municipal governments, plus public concern, has led to the Garry oak ecosystem being identified as one of the most endangered ecosystems in British Columbia. Various programs are being instituted to save the remaining ecosystems from destruction or eradication by non-native flora and wildlife.

Ginseng

In 1982 a two-hectare plot of ginseng was planted in British Columbia's interior near **Kamloops**. Just over a decade later ginseng would emerge as one of the fastest-growing cash crops in the province—potentially poised to outpace fruit farming in cash yield values before the year 2000. Fields planted with ginseng are readily recognizable because of their small size and a low-standing black net or plastic covering that is stretched over the plot.

About 130 growers, centred on the **Thompson**, **Fraser**, and **Okanagan** valleys, currently work about 730 hectares of ginseng fields that in 1994 yielded about 363,000 kilograms of the exotic root. Ginseng yield volumes are low and growing costs are high, but the profit-per-hectare potential makes it the world's most profitable legal agricultural crop.

In 1994, B.C.'s ginseng industry was worth about $30 million, with growers averaging profits of more than $300,000 per hectare. This compares with other crops such as asparagus, which yields profits of about $1,400 per hectare, tomatoes $10,200, and cauliflower $7,200. Approximately $20 million worth of the ginseng was exported to Asia, mostly China and Hong Kong.

In Asia, consumption of ginseng is believed to be beneficial to health—improving short-term memory, lowering blood pressure, regulating cholesterol and blood-sugar levels, reducing menopausal symptoms, increasing lifespan, moderating the body's immune system, and serving as an aphrodisiac. In China, ginseng is often referred to as the "elixir of life" and its consumption dates back at least five centuries.

Ginseng farming is not a get-rich-quick proposition. Although cash returns per area planted are extremely high so too are the costs. It costs between $100,000 and $140,000 a hectare to grow ginseng and takes four growing seasons before the root can be harvested. The root is susceptible to disease and poor weather conditions.

Most of the ginseng grown in British Columbia is North American ginseng, which is natural to the continent and was discovered by Jesuit priest Joseph-Francois Lafitau in Ontario in the early 1700s while he was conducting his famous empirical study of Iroquois laws and customs. Ginseng grew in the woods of central and eastern North America. Because of excessive harvesting, ginseng is now very rare in the wild. There is no record of it being used by **First Nations peoples** for medicinal purposes.

Glaciation

Beginning about one million years ago and continuing until only about seven thousand years ago British Columbia underwent intense glaciation—which was responsible for the majority of the province's physiographic features. The Pleistocene Age saw large areas of the northern and southern hemispheres buried under ice sheets. At its maximum extent, B.C. was almost entirely covered by ice, except for some of the highest mountain peaks, parts of the northern and southern **Rocky Mountains**, and the **Queen Charlotte Islands**.

The ice movement and even the extreme pressure exerted by the glacial weight transformed the provincial landscape. Mountains were scoured to the bedrock as glaciers pressed by on their inexorable spread south from the polar cap. In the softer soil between bedrock peaks, the glaciers gouged out deep valleys. Other mountains were rounded as their peaks were ground away. In front of the ice sheets a mass of soil, gravel, and other loose materials was pushed in the same manner as a bulldozer blade shoves dirt before it.

Throughout this million-year period the ice shifted back and forth across the land as the atmosphere cooled and heated, until finally the earth warmed to present-day temperatures and the last of the great ice sheets melted. This melt took anywhere from three thousand to eight thousand years and ended in some northern and mountain regions only seven thousand years ago. As the ice melted, gigantic rivers and lakes were born, adding the force of their flow to the severe erosion carried out on the landscape by the glaciation. Even today, the mightiest rivers (the **Fraser**, **Columbia**, and **Skeena**) in B.C. derive large volumes of their source flow from seasonal glacial melting. As the ice retreated it also shed debris gathered up within the ice during the southward expansion, creating vast deposits of moraine. The melting waters coursed through these deposits, spreading them and sifting away the lightest parts; scattering in the meltwater's wake the materials that would build plateaus, valley benchlands, the soil for valley bottoms, and alluvial deposits that underlay estuaries and deltas. When the process of glacial retreat concluded at the end of the Pleistocene, a province's topography was in place.

All the erosive forces of wind, water, and chemical decomposition, added to humanity's meagre efforts at land change, have barely scratched the surface of the province by comparison to the impact of the ice age. Had it not been for the Pleistocene the province's landscape would have been vastly different in ways that are impossible to predict.

Glacier National Park

Glacial ice gouged and carved out the 1,350 square kilometres of rugged country comprising Glacier National Park in the **Columbia Mountain**'s Purcell and Selkirk ranges thousands of years ago, and today more than four hundred glaciers and icefields still cover 12 percent of the park's total area. Heavy snowfalls continue to sustain these massive glaciers and every year **avalanches** add new scars to the park's many sheer valley walls. Mountain peaks in this park are jagged and deeply scoured. As the area averages rain every third day, the peaks are often wreathed in clouds. Half of Glacier National Park is alpine tundra, including large stretches of alpine meadows.

Glacier is reputed to have more grizzly bears than any other national park, black **bears** proliferate, caribou sometimes migrate into its valleys and highlands, mountain goats and hoary marmots are common; but high altitudes, deep snow, and lengthy winters make the area a harsh environment for all but the hardiest of wildlife. Below the alpine meadows, Engelmann spruce and alpine fir stands descend the slopes to merge with thick interior **rainforests** of western red cedar and western hemlock. Throughout the park are glacier-fed emerald-coloured lakes, crystalline clear streams, several cave systems created by underground streams, and hundreds of seasonal and continuous waterfalls. A 140-kilometre wilderness trail system provides access to the park's interior regions, with most trailheads found adjacent to the **Trans-Canada Highway**.

The most easily accessible glacier in the park is massive Illecillewaet, an Okanagan Indian word for "big or rushing water." Coincidentally, this glacier reached its most recent maximum extent in 1886, the same year the park was declared, before beginning a long, slow retreat. In recent years it has started inching forward yet again.

The park's western boundary is forty-nine kilometres east of Revelstoke and the Trans-Canada Highway cuts through the park via **Rogers Pass** for forty-four kilometres to reach its eastern boundary forty kilometres from Golden.

Gold Rushes

The telegraph, mass circulation newspapers, and steamboats combined with discoveries of placer (not imbedded in hardrock) gold deposits drew thousands of amateur miners to isolated regions of British Columbia from 1851 to about 1900. Wherever lucky prospectors discovered gold during this period news of the find was soon carried around the world by telegraph and fortune-seekers raced to the area, most coming from the scene of the last mining strike.

The presence of placer gold in British Columbia was first confirmed by American miners prospecting on the **Queen Charlotte Islands** in

Gold panners work alongside the Fraser River near Yale during the 1858 gold rush that drew more than 30,000 prospectors into the B.C. interior in the province's first major gold rush. (BCARS photo A-01958)

1851–52, but the deposits were too small and scattered to spark a rush. In 1858, discoveries in the lower and middle sections of the **Fraser River** caused a rush in the Yale region. Between May and July of 1858, about thirty thousand miners rushed north from the exhausted California fields to the Fraser River region.

The spread of gold rush fever in British Columbia was actively encouraged by Secretary of State for the Colonies Sir Edward Bulwer Lytton despite his contention that the miners were a "motley inundation of immigrant diggers." What Lytton and the B.C. business community saw in the miners, however, was an opportunity to reap a profitable rush of their own by providing services and facilities. It also encouraged the opening of the province's interior to settlement and development, as well as justifying the colonial government in removing from the Hudson's Bay Company much of its authority over the interior lands.

From the Fraser River strike, miners moved into the southern and central interior, causing smaller rushes in the Boundary, Similkameen, **Thompson River**, and **Okanagan Valley** regions. By 1860, however, the richest gold fields were found along the rivers and creeks of the Cariboo. Soon the **Cariboo Gold Rush**, British Columbia's longest and largest, was underway. It would continue until 1871, but its most feverish levels were from 1860 to 1868—the same year that another minor rush occurred along the shores of Omineca River in northern B.C. Finlay, Parsnip, **Peace**, Liard, and **Stikine** rivers were all panned by gold miners and yielded some riches. In 1872 a major strike at Dease Lake drew many of the miners from **Barkerville**'s dying fields farther north to the Cassiar region.

The Cassiar strike was the last of the great placer mine rushes. Although there would be gold strikes and resulting rushes in the Kootenays, and again in the Okanagan-Similkameen region, up until the turn of the century the gold in these finds was lode gold. Lode-mining required hammers, drills, dynamite, mills and smelters, and the ability to engineer a tunnel. This was a more capital-intensive form of mining that required a large waged work force to work a mine. Few of the gold rushers desired to eke out a living as a miner working for a mine owner. The day of the rushes was over.

Government

British Columbia's government derives its structure from British parliamentary tradition. Prior to 1866, B.C. was composed of two British-controlled Crown colonies—one on **Vancouver Island**, the second on the mainland. In 1866, the Union Proclamation joined these colonies to form the Crown Colony of British Columbia. Neither the government the Crown colony replaced nor the colony itself were fully responsible to the citizens of the province—instead it took much of its direction from the colonial office of the British government. The first fully responsible government in B.C. was instituted on July 20, 1871, when the colony entered into confederation with Canada.

Upon entering confederation, B.C. came under the authority of the British North America Act (BNA Act), a statute of the British Parliament. Until 1982, the BNA Act defined the major national institutions and established the division of authority between the federal and provincial governments. In 1982, the BNA Act was incorporated into the Constitution Act. The passage of the Canada Act in 1982 ended the British Parliament's legal right to legislate for Canada.

Canada has a federal government structure. As such the federal government is the supreme governmental body in the country. The legislative powers of the federal and provincial governments are determined through an evolving process of agreements between the central government and the provinces. Since the 1980s, there has been a trend toward decentralization of governmental powers away from the federal government toward the provincial governments. Under Canada's constitutional framework, the province has ownership and jurisdiction over natural resources and is responsible for education, health and social services, municipal institutions, property and civil rights, the administration of justice, and other matters of purely provincial or local concern.

British Columbia's government is modelled after the British system. There are three main branches: the legislature, the executive, and the **judiciary**.

Legislative power is exercised by a single legislative chamber, elected for a maximum of five years. The legislature consists of the lieutenant governor and seventy-five elected members of the legislative assembly. The assembly sits in the **Legislative Buildings** located in the provincial capital of **Victoria**.

The legislative assembly represents the people of British Columbia by conducting the province's affairs and determining its fiscal, political, social, and cultural policies. The assembly is required by law to meet at least once a year with a normal session lasting several months. Special sessions, however, can last a few days or many months, depending on the nature of the government's business.

B.C.'s parliamentary executive is composed of the lieutenant governor and the executive council (normally referred to as the cabinet). The lieutenant governor is the Queen's representative in B.C. and holds a largely ceremonial place in modern provincial government. By constitutional custom, the lieutenant governor is appointed by the Governor General of Canada for a term usually running five years.

Following a general election, the lieutenant governor calls upon the leader of the political party with the largest number of elected members to serve as premier and to form the provincial government. The lieutenant governor, on the advice of the premier, appoints members of the cabinet and is guided by its advice as long as it holds the confidence of the legislative assembly. The lieutenant governor, again on the recommendations of the premier, convenes, prorogues, and dissolves the legislative assembly and gives Royal Assent to all measures and bills passed by the assembly before they become law.

Cabinet is composed of selected members of the ruling party and is headed by the premier. Members of the cabinet usually head government ministries and are members of a variety of cabinet committees. The cabinet is usually composed of the premier and a maximum of about twenty ministers. Members of the ruling political party who are not in the cabinet are referred to as backbenchers. This term derives from the fact that non-cabinet members traditionally sit behind the cabinet in the legislative assembly and are considered to have less power in determining government policy than cabinet members.

The cabinet determines government policy and is held responsible by the legislative assembly for the operation of the provincial government. Deputy ministers are the chief operating officers of the ministries and are appointed by the cabinet. Deputy ministers are responsible for carrying out government policies and for managing the work of their ministries.

The members of the legislative assembly are elected by the constituents of ridings allocated geographically according to a system that strives to balance geographical concerns with equality of population base. The elected member of the legislative assembly (MLA) is charged with representing the concerns and interests of riding constituents. Most MLAs are members of a political party, although there are a few who run as independents. Although the MLA is technically the representative of the riding constituency, the rules of party solidarity may require an MLA to vote for or against a government policy in direct opposition to the prevailing views of the riding constituency or personally held beliefs. Failure to vote in accordance with the party line is usually met with the MLA's ejection from the party. The MLA can then either cross the floor to sit with another party, sit as an independent, or resign.

Because of the small number of political parties in British Columbia and the fact that usually only two or three of these win the majority of votes there is little likelihood of the need for coalition governments in the province. Throughout B.C. history most governments have tended to have a majority—meaning the party in power has more legislative assembly members than all the opposition parties combined. Possession of a majority means the government cannot lose the confidence of the legislature during a vote and therefore cannot fall. When a minority government exists it must maintain the confidence of sufficient numbers of the opposition members to withstand votes of non-confidence. The failure to win such a vote results in the immediate calling of an election no matter how much time remains in the government's elected term of office.

Members of the legislative assembly who are not part of the ruling party are known as opposition members and the leader of the party that won the second most votes is the leader of the opposition.

(*See also* **Government—Local**; **Judiciary**; **Political History**.)

Government—Local

British Columbia's local levels of government consist of incorporated municipalities, school districts, regional hospital districts, and special-purpose investment districts. There are 150 incorporated municipalities in the province, including forty-one cities, fifty districts, fourteen towns, forty-four villages, and one Indian government district. These governments provide local services and facilities such as roads, waterworks, and sewers, as well as a wide range of social, recreational, and protection services.

The province is also divided into twenty-nine regional districts that are incorporated under the Municipal Act. The regional districts encompass municipal and other local areas within their boundaries and negotiate with these more localized governments a division of authority for provision of services. Regional district authority can vary from being quite limited to having broad-ranging responsibility for the overall planning of communities within the district and the provision of essential services such as waterworks and sewers. The **Stikine** region of B.C. is the only unincorporated area in the province.

Localized delivery of primary- and secondary-level education is carried out by the province's seventy-five school districts, which are incorporated under the School Act. These districts cover 98 percent of the province. Each district derives funding from the provincial government and through local school taxes. Many local educational policies regarding curriculum, class size, teacher salaries, and other such issues are determined by the directors of the school board.

The province also has twenty-nine regional hospital districts incorporated under the Hospital District Act. These share the same boundaries as the regional districts and are charged with assisting in planning and construction of health facilities, as well as setting some local policies on hospital operations.

All of the preceding levels of local government are governed by elected aldermanic councils or boards of directors.

Finally, there are three hundred improvement districts, primarily in non-municipal areas, that are incorporated under the Municipal Act or the Water

Act. Services provided by improvement districts include waterworks, fire protection, irrigation, street lighting, drainage, garbage disposal, sewage disposal, parks and playgrounds, dyking, community halls, recreation areas, cemeteries, land acquisition, boat landings, mosquito control, river bank protection, water treatment, electrical energy, and lake level control.

The province is also divided into a comprehensive county system, but the designation of areas into counties has nothing to do with the delivery of government services. Instead, the county system is used for administration of legal services, such as land title designation and the demarcating of jurisdiction of county courts for the hearing of civil and criminal matters.

(*See also* **Judiciary**.)

Grand Forks

Grand Forks is a small community on the western edge of the West Kootenays. At one time, Grand Forks was home to the British Empire's largest copper smelter, and the second largest smelter in the world. The Granby Smelter processed so much copper, gold, and silver during its operational life (from 1898 to 1919) that a huge ten-million-tonne slag deposit was generated. The massive black hills stood undisturbed on the community's edge until 1980, when a new company started converting the slag into an abrasive used for sandblasting.

In 1908, **Doukhobors** travelled west from other Kootenay settlements to establish a colony here. Many of today's residents are descendants of these settlers, giving the community a strong Russian ethnic flavour.

Recent years have brought rapid growth to the small community, with its population growing by about 10 percent annually.

Granville Island

Home to what is usually considered British Columbia's largest fresh-food public market, an art school, theatres, restaurants, and remnants of its original industrial-marine heritage, Granville Island is one of the most popular shopping districts in **Vancouver**. Situated on the south shore of False Creek, beneath Granville Street Bridge, it is reached off West 4th Avenue.

The island was originally created with fill in 1915 to serve as an industrial area. By the 1950s the area was decaying into a district of rundown warehouses and ill-maintained boat sheds. In the mid-1970s, Vancouver city council decided to redevelop the area and work began on the island and adjacent areas of False Creek to create an integrated housing and commercial district. This development is now hailed as one of the most successful inner-city industrial core redevelopments ever undertaken in North America.

Great Central Lake

Found northwest of Port Alberni, a short distance north of Highway 4, Great Central Lake is **Vancouver Island**'s deepest lake—maximum depth of 335 metres. It is a popular lake for canoe trips.

Great White Lodge. *See* Aquarian Foundation.

Green Lake

Approximately forty-eight kilometres long, Green Lake—situated south of 100 Mile House in the Cariboo—is, in a province where lakes so-named occur frequently, the largest of the greens. It is also a lake that has no outlet except via underground drainage. As a result, it has accumulated large deposits of soda, salt, and sulphur, which combine to create its notable green colour.

Greenpeace

In 1970 a small group opposed to nuclear testing in the Pacific Ocean met in Vancouver to form an activist movement they named Greenpeace. The organization has since grown to become one of the largest and best-known environmental organizations in the world, operating in many countries and addressing both international and local issues.

The Greenpeace Council, now based in Amsterdam, provides loose overall control of the organization, but its offices throughout the world operate semi-autonomously—especially when responding to local issues. Membership is difficult to determine as it fluctuates dramatically depending on the issues that are current at the time.

Greenpeace's usual strategy is to attract maximum publicity to generate public pressure on governments and industry to cease or change whatever behaviour it perceives as a violation of ecological principles, such as the equal right of all species to exist and flourish. Past tactics have included using boats to disrupt Japanese and Russian whaling operations and French nuclear tests.

One Greenpeace member was killed July 10, 1985, when French intelligence agents damaged the Greenpeace flagship *Rainbow Warrior* in Auckland, New Zealand, with an underwater bomb. The boat was preparing to sail for Murora Atoll, the French nuclear test site in French Polynesia.

In B.C., Greenpeace's major past campaigns have focused on anti-whaling (the highly successful "Save the Whales" campaign), and generating public support for a seal-hunting ban in Canada's north. Most recently, a major effort by both Greenpeace's provincial and international arms to save **Clayoquot Sound** and other ancient temperate **rainforest** regions from clearcutting is underway. Greenpeace is using public pressure and direct lobbying to convince foreign buyers to boycott any pulp products drawn from timber harvested by clearcut techniques. This strategy has locked Greenpeace in an acrimonious dispute with the provincial government, the B.C. **forest industry**, and pro-forest industry groups, such as SHARE BC and the Forest Alliance of British Columbia.

In what reads like the plot twist of a historical saga, two of Greenpeace's founders are now on opposite sides of this struggle. Patrick Moore is the director of the Forest Alliance of British Columbia and condemns Greenpeace's anti-clearcut campaign. Paul Watson, who broke from Greenpeace, because he believed it wasn't radical enough, to form the Los Angeles-based Sea Shepherd Society, has threatened to use eco-terrorist tactics, such as tree spiking, to disrupt clearcutting in Clayoquot Sound and other ancient rainforests. Tree spiking entails driving heavy spikes into trunks of trees. Chain saws or milling blades striking the spikes are damaged and sometimes workers operating the equipment are badly injured.

Greenwood

With a present-day population of fewer than one thousand, the West Kootenay community of Greenwood is Canada's smallest city. This is a reflection of its past when, as a mining boomtown, it seemed fated to become one of western Canada's major centres. At the time of its incorporation in 1897, two years after its foundation, the population was about three thousand and it bustled with banks, hotels, stores, and other businesses.

It served as the commercial centre for dozens of area mines, including the prosperous Mother Lode Mine, whose thirty-seven-metre-tall brick smelter stack still stands. The stack must have been well constructed as it survived a calamity that led to the mine's abandonment. In 1913, miners seeking new ore bodies for the faltering mining operation drilled five thousand holes and packed them with dynamite. They blew all the holes at once—creating a blast that shattered windows in the nearby community of Deadwood and which, instead of opening up new veins, collapsed the entire mining hole so badly it had to be abandoned.

After World War I the mining boom in the region came to a close and Greenwood became little more than a ghost town. In 1942 the Canadian government was seeking communities willing to serve as Japanese internment camps (*see* **Japanese Canadian Relocation**). Greenwood council agreed to be part of the program and some one thousand of the 20,881 Japanese Canadians interned were moved from the West Coast and forced to take up residence in Greenwood's abandoned houses. After the war, many stayed on and the community continues to have a Japanese Canadian presence today.

Gulf Islands

This cluster of 225 islands and islets in the **Strait of Georgia** east of **Vancouver Island** is protected from Pacific Ocean storms by the **Insular Mountain's** rainshadow. The rainshadow effect limits rainfall on the islands to about one-third that of Vancouver Island's west coast, making it the driest zone on Canada's Pacific coast.

Most of the islands are small, uninhabited, and lack ferry service. Saltspring Island is the largest at 180 square kilometres. About seventy-five hundred of the Gulf Island's total population of approximately 11,400 live on Saltspring. Saltspring is more than three times the size of Galiano—the second largest island in the group—and has several mountain peaks, including Bruce Peak, the Gulf Island's highest, at 698 metres.

The islands' geography results from glacial carving some fifteen thousand years ago. Soil on slopes, especially on **coastlines**, was scraped away to leave the bedrock exposed. Softer rock was pushed up into sandstone ridges or compressed into narrow valleys. The result is that the islands are remarkably scenic with an array of coastal points and coves. **Arbutus** and **Garry oak** stands add to the islands' beauty.

European settlers first arrived on the islands in 1859. Island economies were originally based on **agriculture**, with some island populations creating near self-sustaining, insular economies. Improved ferry access since the 1960s, however, has made **tourism** a vital part of many island economies and also promoted population growth—especially by retirees. Since the mid-1980s island populations have grown by 20 percent and growth rates continue to accelerate. Rising land prices, concerns about overpopulation, and environmental concerns caused by the prospect of over-development are critical issues to many islanders. Such concerns led to the creation in the mid-1970s of the Islands Trust, an elected body that governs the Gulf Islands in much the same manner as a municipal council governs communities elsewhere in British Columbia.

(*See also* **Government—Local.**)

Gwaii Haanas National Park

Protecting all of South Moresby and many adjacent islands and islets at the southern end of the **Queen Charlotte Islands**, Gwaii Haanas National Park is 147,000 hectares in size and includes 15 percent of the archipelago's land mass. It was formally declared a park in July 1988 in what environmental and native people hailed a major victory against pro-logging and **mining** interests. More than 138 islands are encompassed by the park and minimal development is permitted, including the construction of roads and park facilities. The park has no maintained roads, trails, or public facilities and is generally considered to be most easily explored by kayak—although accurate and up-to-date marine charts and ocean experience are recommended. Some of the Sitka spruce in this park are more than one thousand years old and rise to heights of seventy metres.

There are several abandoned Haida villages in the park, including Ninstints, which is located on Anthony Island and was declared a UNESCO world cultural heritage site in 1981. In the late 1800s, the Haida on Anthony Island, known as Kunghit Haida, lost 90 percent of their population to smallpox, and by 1900 the village was abandoned.

Gwaii Haanas includes a vast variety of terrain ranging from tidal pools and islets to alpine meadows on summits rising up to heights of six hundred to nine hundred metres. It is a landscape often cloaked in mists, drenched by rains, and battered by winds and storms. South Moresby has also been identified as the most **earthquake**-prone place in Canada, lying on the terminus of several fault lines. Indeed, the Queen Charlottes are believed by geologists to have been formed by a massive movement of plate tectonics that shifted this small land mass from the South Pacific to its present-day location, which may explain why, of all land masses on North America's west coast, Moresby Island fails to have a continental shelf off its steep western ramparts.

Harrison Hot Springs

Known as the "Spa of Canada," Harrison Hot Springs is a small town of fewer than one thousand that serves as a health and vacation resort focused on two mineral springs adjacent to the waters of Harrison Lake. It is situated north of Highway 7, a short distance from Agassiz in the **Fraser River** Valley.

The hot springs derive from two sulphur-potash outlets that emerge from mountains on the lake's west side. Temperatures at these springs range from 58° to 62° Celsius.

Although legend states that the existence of the springs and the adjacent warmth of the lake's waters was discovered when a miner overturned his canoe and was surprised to discover warm, rather than frigid water, the native name for the lake means "hot water." The lake is seventy kilometres long.

Hazelton

The small village of Hazelton, at the junction of the Bulkley and **Skeena** rivers, traces its roots back at least seven thousand years to when **First Nations peoples** first established a community here. For many centuries it was known by the Gitksan people as Gitanmaks and served as a trading centre.

Today, nearby 'Ksan village reflects this historical tradition. Seven communal tribal houses with totem poles standing in front of each are the village's focal point. There is a treasure room and exhibition centre, carving shed, studio, and various other displays. During the tourist season 'Ksan dancers perform and artists practise traditional arts.

Health Care

The concept of providing the citizens of British Columbia and of Canada with a comprehensive government-administered health care insurance program was first proposed by the federal Liberal party in 1919 as part of its political platform. That same year the B.C. government appointed a Legislative Commission to investigate health care insurance. Although the Commission returned an outline for a state health care system and implementation plan no action was taken. Finally, in response to public pressure, especially from the growing industrial labour sector, the province passed a Health Insurance Act in 1936.

This bill, however, was overwhelmingly resisted by B.C.'s medical profession, which conducted a vote on whether it would accept the act, especially the provisions that set physician fees at a flat rate. Ninety-eight percent of those physicians voting opposed accepting the terms set by the Act. The government indefinitely postponed the Act's implementation.

After 1940, a number of private medical insurance plans were launched in the province, but these were restricted to those who could pay the premiums. Throughout the World War II years, public pressure for a government-administered medical insurance program mounted across Canada.

In 1947, the B.C. government implemented a hospital insurance plan, as did several other provinces. This plan was reformed in 1954 to remove length-of-stay restrictions and to restrict patient costs to one dollar a day. This plan was rolled into a national hospital insurance plan in 1957 and by 1961 all provinces were participating in the national program.

Pressure continued in B.C. for a government-administered medical insurance plan that would guarantee equal access to health care regardless of income, age, existing health conditions, or geographical location. There was also equal demand for such a program at the federal government level. A federal Royal Commission was established in 1961 to study the matter, and its recommendations, delivered in 1964, would lead to an intense national debate that lasted for ten years but ultimately resulted in a comprehensive national and provincial government-administered and -funded health care insurance system.

British Columbia was at the forefront of provinces in creating a provincial government health insurance plan. By 1965, the province started offering the British Columbia Medical Plan in parts of the province where no private- or physician-sponsored plans operated or to people exempted from such plans. In March 1967, the B.C. Legislature introduced a bill to bring all medical insurance plans in B.C. under one public authority, the Medical Services Commission.

Because of these measures, B.C. already had a provincial non-profit health insurance plan in effect when the federal government introduced a national plan on July 1, 1968, which the province immediately joined. Under the national plan, the province received a subsidy from the federal government to help provide medical services, and funded the majority of the remaining program costs through taxes and limited premiums. This plan has remained fundamentally unchanged, although, as health care costs have risen dramatically since the late 1980s, premiums have increased and some physicians have chosen to opt out of the system in protest against what they perceive as far too low remuneration for their services.

Today, provision of health care programs in B.C. accounts for about one-third of all the government's total expenditures. Approximately $6 billion is spent annually, of which about half goes to the provision of hospital care. B.C. has ninety-six acute care hospitals, five rehabilitation care hospitals, ninety-five extended care hospitals, and seventeen diagnostic and treatment centres that service an average of 400,000 acute and rehabilitation patients yearly. The average hospital stay is about seven days.

The Medical Services Plan in B.C. provides health insurance coverage to about 98 percent of British Columbians. Annual expenditures for patient care through the plan are about $1.5 billion. Approximately $1.33 billion of this goes to pay physicians' and surgeons' fees for services.

B.C. also has a program called Pharmacare to assist with paying for prescription drugs and related medical supply costs. This program is not universally available to British Columbians, but, for the majority, 80 percent of expenditures in excess of $500 annually are reimbursed. People aged sixty-five and over receive free drugs and medical supplies. Pharmacare expenditures run about $350 million per annum.

As health care costs continue to rise rapidly, fuelled by higher operating costs and an aging society, the government has been trying to implement a more preventative approach to health treatment. This has entailed such programs as the extension of more home- and community-based health care services to allow for earlier detection of patient illness and less expensive approaches to treatment than hospitalization.

Height of the Rockies Wilderness Area

In August 1987, following a twelve-year campaign by the Palliser Wilderness Society, the Height of the Rockies was established as B.C.'s first Provincial Forest Wilderness Area. Covering 73,000 hectares east of Invermere in the East Kootenays, it is a stunning region of alpine lakes set beneath fifteen **Rocky Mountain** peaks of more than three thousand metres. Height of the Rockies is lush with wildlife, including about eighteen hundred mountain goats, one hundred grizzly **bears**, two thousand deer, and two thousand elk.

The wilderness area is accessible by gravel roads that lead to four separate trailheads from which hiking access into the area is possible. Commercially operated horse-pack trips into the wilderness area are also available.

Hell's Gate

Hell's Gate is a rocky gorge of the **Fraser River Canyon** south of Boston Bar that funnels the powerful river through a narrow glacially carved chasm with rock walls thirty-four metres high. When explorer Simon Fraser reached the passage in 1808 he described it as resembling the "gates of hell." Fraser opted not to try shooting the furious rapids that run at speeds averaging twenty-eight kilometres per hour, but can reach forty-seven kilometres per hour. Even the portage Fraser carried out, however, was extremely difficult given the steep, virtually sheer, cliffs that had to be surmounted to get to the western side of the passage.

Whether Hell's Gate derives its name from Fraser's description or from other causes is unknown. An alternative explanation is that the gorge was so named by miners whose comrades drowned trying to navigate their rafts through the narrow gorge.

Between 1913 and 1914, construction of the Canadian National Railroad along the side of the gorge caused several severe **landslides**, which blocked much of the waterway, making the rapids even more hostile. The sockeye **salmon** run up the river was disrupted, resulting in a serious decline in the salmon harvest of subsequent years. The problem was not effectively cured until 1944 when fishways were constructed to permit spawning salmon to get past the rapids.

Today, Hell's Gate is a major tourist attraction. An aerial tram descends 153 metres, then swings across the Fraser River and Hell's Gate Fishway in a three-minute sweep to the other side. The gorge is also a popular river **rafting** route and several private companies offer rafting runs that are among the most exhilarating in the province.

Helmcken Falls

Situated in **Wells Gray Provincial Park**, Helmcken Falls is Canada's sixth-highest falls. The falls have a vertical drop of 137 metres as the Murtle River cascades off the edge of Murtle Plateau to join Clearwater River. This is considered one of the most spectacularly beautiful falls in Canada and is the park's main attraction. In winter the falls freeze into a massive ice cone, known as "the Bookmark," which stands taller than a twenty-storey building and is broader at its base than a football field. The frozen column of spray can rise up to a height of 305 metres.

Heritage. *See* Cultural History.

Highways

British Columbia's major transportation system is via highways. There are approximately twenty-two thousand paved kilometres of provincial highways and twenty-one thousand unpaved kilometres. This network of highways crosses about twenty-seven hundred bridges. Some of these bridges are among the longest in the world.

East-west highways crossing the province include Highway 16 running east from the coast at **Prince Rupert** to McBride; **Trans-Canada Highway (Highway 1)** from **Victoria** to the Alberta border near Field; and Highway 3, the most southerly route, which begins off Highway 1 at Hope and runs east to the Alberta border inside the **Crowsnest Pass**. The province's only highway running its length from south to north is Highway 97, which enters B.C. at Osoyoos in the **Okanagan Valley** and exits the province just south of Watson Lake, Yukon.

Even with this vast network of roads, much of the province is accessible only by water, air, or **hiking** trail.

Hiking

With one of the most varied and rugged wilderness landscapes in the world, British Columbia offers almost limitless opportunities for hiking—ranging from outings of a few minutes to gruelling month-long expeditions that are among the world's most demanding.

The province's most famous hiking trail is the **West Coast Trail** on **Vancouver Island**. **Cape Scott** Provincial Park, also on the island, is often cited as an excellent hiking route, although it is also one of the wettest regions in the province.

Two historic routes—the **Alexander Mackenzie Heritage Trail** and the **Chilkoot Trail**—allow hikers to follow in the path of alternatively an early explorer or gold stampeders en route to the Klondike Gold Rush.

The best beach hiking in the province is found at Naikoon Provincial Park's East Beach Trail in the **Queen Charlotte Islands**, which takes five to seven days to hike and is mostly along beach terrain.

Most of the province's hiking trails, whether in national, provincial, regional, or municipal parks, or on Crown land, are generally through what should be considered wilderness area. Hikers should have adequate equipment and experience for all but the shortest of hikes. As weather in B.C. is unpredictable, especially in coastal regions, appropriate changes of clothing should be carried. Most streams and lakes in the province are considered unsafe to use as untreated drinking water. Hikers should carry sufficient drinking water with them, or use purification tablets or boil stream water before drinking. In more remote hiking areas, carrying a relevant topographic map is advisable.

Historical Overview

Although British Columbia was one of the last North American frontiers to be discovered by Europeans, most of the province had been populated by **First Nations peoples** for between ten thousand to fifteen thousand years prior to the arrival of the first Spanish explorer, Juan Perez Hernandez, in 1774. Perez did not land, but he laid claim to British Columbia for Spain.

Four years later, James Cook took his two ships under British flag into **Nootka Sound** on the west coast of **Vancouver Island** and, despite the Spanish possession claim, within a few years British traders were arriving by sea and engaging in fur trading with the First Nations peoples. In 1789, Spain and Britain disputed ownership of the west coast of North America. The Spanish established a trading post at Nootka Sound and seized British ships stationed there. The Nootka Sound Controversy, as this was called, was settled in 1792 by the Nootka Conventions, which gave equal trading rights to both countries and left the subject of ownership unsettled. By 1792, however, Britain's claim to the region was strengthened by Captain George Vancouver's meticulous three-year mapping of the coast from Oregon to Alaska. Many of the bays, inlets, and coastal landform features of B.C. still bear the names given them by Vancouver.

In 1793, Alexander Mackenzie of the North West Company entered the region from the east by travelling the **Peace River** and Upper **Fraser River**. He reached the Pacific Coast by following a traditional **oolichan** fish-trading route through the **Coast Mountains** to Bella Coola. This trail is now known as the **Alexander Mackenzie Heritage Trail**. Soon after, David Thompson and Simon Fraser, also members of the North West Company, explored other parts of the interior and opened it to the fur trade.

Throughout the first half of the nineteenth century, British Columbia remained little populated or known by Europeans and underwent no settlement boom similar to that occurring in the eastern part of Canada or even on the prairies. The fur trade throughout this period was controlled primarily by the Hudson's Bay Company (HBC), which extended its operations into part of what is today Washington and Oregon states. Controversy over American and British territorial claims on the west coast produced the Oregon Treaty of 1848 which extended the **49th Parallel** border demarcation west from the **Rocky Mountains** to the **Strait of Georgia** and included all of Vancouver Island as British territory. The Hudson's Bay Company had established its headquarters for this region at Fort Victoria on the island in 1843 and the U.S. agreed to this location to the south of the 49th parallel remaining British.

In 1849, Britain opened Vancouver Island to colonization by the HBC. Two years later a company official, James Douglas, became the colony's first governor. He established a legislative assembly for Vancouver Island in 1856, although the island's European population was still very small and virtually no Europeans lived on the mainland other than at fur trading forts, such as **Kamloops**, Fort George, and Fort St. James.

Two years later, in 1858, gold was discovered in the sand bars of the lower Fraser River. The period of **gold rushes**, which opened up the interior of B.C., had begun. By the early 1860s, **Barkerville**, with a population of about twenty-five thousand, was the largest community in western Canada.

Trying to establish government and maintain law and order on the mainland, the British government created the colony of British Columbia in 1858 with Douglas, still governor of Vancouver Island, serving as its governor. **New Westminster** was declared the new colony's capital in 1859. The two colonies were united in 1866 to reduce administrative costs, and in 1868 **Victoria** was declared the capital.

A year earlier, the eastern provinces of the North American British colonies had united in the Confederation known as Canada, and B.C. was soon debating whether it should also join. In 1871, the twelve thousand white residents agreed to enter the Dominion of Canada on condition that the federal government link B.C. to the east via a transcontinental railway. It would be fifteen years before the federal government made good on this promise and the delay sowed the seeds of a distrust of eastern promises and intentions that persists today.

Throughout the 1880s the province stagnated economically. Its population, after the gold rushes, grew slowly so that in 1881 the twenty-four thousand whites were outnumbered by the estimated twenty-five thousand First Nations peoples. Some prosperity did develop around **Vancouver**'s port upon completion of the Canadian Pacific Railway in 1885, so that by 1901 about twenty-seven thousand people lived in Vancouver, outnumbering Victoria's population of approximately twenty-four thousand. The rest of the province remained barely populated by European settlers.

After 1900, the province's natural resource wealth was fully recognized, however, and aggressive exploitation began. A **salmon**-cannery industry, sawmills, pulp and paper mills, and other fish and **forest industry** operations soon developed along the West Coast and to a lesser extent in the interior. After World War I, the opening of the Panama Canal allowed for expanded export trade markets for the forest industry, and forestry soon emerged as the dominant economic force in the province's **economy**.

Interior settlement during this period concentrated in valleys that contained arable land, such as the **Okanagan** and **Thompson** valleys, and in the Kootenay regions where mining operations were established. Growth extended outward from these initial communities as transportation systems were moved into the rest of the province, but the historical development of B.C.'s **population** base set the continuing pattern that resulted in its concentration in the Georgia Basin areas of the Lower Mainland and southern Vancouver Island, and the Okanagan Valley.

Construction of the Grand Trunk Railway from Edmonton through the Upper Fraser, Bulkley, and **Skeena** valleys between 1907 and 1914 was intended to give Canada a second gateway through the mountains of B.C. to the Pacific Coast. This rail access established **Prince George** as a small sawmilling community. The port and rail terminals at **Prince Rupert** never achieved anticipated shipping volumes and the second gateway remained largely unused.

The Great Depression of the 1930s caused an economic decline that persisted until 1945 due to loss of world markets resulting from first the depression and then World War II. Not until the early 1950s, when transportation systems in the province were greatly extended, did B.C. start to expand its natural resource extraction industries within the interior and integrate these with coastal collection, processing, and management centres. Since the 1960s, the provincial economy and population have grown primarily as a result of immigration and migration to B.C. from other parts of Canada. The economy, however, remains firmly footed on natural resource-based industries and continues to lack sufficient diversity and internal strength to be free of the effect of world market trends.

For more history see especially the following listings: **Barkerville**; **Cariboo Gold Rush**; **Cariboo Road**; **Chinatowns**; **Columbia River Treaty**; **Craigellachie**; **Cultural History**; **Doukhobors**; **Ethnicity**; **First Nations Land Claims**; **First Nations Peoples**; **Gold Rushes**; **Health Care**; **Japanese Canadian Relocation**; **Political History**; and **Potlatch**; as well as individual listings on communities, parks, and regions.

Hockey. *See* **Cultural History; Vancouver Canucks.**

Hope Slide

On January 9, 1965, the most devastating slide in recent British Columbian history took place eighteen kilometres east of Hope on the Hope-Princeton Highway. Without warning, the entire side of a 1,983-metre-high and one-kilometre-wide mountain suddenly began to move. Within minutes, forty-six million cubic metres of earth, rock, and snow bore down into the narrow valley below at speeds exceeding 160 kilometres per hour. The highway ran directly along the mountain's foot and four motorists were killed by the slide, which buried the road under debris with depths of up to one hundred metres. Two of the bodies were never found. It took twenty-one days to build a temporary road through the disaster area.

Without warning on January 9, 1965 a large section of a mountain roared down in a massive avalanche that buried a section of Highway 3 east of Hope. This photo was taken within hours of the disaster. (BCARS photo H-04745)

Today, the highway curves in a wide arc around the vast spray of rock debris jumbling the valley floor, which has been left largely undisturbed.

Hornby Island

This northern **Gulf Island** just off the east coast of **Vancouver Island** south of Courtenay is the only place in the world where the primitive six-gill shark comes into shallow water. Normally these sharks, averaging six metres in length, live deep in the ocean, but from June to September they move slowly along an underwater ledge at the south end of Flora Islet, off the southern tip of Hornby Island. In places, the water at this ledge is only fifteen metres deep, but usually the sharks stay below twenty-seven metres. Scuba divers from around the world come to mingle with the sharks. For some reason the six-gill sharks are remarkably somnolent during the time they spend at Flora Islet and can be safely approached, even touched. Some researchers believe the sharks are lulled by the water's unaccustomed warmth. Why the sharks return here each year is unknown.

Hostels

There are five hostels in British Columbia operated by Hostelling International—Canada—B.C. Region. These hostels are located in **Kamloops**, Penticton, **Vancouver**, **Victoria**, and **Whistler**. They are open year-round.

In addition to those operated by Hostelling International, there are ten privately operated hostels that are licensed for operation by Hostelling International. These are located at **Alert Bay**, **Chemainus**, Fernie, Iskut, Nanaimo, Nelson, Powell Lake, Saltspring Island, Squilax, and **Victoria**. Operating seasons for the private hostels vary.

Hot Springs. See Ainsworth Hot Springs; Harrison Hot Springs; Invertebrates; Radium Hot Springs.

Hugh Keenleyside Dam

Located eight kilometres west of Castlegar, this fifty-metre-high earthfill and concrete dam is part of the **Columbia River** System. Completed in 1965, the dam holds back Upper and Lower **Arrow Lakes** and has created a controlled drainage area totalling 3.65 million hectares known as the Arrow Lakes Waterway.

This waterway includes the Arrow Lakes and extends for 232 kilometres north to Revelstoke. To the south, the waterway stretches 230 kilometres to Grand Coulee Dam in Washington State. The waterway is a popular pleasure boating destination, with excellent fishing for kokanee and other fish. Construction of Grand Coulee Dam in the 1930s doomed the Columbia River **salmon**-spawning grounds north of the dam, as the migrating fish were unable to get past the 108-metre concrete structure. Due to its height, a fish-ladder was deemed impossible to construct and one of the Northwest Pacific's major spawning grounds was sacrificed to the demand for hydroelectric power, flood control, and provision of an irrigation source for agricultural development of eastern and central Washington State. Dam control of water levels, both by Hugh Keenleyside and Grand Coulee, can vary water levels by up to twenty metres, with daily levels rising or dropping as much as thirty centimetres.

The dam has one of western Canada's only navigation locks. The lock is fifteen metres wide and stretches eighty-eight metres between the lock gates. River traffic is lifted twenty-three metres from below the dam to enter the Lower Arrow Lake reservoir. Tugs pulling log booms downstream to the sawmill and pulp mill at Castlegar share the lock with pleasure craft.

(*See also* **Columbia River Treaty**; **Mica Dam**.)

Hunting Regulations

Anyone wishing to hunt or carry firearms in British Columbia must obtain the required licences. It is illegal for anyone under the age of ten to carry a firearm or hunt in B.C. Children aged ten to fourteen must hold a Junior Hunting Licence and hunt only when accompanied by an adult possessing a hunting licence. Hunters aged fourteen to nineteen must have a valid hunting licence and be accompanied by a person over nineteen who holds a valid hunting licence.

Hunting is prohibited in all **national parks**, most **provincial parks** and recreation areas, and in all **ecological reserves**. The hunting season for specific species often varies from one region of the province to another, as does the bag limit. Special licences are required for the hunting of some animals. These licences are in addition to the basic hunting licence.

Non-residents of B.C. hunting big game must be accompanied by a licensed B.C. guide. When purchasing big game licences, non-residents must provide the licensing office with the name of the guide outfitter, the guide's licence number, the location in which the hunt will take place, and the dates of the hunt. Canadian citizens from outside B.C. may hunt big game only in the company of a licensed guide or a B.C. resident holding a valid Permit to Accompany. It is not necessary for a non-B.C. resident to be accompanied by a licensed guide when hunting for small game.

Ice Age. *See* **Glaciation.**

Immigration. *See* **Cultural History.**

Imports. *See* **Economy.**

Indian Art; Indian Basketry and Weaving; Indian Land Claims; Indian Religion. *See listings under* **First Nations.**

Insects. *See* **Invertebrates.**

Insular Mountains

The majority of the Insular Mountain range is submerged beneath the waters of the Pacific Ocean, but this range extends from the towering summits of the Olympic and Cascade Mountain ranges on the Washington State coastline to the tip of Graham Island in the **Queen Charlottes.** Above the ocean surface, the Insular Mountains exist as the Queen Charlotte Mountains and the **Vancouver Island** Mountains.

Almost all of the Queen Charlottes, except for the northeastern part of Graham Island, are part of this mountain range. Maximum altitude of peaks on the islands reaches about 1,130 metres, but the mountains are extremely rugged with serrated peaks cut by ice-age glaciers. The mountains on the islands' western edge protect the eastern portions from the worst of Pacific Ocean storms.

All of Vancouver Island, other than a narrow strip of lowland along the eastern and northern coast, is encompassed by the Vancouver Island Mountains. The island has many impressive mountain peaks, including **Mount Golden Hinde** (elevation 2,200 metres), Elkhorn Mountain (2,195 metres), Mount Victoria (2,163 metres), and Mount Colonel Foster (2,134 metres). All of these highest peaks are located in the central part of the island in the vicinity of **Strathcona Provincial Park.** Summit elevations decline to the northwest and southeast of these peaks, with no peaks higher than 1,525 metres found northwest of Nimpkish Lake or southeast of Cowichan Lake.

Insurance Corporation of British Columbia (ICBC)

In 1973, the provincial New Democratic Party **government** introduced a compulsory one-corporation automobile insurance program providing basic liability coverage and benefits to all licensed motor vehicle owners in the province. The government-owned corporation was called the Insurance Corporation of British Columbia (ICBC). Initially ICBC was operated in total exclusion from the traditional insurance agencies and services it replaced, but within a few years premium collection was turned back to private insurance agencies and private insurance companies were allowed to compete with ICBC in provision of extended coverage, such as collision protection.

Government policy is that the premiums paid by B.C. motorists must cover the cost of claims incurred and, in recent years, premiums have risen steadily to offset rising claim settlement costs.

Interior Plateau

Covering an immense expanse of terrain running from north to south for 901 kilometres and east to west for 378 kilometres at its widest point, the Interior Plateau is one of the major physiographic features of British Columbia. Encircled by mountains, it is flanked to the west by the **Coast** and **Cascade** mountains, to the north by the Skeena and Omineca mountains, to the east and southeast by the **Rocky** and **Columbia** mountains. Narrow belts of highlands and deeply carved valleys provide the only accesses through these mountains to connect the Interior Plateau with the rest of the province and the world. The Interior Plateau runs from the northernmost reaches of **Babine Lake** to a narrow neck centred on the **Okanagan Valley** at the **49th parallel**. The plateau itself extends a short distance into Washington State.

The Interior Plateau is almost completely drained by the **Fraser River** and its tributaries; the **Skeena**, **Peace**, and **Columbia** rivers, and their many tributaries provide only minor alternative drainage routes. Average altitudes of the plateau seldom exceed one thousand metres.

Contained within the Interior Plateau is the majority of the province's population outside of the Georgia Basin on the coast. This is a region with a wealth of resources—**forests**, mineral deposits, and soil capable of supporting **agriculture**. The **Cariboo**, Thompson Valley, Okanagan Valley, and other major parts of the province lie within the boundaries of the Interior Plateau. Major B.C. cities, such as **Prince George**, **Kamloops**, and **Kelowna** are situated on the Interior Plateau.

Interior System

One of four divisions of the Canadian Cordillera (*see* **Physiography**) as commonly designated by physiographers, the Interior System is a vast part of the province that is strewn with a diversity of landforms. These include low-lying plains and basins, plateaus, highlands, and an array of small mountain ranges.

At first glance, designating these landforms as part of one cohesive system seems little more than a random convenience. A closer look, however, reveals common geological denominators and a similarity in development that distinguishes this system from those to its east and west.

On the west, the Interior System is bordered by continuous mountains— the ranges of the **Cascade** and **Coast**—stretching from the **49th parallel** to the Yukon boundary. To the east, the extreme northern portion of the Interior System is bordered by the Liard Plateau north of the Liard River and south of the river by the **Rocky Mountains**, which continue down to the B.C.-U.S. border.

The Interior System encompasses a large part of the province and extends into the Yukon. Its sheer size creates the physiographic diversity that characterizes the system. Basically, the system breaks down into three distinctive subdivisions running from north to south, with a fourth region—the **Rocky Mountain Trench**—to the east. In the province's north and Yukon Territory lies the Northern Plateau and Mountain Area. Only part of this area extends into British Columbia, a section referred to as the Yukon Plateau and Liard Plain. This region was among the last in the province to be freed of glacial ice and its topography is typified by glacial deposits, low depressions, gently rolling hills, basins, widely flared valleys, and mountain peaks that seldom exceed two thousand metres. This area is among the most isolated and least developed in the province.

South of this region lies the Central Plateau and Mountain Area, most of it north of the 55th parallel. This region contains the Stikine Plateau, Skeena Mountains, Nass Basin, Hazelton Mountains, Cassiar Mountains, and Omineca Mountains. It is a wild, mountainous, often extremely isolated, mineral-rich, and rugged region. Mountains range from high peaks, such as the Seven Sisters grouping in the Bulkley Range, to the rounded mounts surrounding the Dease Plateau. Glaciers during the Pleistocene determined the shape of this region, the extent of **glaciation** varying in accordance with the presence of granite and other impermeable and immovable stones.

Running south from the Central Plateau and Mountain Area to the 49th parallel lies the Southern Plateau and Mountain Area. This area is the most accessible portion of the interior of British Columbia, the most populated, and the most developed. This region contains the massive **Interior Plateau**, the Cariboo, and the **Okanagan Valley**. The most western portion of this area is a region of basins, plateaus, highlands, and low-ranging mountains. The eastern portion is rugged, containing the **Columbia Mountain** ranges broken by steep valleys. The eastern flank of the Columbia Mountains borders the Rocky Mountain Trench.

An almost universal feature throughout most of central B.C. is the flat or gently sloping surfaces characteristic of plateaus and highlands—the product of stream erosion, glacial action, uplifting, and volcanic lava flows. Glaciation left deep drifts of soil and rock debris across the plateaus, as well as cutting many of the valleys, such as the Okanagan and Similkameen. The massive rivers of the **Fraser**, **Thompson**, and **Nechako** later cut their own paths through the porous plateaus. Other channels were cut through the plateaus by glacial-melt rivers that have long since disappeared from the region or remain now only as minor streams. The area's many lakes lie in depressions and blocked valleys created by glacial scouring and deposits.

Internment. *See* **Japanese Canadian Relocation.**

Invertebrates

Species of invertebrates in British Columbia are believed to number between fifty thousand and seventy thousand. Invertebrates are animals lacking a backbone. More than 90 percent of all living animals are invertebrates. Apart from the absence of a backbone, invertebrates have little in common. They are generally soft-bodied animals without a rigid internal skeleton, but often have a hard outer skeleton (true of most molluscs, crustaceans, and insects) that serves, as well, for body protection. The most numerous subgroup of invertebrates is the arthropods, comprising insects, crustaceans, spiders, and their relatives.

A tidal pool at Botanical Beach Provincial Park on Vancouver Island thrives with invertebrate life, such as a sea star. (Mark Zuehlke photo)

In British Columbia about twenty-five thousand arthropod species have been identified; researchers believe, however, that the actual number of arthropod species may be closer to fifty thousand. This compares to the presence of only 454 bird and 143 mammal species.

No region of B.C. has been thoroughly surveyed for invertebrates, so little is known about their role in the province's diverse ecosystems. They are known, however, to be essential to maintaining ecosystem resiliency and preservation. Many insects, including bees, flies, butterflies, and beetles, are key players in the pollination process. As a critical component in the food chain, invertebrates provide food for other animals. Insects and other soil-inhabiting creatures help create productive soil. Other predator and parasitic invertebrates are vital for controlling plant and invertebrate species that are viewed as pests by humans.

Specific areas or environments in which some B.C. invertebrate populations are endangered or where scientific knowledge is particularly limited are the coast's ancient temperate **rainforests**, the **Okanagan Valley** and southeastern **Vancouver Island** drylands, hot springs, and caves. Initial surveys of the west-coast rainforests have revealed a very high invertebrate **biodiversity** that is still little understood or catalogued. A number of species appear to be rare or endangered, especially species of segmented worms, crustaceans, millipedes, springtails, spiders, and mites. The invertebrates in the soil and forest canopy of these **forests** are particularly poorly known.

Butterflies and moth populations in the Okanagan Valley and southeastern Vancouver Island are especially numerous and diverse. These are also two of the province's most endangered ecosystems. Experts believe that there are probably one hundred species of moths alone confined to the south Okanagan—an area where the natural ecosystem is being rapidly displaced by urban and agricultural development.

Springs, especially hot springs, are one of the province's most endangered and rare habitats. They are also home to some of the province's most unique invertebrates, including several species that are known nowhere else in the world. The entire world distribution of the freshwater snail, *Physella wrighti,* for example, is confined to the warm outlet of Alpha Pool at the Liard River Hot Springs. Other invertebrates in springs include caddisflies, beetles, midges, dragonflies (such as the Vivid Dancer damselfly that lives only in the Liard Hot Springs), and small crustaceans.

In the province's more than one thousand charted cave systems many invertebrate species exist that are found in no other environment. The only members of the amphipod crustacean *Styobromus quatsinensis* species in the world are found in Thanksgiving and Hourglass caves on Vancouver Island. B.C.'s caves have been barely examined for what unknown and possibly singular species may inhabit them.

Most of B.C.'s mollusc species are found in the southern part of the **Rocky Mountain Trench**, Thompson-Okanagan Plateau, eastern Vancouver Island, and the Lower Mainland. There are at least fourteen species of rare and endangered freshwater molluscs in the province. Freshwater molluscs are particularly vulnerable because the province's freshwater habitats are threatened by over-exploitation, pollution, and hydroelectric development.

About fifty invertebrate species or subspecies are known to be very rare or endangered in B.C. Only thirteen specimens of Lucas butterfly have been found in the world, all of them from two populations on Vancouver Island at Langford and **Victoria**, and one on Gabriola Island. Another butterfly, *Euphydryas chalcedona perdiccas,* existed in two populations on southern Vancouver Island, one on Mount Finlayson (north of Victoria), the other on Mount Tzouhalem (east of **Duncan**). The Mount Finlayson population has been extirpated and it is feared the Mount Tzouhalem population has also disappeared.

One of the most endangered species in the province is curiously enough a type of black fly—*Prosimulium constrictistylum.* Known to exist only in a very small stream one kilometre east of Osoyoos, this fly is endangered by the threat of human destruction of its stream environment.

Islands

The **Insular Mountains** lying seaward of the **Coast Mountains** of B.C. are mostly underwater. Their summits, however, rise from the Pacific Ocean to form the province's 6,500 islands and islets. **Vancouver Island** is the largest island in the province, as well as in North America. The 150 islands that constitute the **Queen Charlotte Islands** form the westernmost edge of Canada. With about 100 islands clustered within 130 square kilometres, the **Broken Group Islands** on Vancouver Island's west coast is one of the most concentrated island groupings on the west coast of North America. The 225 islands and islets lying in the Strait of Georgia, known collectively as the **Gulf Islands**, experience some of the most sheltered and moderate weather in the province. They are also, after Vancouver Island, the only islands in the province that are well populated.

(*See also* **Broken Group Islands; Gulf Islands; Hornby Island; Insular Mountains; Meares Island; Queen Charlotte Islands; Race Rocks; Ripple Rock; Vancouver Island.**)

Jade. *See* Symbols.

Japanese Canadian Relocation

The World War II mass relocation of Japanese Canadians in British Columbia away from coastal areas to camps in the province's interior, Alberta, Manitoba, and Ontario was the culmination of a long history of racism against people of Japanese descent or origin. Japanese immigration to B.C. began in 1877 and by 1914 ten thousand Japanese were permanently settled in Canada, almost all in British Columbia.

This first wave of immigrants were known as Issei. The Issei were usually young and literate, and came from poor and overcrowded fishing and farming villages on the islands of Kyushu and Honshu. They settled primarily in or near **Victoria** or **Vancouver**, on Fraser Valley farms, or in Pacific coast fishing villages and pulp towns.

By 1907, due to agitation by B.C. politicians, the federal government pressured Japan to limit emigration of males to Canada to 400 per year. Subsequent immigration was consequently of women joining husbands who had arrived earlier. In 1928, again at B.C. political insistence, the government restricted Japanese immigration to 150 persons per year. Given the racist climate existing in the nation even this net quota was rarely met. With the outbreak of World War II in 1939 all immigration from Japan ceased.

Both Issei immigrants and their Canadian-born children, the Nisei, faced massive discrimination. B.C. politicians, pressured by white supremacists, passed a series of laws intended to force Japanese Canadians to leave Canada. All Japanese Canadians, including Nisei and World War I veterans, were denied the right to vote. They were legislatively excluded from most professions, the civil service, and teaching posts. Labour and minimum-wage laws ensured Asian Canadians could work only in menial jobs and at rates of pay lower than those paid Caucasian employees. In the 1920s the federal government sought to exclude Japanese Canadians from fishing livelihoods by limiting the number of fishing licences awarded either Issei or Nisei. During the 1930s Great Depression, Japanese Canadians were allowed social assistance that was only a fraction of that paid Caucasians. Nisei were barred from service in the military until 1945 because allowing such service would require them being given the vote.

The discriminatory practices of B.C. society against the Japanese encouraged them to congregate in exclusive enclaves where they could develop their own social, religious, and economic institutions. On Powell Street in Vancouver, in Steveston, Mission City, and other Fraser Valley villages, in Victoria, and in coastal centres such as Tofino and **Prince Rupert**, Japanese Canadians built churches and temples, established Japanese-language schools and community halls, and built hospitals staffed by Japanese doctors and nurses. They formed cooperative associations to market fruits, vegetables, and fish, and community and cultural associations for self-help and social events. By 1941, there were more than one hundred clubs and organizations within the tightly knit community. So pervasive were the discriminatory practices against Japanese Canadians that even Nisei who were fluent in English and possessed **post-secondary education** could attain only minimum-wage labourer positions outside the Japanese Canadian enclaves.

The existence of a cohesive and virtually self-sustaining social system in the Japanese enclaves was held up by the anti-Japanese lobby in B.C.—who had forced its creation in the first place—as further proof that neither Issei nor Nisei could be assimilated successfully into the province's white culture. At various times they clamoured for all Japanese in Canada to be deported back to Japan.

With the outbreak of World War II, and immediately following the Japanese bombing of the U.S. naval base at Pearl Harbor on December 6, 1941, the federal government acquiesced to pressure from the provincial government and B.C. federal politicians by using provisions of the War Measures Act to order all Japanese Canadians residing within one hundred miles (160 kilometres) of the Pacific coast relocated. This move came a scant twelve weeks after the attack on Pearl Harbor.

The official justification was that the Japanese Canadians posed a national security risk, although the order was opposed by Canada's senior military and police officers who said there was no evidence that Japanese Canadians posed any such threat. No Japanese Canadian was ever charged with disloyalty to Canada. Later in the war, the federal government justified the relocation as a means of protecting Japanese Canadians from mobs in B.C., but there was no proof that any such mob action would have occurred. Indeed, only 150 anti-Japanese letters and resolutions were received by the federal government prior to the relocation being ordered.

In 1942, the shelling of the Estevan Point lighthouse on Vancouver Island by a Japanese submarine was used as the final justification by politicians for ordering the removal of 20,881 Japanese Canadians—about 75 percent of whom were Canadian nationals—from their homes. They were processed through a temporary holding camp in Vancouver, and shipped to internment camps in B.C.'s interior or to sugar beet farms in Alberta and Manitoba. Between 1943 and 1946 the federal government sold off all Japanese Canadian property— homes, farms, fishing boats, businesses, and personal property—and deducted from the proceeds any welfare received by the owner while confined and consequently unemployed in the internment camps. Most of the property sold for well below its commercial value. In 1945, Japanese Canadians were forced to choose between deportation to Japan or dispersal east of the **Rocky Mountains**. Most chose the latter and were dispersed to Ontario, Quebec, and the Prairie provinces.

With war's end the federal government's punitive measures continued. In 1946, again at B.C. political instigation, the federal government attempted to deport ten thousand Japanese Canadians. It abandoned the plan only in the face of massive public protest from across Canada by non-Japanese. Finally, in 1949, Japanese Canadians regained their freedom and were given the right to vote. But the damage to the Japanese Canadian community was done. The cohesive enclaves were permanently devastated by the relocations and the subsequent dispersal east of the Rockies left the population scattered thinly across Canada. Despite gaining the right of citizenship and their freedom, Canada retained an anti-Japanese policy by continuing to block immigration from Japan until 1967.

The major force that united Japanese Canadians after World War II was a movement aimed at seeking redress for the suffering and loss of property caused by the relocation. The National Association of Japanese Canadians (NAJC) served as the fulcrum for this movement. In 1988 the federal government finally issued a formal apology to Japanese Canadians and paid about $300 million in compensation.

One of the Japanese Canadian internment camps was located at **Kaslo** on the west shore of Kootenay Lake. In 1994 this small community, population of about 870, opened a free museum and archival display that traces its role as a camp in the internment years.

Juan de Fuca Strait

Juan de Fuca Strait runs between **Vancouver Island** and Washington State for its entire 160-kilometre length. The strait connects the **Strait of Georgia** and Puget Sound to the ocean. The many deepwater ports, including those of **Vancouver**, **Victoria**, and Seattle, make this a heavily travelled body of water. Tidal currents in the strait are complex and dangerous.

Juan de Fuca derives its name from Greek mariner Apostolos Valerianos, nicknamed Juan de Fuca, who in 1596 met English trader Michael Lok in

Venice. Juan de Fuca described to Lok a voyage he alleged to have commanded on behalf of the Viceroy of Mexico up the Pacific Coast in pursuit of a northern route to the Atlantic. Juan de Fuca claimed to have discovered a strait between 47 and 48 degrees latitude.

In 1787 Captain Charles Barkeley also explored a strait in that location, and, having read Lok's account of Juan de Fuca's tale, named it after Juan de Fuca. Most historians believe Juan de Fuca made up the entire story of his voyage up the Pacific coast and that the fact the strait so closely matched his description, including the precise details of its location, is mere coincidence. No records exist of the sailor being commissioned to carry out any voyage.

Judiciary

The British Columbia judicial system is composed of the Court of Appeal of British Columbia, the Supreme Court of British Columbia, and the Provincial Court of British Columbia, which includes Small Claims Court and Family Court. Judges are appointed to the B.C. Court of Appeal and Supreme Court by the federal government and to the Provincial Court by the provincial government.

The federal judicial system includes the Tax Court of Canada, the federal Court of Appeal, the Federal Court of Canada, and the Supreme Court of Canada. The Federal Court of Canada hears cases in limited areas of law that fall exclusively under federal jurisdiction; for example, reviewing decisions made by federal tribunals such as the Canada Labour Relations Board. The Supreme Court of Canada is the court of final resort and hears selected appeals from the federal Court of Appeal and provincial Court of Appeal.

Provincial Court deals with lesser criminal matters, including trials of minor or summary conviction offences, trials of serious (indictable) offences where the accused elects to be tried in Provincial Court, and preliminary inquiries of indictable offences to determine if sufficient evidence against the accused exists to warrant a trial. The Family Court division of the Provincial Court deals with matters arising out of Family Law, such as child custody disputes and adoption issues. Family Court in Canada does not have jurisdiction over divorce cases and their consequences. These are a Supreme Court of British Columbia matter because they involve the division of property—a higher court jurisdiction. Small Claims court hears civil disputes over issues of indebtedness up to the amount of $10,000. Traffic disputes are handled in traffic court.

There are 101 Provincial Court, 33 Supreme Court, and 3 Appeal Court locations across the province. It costs the provincial government about $387 million per annum to operate B.C.'s criminal and civil court system.

Approximately 90 percent of all B.C. criminal cases are decided in Provincial Court. The remaining 10 percent are heard in Supreme Court. The Provincial Court also handles cases involving juveniles that fall within the jurisdiction of the Young Offenders Act. In an average year the Provincial Courts will hear about 110,000 criminal cases, 19,500 youth cases, 18,500 family law cases, and 46,400 civil cases.

The Supreme Court of British Columbia hears about 44,000 civil cases and 4,500 criminal cases. Total new cases of all kinds in B.C. average about 315,000 per year.

Kamloops

In terms of land coverage, Kamloops, with an approximate population of 67,000, is the province's largest city. Kamloops sprawls across 310 square kilometres of the Thompson River Valley, assuming a ragged star-like shape. The convergence of the South and North **Thompson** rivers here was known by Secwepemc (formerly Shuswap) natives as *Kamloopa,* meaning "where the rivers meet." First European settlement here was in 1812 by fur traders. Today, the city is a transportation, mining, and pulp milling economic centre. Kamloops hosted the Canada Summer Games in August 1993.

Kaslo

A small community of about eight hundred on the edge of **Kootenay Lake**, Kaslo endured two major disasters in 1894. At the time it was a thriving silver-mining boomtown with a population of about seven thousand. On February 25, 1894, fire broke out and destroyed most of one of the town's busiest streets. Later the same year a storm whipped up by hurricane-force winds struck. The winds blew the front out of a hotel and flattened the town jail. A bridge and log jam upriver gave way and the swollen Kaslo River tore through the town, sweeping away many buildings.

The townspeople rebuilt but soon the silver mines played out and the population dwindled away to its present-day levels. Many of the historic buildings have been restored.

During World War II Kaslo was the site of a **Japanese Canadian** internment camp. Today, the community has a small museum that relates the experiences of the camp internees.

Kelowna

Kelowna is the largest B.C. city outside of the Georgia Basin region of the Lower Mainland and southern **Vancouver Island**. City population is approximately 76,000; area population about 120,000. In 1961 barely twenty-seven thousand people lived in this same area of the **Okanagan Valley**, but by the early 1970s growth became rapid and shows little sign of abating despite a fragile economic base centred on **tourism**, forestry, **agriculture**, and the servicing of a growing retirement **population**.

Between 1988 and 1994 the population swelled by twenty thousand, or 38 percent. With the growth came rapid development of strip malls, walled community subdivisions, and heavy traffic congestion. These and other developments have led to concerns that the very quality of life that draws people to move here might be threatened by the continued population growth.

Situated on the shores of Okanagan Lake, Kelowna is a popular tourist destination, particularly in summer because of its warm temperatures and proximity to the lake. In winter, nearby ski hills also draw tourists.

Kemano

Seventy-five kilometres southeast of **Kitimat**, across the **Coast Mountains**, Kemano is the site of a massive 896-megawatt hydroelectric generating station providing power to the Alcan aluminum smelter in Kitimat. The Kenney Dam constructed on the **Nechako River** in 1952 diverted much of the river's water through a sixteen-kilometre-long tunnel to Kemano.

In 1987, the federal government authorized Alcan to further divert the flow of the Nechako as part of a $1.3 billion mega-project—known as the Kemano Completion hydroelectric power project. That plan called for reducing the river's flow to 12 percent of its pre-1950 level by diverting the water through a tunnel adjacent to the current one to power four additional generators.

The plan faced stiff resistance from environmentalists, the **fishing industry**, and many locals afraid the Nechako-flow reduction would cause irreversible environmental damage and harm the salmon fishery. In January 1995, the provincial government cancelled the project. At the time, Alcan had already spent $535 million on construction.

Khutzeymateen Valley Provincial Park

The Nisga'a named this valley Khutzeymateen, which means "a confined space of **salmon** and **bears**." It is the presence of a large spawning-salmon population and thick berry growth on the hillsides in spring that draws about fifty grizzly bears into the valley, giving it the most heavily concentrated grizzly population in British Columbia. In 1994, the isolated valley, to the north of **Prince Rupert**, was upgraded from its status as Canada's only official grizzly bear sanctuary to provincial park status.

The four-hundred-square-kilometre valley contains a dense rainforest that includes stands of Sitka spruce. In the shadows of the forest, grizzlies averaging four hundred kilograms feast on salmon from the valley streams (often eating only the nutritious brains), rub against favourite trees, dig up skunk cabbage to munch on the roots, and wallow in black mud holes on the valley's estuary flats.

From May to October, they roam the estuary meadows near Khutzeymateen River, Kateen River, and Carm Creek. The approach of denning time coincides with the spawning runs of pink, coho, chum, and chinook salmon, which, in addition to attracting grizzlies, draws black bears, **wolves**, and swarms of bald eagles into the valley.

Despite its status as a provincial park, Khutzeymateen is still a protected grizzly bear sanctuary and the public may only enter the area with government authorization or as part of an authorized guided group.

Killer Whales

Killer whales, or orcas, are found in the waters of the province's Pacific coast. There are nineteen known resident pods totalling approximately 275 whales that live permanently in B.C. waters. Three of the pods are resident to the southern half of **Vancouver Island**, ranging from Campbell River south to the waters around Washington State and up the west side of Vancouver Island as far north as Tofino.

The remaining sixteen pods loop around the northern half of Vancouver Island from Campbell River to Tofino. These whales concentrate most of the year in Johnstone Strait and Robson Bight off the east coast of the island.

Resident killer whale pods lead a relatively placid life and feed on fish, especially **salmon**, within their well-defined home territories during the summer seasons. When winter comes and the salmon are scarce they move far out to sea in search of better feeding opportunities.

In addition to the salmon-feeding residents, about one hundred transient killer whales roam the B.C. coast, hunting sea **mammals** as they travel between southern Washington State and Alaska. These whales appear more fearsome than their resident pod relatives because of the ferocity and savage suddenness of their attacks upon sea mammals.

Killer whales never grow larger than 9.5 metres. The killer whale is a member of the dolphin family *Delphinidae* and is the largest of the oceanic dolphins. It is black, with white on the underparts, above each eye, and on each flank. The snout is blunt, and the jaws are equipped with forty to fifty large, razor-sharp teeth. The flippers are rounded and the dorsal fin is triangular. Fin, flippers, and tail flukes enlarge with age in the male, the dorsal fin eventually forming a tall triangle up to 1.8 metres high.

Killer whales live in groups, usually of a few to about fifty individuals. They often swim in formation, either in a line or in rows, and sometimes leap out of the water (breaching). They are well adapted for hunting by virtue of their build, teeth, strong jaw muscles, and their organized behaviour when hunting in packs.

Until the late 1960s killer whales were usually feared by humans, considered to be as dangerous as the most deadly types of sharks. Fishermen traditionally hated killer whales, often shooting them on sight. Beginning in the late 1960s, however, research revealed that killer whales possibly were highly intelligent, formed strong kinship ties within their pod, and possessed a gentler spirit and nature than had been traditionally attributed to them. Undoubtedly, too, the fact that most other whale populations on the Pacific coast had been slaughtered off or were in serious decline contributed to growing public fascination with, and sympathy for, killer whales.

Researchers today have assigned identification numbers to the resident pods of killer whales plying B.C. waters and have even identified and assigned ages to individual whales in many of the pods.

(*See also* **Pacific Grey Whales**; **Whales**.)

Kimberley

At an elevation of 1,113 metres, Kimberley, with a **population** of about sixty-five hundred, is Canada's highest city. Situated in the **Rocky Mountains** on Highway 95A west of Cranbrook, the community is trying to shift its economic base from **mining** to **tourism** before the scheduled closure of Cominco's Sullivan Mine in the year 2000. The community is pinning its tourism-industry hopes on becoming a major ski destination. Part of this strategy has entailed dressing up its downtown core with a Bavarian alpine theme for store fronts. Kimberley claims the world's largest operating cuckoo clock, situated in the pedestrian-only "Platzl" shopping area.

Kinbasket Lake

Kinbasket Lake is about two hundred kilometres long and seldom exceeds two kilometres wide. It is actually part of the **Columbia River** backed up into a reservoir lake by the **Mica Dam**. Much of its length is bordered on one flank by the western reaches of the **Rocky Mountains**, providing the lake with incredible scenery. The lake's gentle currents and sheltered waters make it an increasingly popular canoeing route for paddlers of all skill levels.

Kispiox

At the junction of the Kispiox and **Skeena** rivers, Kispiox is the traditional Gitksan home of the Frog, Wolf, and Fireweed clans. The name means "people of the hiding place." A legend holds that the village was once massacred by hostile Indians and that only one woman survived. The totem poles in this small Gitksan village are among the best in the province.

Kitimat

In 1948, Kitimat, located south of Terrace at the head of the ninety-kilometre fjord Douglas Channel was selected by the Aluminium Company of Canada (Alcan) as the site of a massive aluminum smelter. The decision to locate at Kitimat resulted from the availability of hydroelectric power if nearby **Nechako River** was dammed and the fact that Douglas Channel was deep enough to serve as a sheltered deepwater port to allow shipping of product to international markets.

At the time, however, hardly anyone lived in the Kitimat area, so between 1951 and 1954, Alcan built a community designed to house and support a population of 13,500. Utilizing 1950s concepts of social organization, Alcan created a town that was both remarkably liveable and ordered—a fact which continues today to give the community its unique character.

Commercial and industrial areas were located well out of view of residential areas. Residential neighbourhoods were precisely measured and built to achieve an individual conformity that reflected the status of each worker's position in the plant. Streets were named in alphabetical clusters that feature uniform neighbourhood themes—fish for one area, birds for another, pioneers yet another.

One radical departure from 1950s subdivision planning was a decision to face yards toward green space cut by walkways rather than a street (the streets run between the lawns of backyards). The result of this innovation was creation of what is even today a community that has more than average greenspace within its neighbourhoods.

To find workers for its new operation, Alcan recruited in Scandinavia, Portugal, and much of southern Europe. Consequently, Kitimat has a richly diverse **ethnicity**. Close to one-third of the town is of Portuguese descent. In recent years, Kitimat has begun to diversify its economy away from singular dependency on the Alcan plant. A large pulp and paper mill, operated by Eurocan Pulp and Paper, is now a major employer.

Kitlope Valley

Situated on B.C.'s central coast between **Kitimat** and Bella Coola, the Kitlope Valley is the earth's largest remaining untouched coastal temperate **rainforest**. In 1994, its 317,000 hectares were granted protected status, a move that following resolution of **First Nations land-claim** negotiations will lead to the valley being granted provincial park status. Kitlope is a pristine wilderness of eight-hundred-year-old trees and glacial green rivers that survived the devastation of industrial logging because of its isolation and difficult terrain.

Before the granting of protected status the valley had been slated for eventual logging by West Fraser Timber Company, which held the cutting rights to the valley. But after years of low-profile negotiations between the company, the provincial government, and the Haisla nation, West Fraser voluntarily surrendered its cutting rights to the valley, estimated to have been worth a potential profit of $12 million. The company received no compensation under the agreement.

Kitlope is now jointly managed by the province and the Haisla nation.

Knapweed

Knapweed infestation is causing major environmental deterioration of the grasslands of the province's southern interior and a resultant loss of beef production. If it continues to spread unchecked, scientists fear B.C.'s grasslands could be destroyed as the knapweed replaces native grasses.

There are two types of knapweed in B.C. The most common is diffuse knapweed; the other, spotted knapweed. Diffuse knapweed has a single upright stem of twenty to one hundred centimetres height and numerous spreading branches. It is easily recognized by the short rigid spines on the flower heads, which are white or sometimes pinkish. A short-lived perennial, it propagates through the spread of over nine hundred seeds per plant under rangeland conditions. In irrigated areas, however, each diffuse plant can release up to eighteen thousand seeds.

Spotted knapweed is also a short-lived perennial. It has a thistle-like purple flower; produces about four hundred seeds in rangeland conditions and over twenty-five thousand seeds under irrigation. It grows from twenty to 120 centimetres tall.

Knapweed was introduced to B.C. from Eurasia in the early 1900s. It has no natural enemies or parasites in North America to keep it in check. People unwittingly help spread knapweed great distances in the undercarriages of vehicles, trains, and light aircraft. Florists, who use knapweed in dried floral arrangements, also contribute to its spread.

Knapweed is highly competitive, capable of invading grassland sites and forcing out all native vegetation. Domestic animals and wildlife, such as elk, rely on range grasses and herbs for up to 80 percent of their diet. Encroachment by knapweed destroys the forage base, resulting in significant declines in deer and elk numbers in affected areas.

More than forty thousand hectares of B.C.'s southern interior grasslands are knapweed infested, with forage potential in these areas reduced by up to 90 percent. Unchecked, knapweed could spread to infest one million hectares of grassland and undetermined areas of fringe forest. If spread to its ecological limit, knapweed could infest up to ten million hectares in western Canada.

Economically, knapweed causes the annual loss of about $400,000 in equivalent hay production. If spread to its limits throughout the province, the loss would be more than $13 million. The heaviest areas of knapweed contamination are in the **Okanagan**, Thompson, and Similkameen valleys. There are also serious infestations in the Kootenays and following close to Highway 97 in a finger that extends from Cache Creek north to Quesnel in the Cariboo. To date, knapweed has not become a serious problem in the Cariboo's rich grasslands but this salient infestation near roadways poses a major risk of spreading.

Knapweed control is being coordinated by the provincial agriculture ministry utilizing a blend of cultural, chemical, and biological control methods. To fight knapweed, a European fly, *Urophora quadrifasciata,* was first released in B.C. in 1972. This fly galls (causes a tumour) on the knapweed seed heads and also plants its eggs in the knapweed flower head upon which the larva then feed. Combined with another biological control agent, *Urophora affinis,* several sites formerly infested with knapweed have been about 95 percent deinfestated by the seed-reducing effects of these insects.

Kootenay Lake

Located in the Nelson-Creston region of the Kootenays, Kootenay Lake is more than one hundred kilometres long and ranges from two to six kilometres wide. It runs through the heart of the Purcell and Selkirk ranges of the **Columbia Mountains**. The lake is famous with anglers for giving up the world's largest rainbow trout catches—some specimens have weighed up to sixteen kilograms.

Kootenay National Park

The land encompassed within Kootenay National Park's 140,600 hectares is incredibly diverse. This park is the only Canadian national park where cactus grows and glaciers calve. The park is located on the western slope of the **Continental Divide** and runs 104 kilometres from north to south. Home to **Ra-**

dium Hot Springs, the parkland was traditionally a major travel route, as well as a hunting and gathering and spiritual celebration region, for native peoples living in the plains country of southern Alberta, and British Columbia's **Rocky Mountains** and Kootenays.

This region was declared a national park in 1920 when the provincial government deeded it to federal authority in return for construction of a road through the central Rockies. The road (now designated Highway 93) completed in 1923 through Vermilion Pass with an elevation of 1,651 metres was one of the province's highest roadways. It passes directly through the heart of the province, running from Radium Hot Springs in the northeast Kootenays to Castle Junction in Alberta, south of Lake Louise.

Today the park is visited by more than 1.2 million people annually—a number exceeded in Canada only by Banff and Jasper national parks. Many tourists come for the hot springs, others for the outdoor recreation opportunities that range from **hiking** to boating and **skiing**. The park has a large wildlife population, including black **bears**, grizzlies, elk, deer, mountain goats, moose, coyotes, and **wolves**, as well as more than 150 species of birds.

Even more than wildlife, however, what the park offers visitors is the grandeur of one of the greatest concentrations of peaks in the Rocky Mountain park system. Summits stand literally everywhere in seemingly random abandon. Most of these summits range between twenty-eight hundred and thirty-one hundred metres.

'Ksan. *See* Hazelton.

Kutenai Canoe

The Kutenai **First Nations people** of the Lower Kootenay Lake country built a style of canoe unique to the rest of North America. Instead of the bow and stern curling up or remaining flat as is true of other canoes, the Kutenai Canoe pointed downward at either end. The only other place in the world where such canoe construction is known to have occurred was in the Amur River Basin in Russia, among the Gilyaki peoples, near the Sea of Okhotsk, separated from Bering Strait by the peninsula of Kamchatka. As the Kutenai's language has no close relationship to other native American languages, the similarity in these two canoe designs has led some researchers to speculate that the two peoples are related and that the Kutenai must have crossed to Canada in an isolated migration across the Bering Sea.

A replica of the Kutenai canoe is on display at the Creston Valley Museum in Creston.

Labour Force

About 1.5 million of B.C.'s 3.2 million people are employed, with approximately a further 10 percent actively seeking employment. Fifty-nine percent of all women between the ages of fifteen and sixty-five work, as do 74 percent of all men in the same age bracket.

About 52 percent of the province's work force has attended a post-secondary institute; about 38 percent of these have completed some type of **post-secondary education**. This is a significant increase over the 1982 figures, when only 36.2 percent of the labour force had any post-secondary schooling at all.

Since the mid-1980s, the service-producing sector of the province has grown more rapidly than the goods-producing sector, similar to the trend in the rest of Canada and most other developed nations. Between 1982 and 1992, employment in the province's service sector increased from 875,000 to 1.158 million. In contrast, goods-producing employment rose from 327,000 in 1982 to only 359,000 in 1992. In this period, then, the service-producing sector's share of total employment rose from 72.8 percent of all employees to 76.3 percent. This upward growth trend is expected to continue.

The concentration of jobs in the service sector is increasing the amount of employment available in the urban centres and decreasing employment availability in the more rural regions of the province, which are traditionally dependent on natural resource extraction employment in the goods-production sector. The Lower Mainland's share of employment in the 1982 to 1992 period grew from 56.8 percent of all employment to 60.2 percent. This trend, too, is expected to continue and is slowly drawing **population** away from the other parts of the province, except for the **Okanagan Valley** and the southern and eastern portions of **Vancouver Island**.

Unemployment in B.C. is usually about one percent lower than the Canadian national average. The number of unemployed women and men is usually fairly equal.

Although most of the employment in the province is found in the service sector, it is the goods-producing sector that enjoys the highest wages. Average weekly wages in B.C. in 1992, for example, were about $549.00—the highest in Canada outside Ontario—but wages paid in the **mining industry** averaged the province's highest rates at $965.21 per week. Forestry and logging paid the second highest rates—$748.89. The average personal income for British Columbians was about $23,516 per annum, unchanged from the previous year. Average wages paid to women are considerably lower than those paid to men. In 1990, for example, women earned an average of only $18,357 compared to earnings paid to men of $31,162. Wages in recent years have continued to grow only slowly, despite continuing improvement in the state of the province's economic health. The margin of difference between the salaries of women and men is closing, but only gradually.

Ladysmith

Had **Vancouver Island** not been excluded from the **49th-parallel** clause of the Oregon Treaty of 1846, Ladysmith would have been a border town as the 49th parallel crosses Vancouver Island right through the community's heart. The agreement between the American and British governments, however, declared all lands north of the parallel to be British, all land south to be part of the United States—except for Vancouver Island, because the southern tip was already home to the important British Empire community of **Victoria**.

Ladysmith, originally called Oyster Harbour due to the presence of massive oyster beds, was renamed Ladysmith by B.C. coal-mining magnate and eventual provincial premier James Dunsmuir. He designed the town as a recreation area and dormitory for miners recovering from the rigours of working his island mines. The town's new name honoured the British breaking of a Boer forces siege on the South African community of Ladysmith—known as the Relief of Ladysmith. In keeping with his homage to British military exploits in the Boer War, Dunsmuir named the town's streets after Empire-forces generals of that war, such as Kitchener, BadenPowell, Roberts, and French.

Lakes. *See* **Arrow Lakes; Bowron Lakes; Cultus Lake; Great Central Lake; Green Lake; Kinbasket Lake; Kootenay Lake; Nitinat Lake; Okanagan Valley; Quesnel Lake; Shuswap Lake.**

Land Claims. *See* **First Nations Land Claims.**

Land Ownership and Use

British Columbia has a total area of 94.78 million hectares, of which only about 6 percent is privately owned. The following is a breakdown of the province's land status.

Land Status Category	Area (hectares)	Percent
Federal Land		
National parks	475,999	0.5
Indian reserve	341,077	0.4
Defence lands	57,266	0.1
Transportation	15,477	-
Miscellaneous	31,579	-
Total Federal Land	**921,398**	**1.0**
Provincial Land		
Provincial forests	73,897,568	78.0
Tree farm licences	6,440,779	6.8
Community pastures	167,699	0.2
Provincial parks	5,364,501	5.6
Regional parks	8,128	-
Crown land under		
Land Act tenure	379,606	0.4
Ecological reserves		
(land only)	107,321	0.1
Total Provincial Land	**86,365,602**	**91.1**
Private Land	**5,686,000**	**6.0**
Total Land Area	**92,973,000**	**98.1**
Total Water Area	**1,807,000**	**1.9**
Total Area	**94,780,000**	

Landslides

British Columbia's mountainous terrain creates a landscape prone to mass movements of rocks and soil commonly referred to as landslides. The province's slopes are primarily composed of heavily faulted sedimentary and igneous rock that has been sheared to a radical steepness by glacial erosion. This weakened rock surface is often heavily covered by sediment soils left during the glacial retreat. Neither the soil nor the rock beneath it is anchored in place— so heavy precipitation or seismic tremors can cause it to move. Sometimes contributing to the land's overall instability is the presence of rivers or tidal forces that further undercut the unstable soil and rock. Logging operations on or near these locations can also disturb their stability by increasing erosion from rainfall.

All these factors make landslides fairly commonplace throughout much of the province. Most of the slides are small and usually occur in isolated areas where property damage and human injuries are rare. There have, however, been some major slides in the twentieth century that have caused loss of life or serious property and environmental damage.

In both 1913 and 1914, major rock slides near **Hell's Gate** in the **Fraser Canyon** dumped huge amounts of debris into the **Fraser River**. The rock clogging the river's flow greatly impeded the annual upriver **salmon** runs in those years. As a consequence, spawning was reduced, resulting in a fishing industry loss worth millions of dollars.

There has been loss of life throughout the century resulting from landslides. Between 1967 and 1987, for example, thirty-four people died in landslides. Damage caused in this period was in the tens of millions of dollars.

The worst slide in recent provincial history occurred on January 9, 1965, when the **Hope Slide** buried a section of the Hope-Princeton Highway and four motorists were killed. The greatest loss of life caused in recent history by landslides occurred in the winter of 1981–82 in the area between Squamish and **Vancouver**. Ten people were killed by debris torrents and one rock fall here.

Two areas of the province have been uniquely affected by landslides and in each case the provincial government undertook unusual strategies to reduce the risk of property damage and injuries. On the northwest coast of **Vancouver Island**, the small community of Port Alice was erected in 1965 at the head of Neroutsos Inlet to replace a post-World War I pulp and logging company town that had been constructed four kilometres farther down the inlet in Quatsino Sound. The community of about thirteen hundred was located at the foot of some mountains on what proved to be a debris fan coming off the adjacent slopes. On December 15, 1973, a mud flow, originating at the seven-hundred-metre level on the steep slopes overlooking the town, poured into the community and caused $800,000 damage but no fatal injuries. Two years later there was another large slide into Port Alice. Smaller slides were frequent.

Provincial engineers and geologists descended on the town to try and save it from further damage. Eventually, to understand the forces at work, a scale model of the town and adjacent slopes was constructed. Using bentonite mud with a similar viscosity to the coarse, bouldery gravel found on the slopes overlooking Port Alice, mud flows were reproduced to identify a movement pattern. From findings derived from the model's mud slides the provincial government constructed a mud-dyking system for $250,000. The dykes were designed to protect the town from flows of up to 2.5 times the volume of the 1973 to 1975 slides by diverting the mud into unsettled areas. To date the system has worked and Port Alice has been spared further mud-slide damage.

In another region of the province, government engineers could not develop a solution to the landslide risk and authorities ultimately ordered the threatened homes and properties abandoned. This was in an area adjacent to Mount Garibaldi, some thirty kilometres northeast of Squamish. The specific location was on the east side of Cheakamus River, extending up Rubble Creek to a geological formation called the Barrier. It was an area that had been subject to a large number of rock slides. In May 1971, a private land development company applied to construct a 288-lot residential development astride the Rubble Creek rock fan. The government reviewed the application and rejected it as unsafe, a decision sustained by the Supreme Court of British Columbia. After a detailed analysis by a special advisory panel the environment ministry invoked powers provided by the Emergency Program Act. Under the act, the area was declared a civil defence zone and land and buildings existing within it were compulsorily purchased by the minister of environment for a sum that was not to exceed $7 million in compensation. The decision directly affected 102 property owners. Against enormous local opposition, the land was acquired and threatened buildings were demolished.

Languages

The multi-**ethnicity** of British Columbia's **population** is reflected in the major languages spoken by its citizens. The dominant language is English, one of Canada's official languages, with about 2.6 million of the province's 3.28 million people claiming this as their language of choice.

After English, the next most spoken language in the province is Chinese— the language of choice for about 141,000. Chinese is followed by German, spoken by approximately 81,000. Punjabi, an East Indian language, is spoken by about 58,000 British Columbians. The fifth most spoken language in B.C. is French—the first language for about 45,000 people—and Canada's second official language.

Legal System. *See* Judiciary; Police Forces.

Legislative Buildings

The province's Legislative Assembly meets and is officed inside the Legislative Buildings, an ornate structure that dominates the downtown of **Victoria**. Built at the then exorbitant cost of $923,000, the Legislative Buildings were designed by a twenty-five-year-old architect, Francis Mawson Rattenbury, who had moved to Canada and Victoria only the year before, and was virtually unknown. The buildings were constructed hastily to be ready for Queen Victoria's Diamond Jubilee in 1897 and were opened in time despite many construction problems. The east and west wings, parallel to the Legislative Chamber, and the south wing, housing the Legislative Library, were completed in several phases from 1911 to 1915.

B.C. materials were used in the construction of the buildings. The foundation and steps are of granite from Nelson Island, the facing stone of andesite from Haddington Island, and the original roofing slate was from Jervis Inlet. Native woods panel much of the interior.

The many stained- and art-glass windows were designed and manufactured for a total cost of less than $12,000. The front area of the buildings is decorated with a number of statues, notably the two-metre-tall gilt figure of Captain George Vancouver atop the central dome.

Since 1897, the tradition of illuminating the exterior of the buildings has been maintained. Today, some thirty-three hundred lightbulbs highlight the façade in a brilliant night-time display.

In 1973, the B.C. government began restoring the buildings, some of which had undergone a number of renovations and alterations over the years. Some had also fallen into disrepair. Architects and designers returned to Rattenbury's original drawings to ensure accuracy of detail. The exterior was restored from the foundations to the top of the George Vancouver statue, which was regilded with fourteen-karat gold. Stained- and art-glass windows were repaired. Mosaic tiles and ornate plaster work were restored.

Lighthouses

The rugged **coastline** of British Columbia has long been considered treacherous for ocean-going vessels and pleasure craft seeking safe harbour. To provide protection for the mariner, forty-one lightstations maintained by the **Ca-**

nadian Coast Guard have been established from the southern tip of **Vancouver Island** north to the Alaska border.

The oldest lightstation on the west coast of Canada is at **Race Rocks**, about sixteen kilometres west of **Victoria** in **Juan de Fuca Strait**. Built in 1860, at a time when most Canadian lightstations were of wood construction, Race Rocks was constructed of stone blocks up to two metres thick, which were quarried and cut in Scotland and

Canada's oldest west coast lighthouse is the station at Race Rocks. The tower was constructed in 1860 using blocks of stone taken from quarries in Scotland and shipped around Cape Horn. (BCARS photo I-03698)

transported as ballast by ships travelling around Cape Horn. This original structure is still operating.

Cape Beale lightstation, built in 1874, was the only aid to navigation on the storm-torn west coast of Vancouver Island until 1891. Egg Island, built in 1898, was the first lightstation in Queen Charlotte Sound. Pointer Island lightstation, on an island so small that it shrinks by a third every time the tide washes in, was constructed in 1899.

Green Island, established in 1906 at the northern entrance to Chatham Sound, is the province's most northerly lighthouse. Winds here occasionally reach one hundred knots.

Pachena Point was built in 1907, following B.C.'s most disastrous shipwreck—the sinking of the passenger liner *SS Valencia*.

Estevan Point is the tallest lighthouse on the Pacific coast. Appearing like a skyscraper on its lonely beach, it is 38.7 metres from its base to the focal beam of the light. A masterpiece of architecture, it is designed to sway in high winds. For added strength, flying buttresses—arched supports built between the wall of a building and a supporting column to take some of the upper-weight off the main supporting foundation—were used in the design.

Triangle Island, eventually abandoned, was built in 1910 and declared the tallest lighthouse in the world. This was not because of its height—only fourteen metres—but because it was located on the island's highest point, which was 213 metres above sea level. The lighthouse was double the elevation of any other Pacific coast station and its one-million-candle-power beacon was visible fifty-four kilometres out to sea. Unfortunately, Triangle Island was obscured in low-lying cloud and fog for half the year, so the powerful light was usually invisible to mariners. This led to the station's abandonment and the construction of a new station at nearby **Cape Scott** in 1927.

Langara Island, built in 1913, is the most westerly lightstation in Canada, as well as the most isolated on the northern coast.

Since the early 1990s, the manned lightstations on the Pacific coast have been at the centre of a major controversy. Federal cost-cutting initiatives have called for all lightstations to be automated and the lighthouse keepers removed. The plans have been resisted by the keepers, most mariners, and recreational groups, who all maintain that, besides keeping the lights operating, the lightkeepers are a vital factor in lifesaving in isolated waters and terrain.

Lillooet

Lillooet dates back to the **Cariboo Gold Rush**, when it served as a terminus for the boat route north via Harrison and Anderson lakes and later as starting point of the **Cariboo Road**. A cairn on Main Street marks Mile 0 of the road.

All Cariboo communities incorporating mileages into their names measure their distance reference from this point. 100 Mile House, then, is one hundred miles from Lillooet by the Cariboo Road.

Lions Gate Bridge

Lions Gate Bridge crosses the First Narrows waterway to connect **Vancouver** with North Vancouver. The bridge's Vancouver end is at **Stanley Park**. Completed in 1938, the bridge was built privately by the wealthy Guinness family of British brewing fame. A suspension bridge modelled after Golden Gate Bridge in San Francisco, which was completed a year earlier, Lions Gate is an impressive visual Vancouver landmark under which most commercial shipping traffic entering the city's port passes to enter Burrard Inlet. Use of the bridge, which provided a short cut between communities on the First Narrows north shore and Vancouver, originally required payment of a toll. In 1955 the B.C. government paid $6 million for the 473-metre span and the toll was no longer charged.

With only three lanes (the middle lane's direction of travel is adjusted to meet rush hour traffic patterns), the bridge is now considered hopelessly inadequate to meet present-day traffic volumes. Some traffic flow improvement plans have recommended replacing the bridge with a more modern span, but it is doubtful that Vancouverites would any more agree to the loss of this magnificent landmark than San Franciscans would see the Golden Gate replaced.

Lions Gate is the name of the body of water at the mouth of Burrard Inlet over which the bridge crosses. The passage derives its name from the Lions Mountains that overlook the water on the northern shore.

Liquor Laws and Regulations

It is illegal in British Columbia for anyone under the age of nineteen to purchase or be in possession of alcoholic beverages. Operation of a motor vehicle while impaired by alcohol is also an offence. So, too, is public drunkenness. All of these are considered criminal offences and are punishable by one or more of the following: imprisonment, fines, and the suspension of drivers' licences.

Driving while impaired is a serious offence in B.C., punishable by heavy fines, jail terms on second offences, and automatic driving suspensions that increase in duration for repeat offenders. Refusing to take a breathalyser test is also an offence. The impairment level is .08 percent (eighty milligrams of alcohol in one hundred millilitres of blood).

The sale and purchase of liquor products in the province is subject to relatively strict government regulations. Beer and wine products are available at government liquor stores and through about 245 cold beer and wine stores, through off sales at bars and pubs, and at industry agency stores, usually operated on-site at wineries and breweries. All other alcoholic beverages are sold for off-premise consumption only through the two hundred government-owned liquor stores, licensed rural agency stores, or at specially-licensed distillery outlets.

In all, there are about sixty-four hundred licensed establishments in the province that can serve or sell alcohol products. These include such outlets as stores, pubs, restaurants, cabarets, and sport stadiums or concert halls. The sale of alcohol without a licence from the provincial government is prohibited.

Logging. *See* **Forest Industry.**

Mammals

Only 143 of British Columbia's fifty thousand to seventy thousand native species of animals are mammals. These mammal species break down into 175 subspecies. For example, the **bear** species in B.C. comprises two subspecies: black bear and grizzly bear. The province also has twelve exotic species of mammals, divided into twenty-six subspecies.

Mammals are generally regarded as the most evolved or advanced of the vertebrates (animals having a backbone). They have a number of shared characteristics, including being warm blooded and having mammary glands which produce milk for nourishing their young. Mammals range in size from tiny shrews and **bats** that have virtually no discernible weight to the largest animal on Earth—the blue **whale**, measuring over thirty-five metres and weighing more than one hundred tonnes.

Many of B.C.'s mammal species and subspecies are at risk. One subspecies of caribou—the Dawson caribou—is extinct in B.C. A further thirty-three species and subspecies are on the province's ministry of environment Red List (legally designated or being considered for designation as endangered) and twenty-nine species and subspecies are on the Blue List (considered sensitive or vulnerable). Most of these threatened mammals are quite small. There are, for example, three subspecies of chipmunks on the Red List, and three shrew subspecies. The wood bison and Dall's sheep, both large mammals, are also on the Red List. Blue List mammals include three subspecies of sheep, the Roosevelt elk, plains bison, both the black and grizzly bear, three subspecies of mice, and the badger.

Meares Island

Just off Tofino on **Vancouver Island**'s west coast, 8,477-hectare Meares Island is at the centre of a major land-use controversy. The island is home to massive stands of ancient western red cedar and hemlock trees and is a traditional home of the Nuu-chah-nulth peoples. The Nuu-chah-nulth village of Opitsat is situated on the island.

Logging of the island's forest started in 1905, but the first clearcutting began in 1955. In the early 1980s, MacMillan Bloedel Ltd. obtained provincial government approval to log much of Meares Island, including parts that were highly visible from Tofino. The approval sparked massive protests from environmentalists, native groups, and residents of local communities—particularly in Tofino. In November 1984, protesters blocked the first attempts by loggers to get to the island to begin cutting. The Nuu-chah-nulth declared the island a "native park" and the entire issue of Meares Island's fate was sent to the B.C. Supreme Court. All decisions on the future of Meares Island are now subject to a **First Nations land claim** to the land. If the island is returned to the Nuu-chah-nulth it may or may not be saved from logging. Native leaders have refused to commit themselves one way or the other, citing the negotiating of an agreement as being of greater immediate import. They also reserve the right to implement whatever economic strategies their people approve to raise Nuu-chah-nulth living standards.

Measurement. *See* **Metric System.**

Medical Care. *See* **Health Care.**

Metric System

British Columbia, as is true of Canada as a whole, uses the metric system to measure distance and all other measures.

The decision to replace the historic British imperial system of units (based on yards, pounds, gallons, etc.) with a metric system was made by the Canadian government in 1971. The metric system decided upon was the latest evolution in the system known as the Système international d'unités (SI). Conversion to metric measure was prompted by rapidly advancing technology and expanding world-wide trade, both of which made it clear that a country as dependent upon import and export trade as Canada needed to operate with an international measure system that was readily adaptable to a world market.

Converting to the metric system in Canada was a gradual process allowing for the re-education of a public used to the British imperial system. The first extension of metric unit measure into the realm of everyday Canadian life had the unfortunate timing of being introduced on April Fool's Day (April 1), 1975, when all temperature announcements were given only in degrees Celsius during weather forecasts. In September 1977, road signs showed distances in kilometres and speed limits in kilometres per hour. The national process of converting to metric was not completed until December 1983.

The adoption of the metric system has been controversial from the outset, both because of the mandatory nature of the government regulations and the fact that it was seen by many Canadians as an attack on the British Canadian heritage. In the mid- to late-1980s some of the regulations were relaxed so that the two measures could be posted side by side and small businesses could continue to operate to a limited degree in the imperial system. But the metric system is clearly here to stay.

The following chart shows some common conversions.

To Change	To	Multiply by
centimetres	inches	.39
metres	feet	3.28
kilometres	miles	.62
square metres	square yards	1.20
square kilometres	square miles	.39
hectares	acres	2.47
kilograms	pounds	2.21
kilometres	nautical miles	.54

To Change	To	Multiply by
inches	centimetres	2.54
feet	metres	.30
miles	kilometres	1.61
square yards	square metres	.84
square miles	square kilometres	2.59
acres	hectares	.41
pounds	kilograms	.45
nautical miles	kilometres	1.85

Mica Dam

The last of the dams constructed as part of the **Columbia River Treaty** hydroelectric- and water-reservoir creation agreement between British Columbia and the United States, Mica Dam is also the highest earth-filled dam in North America and the eleventh highest in the world. The dam rises 242 metres above the Columbia riverbed. It began storing water in 1973, nine years after the signing of the treaty agreement.

Mica Dam is located about 150 kilometres north of Revelstoke at the end of Highway 23. It is situated at the mouth of now greatly enlarged **Kinbasket Lake**, which serves as the dam's reservoir.

Mining Industry

More than 85 percent of British Columbia lies within the Western Cordillera, a geological formation containing a wide variety of valuable minerals that encompasses all of B.C.'s mountain ranges and plateau regions. Only the northeastern plains portion of the province that lies to the east of the **Rocky Mountains** is outside the Cordillera.

The province can be divided geologically into six distinct regions that extend in north-south strips for roughly its entire length in a line that generally coincides with the north-south line of the major mountain ranges. The most westerly region is composed of the **Insular Mountain** range islands of **Vancouver Island** and the **Queen Charlotte Islands**. This area is known for coal deposits and minerals such as copper and iron ore. Bordering the mainland coast, and including the **Coast Mountains**, the next region is rich in a wide range of metal ores, including gold. To the east of the Coast Mountains, a large band of unmetamorphosed sedimentary and volcanic rock has been eroded by streams, exposing what are known as intrusive complexes, rich in copper and molybdenum. The next area, dominated by the **Rocky Mountain Trench** and its bordering mountain ranges, consists of very old sedimentary rock, primarily schists and granitic intrusions. Most of the major lode metals in the province are found here, especially the historic Kootenay mineral deposits of copper, lead, silver, and zinc. The Rocky Mountain Belt, as the next area is known, follows the line of this mountain range the length of the province, and is centred on the range's eastern slopes. Composed of mostly sedimentary carbonate rock, the area features metallurgical-quality coal deposits. To the north of **Fort St. John** and the **Peace River**, in the northeastern part of the province, and lying outside the Cordillera, is a sandstone and shale region that contains the province's only known significant natural gas and petroleum deposits.

Although the mining industry is still one of the most important sectors of the B.C. economy, historically it was even more significant—serving as the primary reason for European settlement of the province's interior in response to **gold rushes**, and drawing settlement into the Kootenays and other geographically isolated regions of the province.

The earliest mining took place on the province's coast. A coal mine opened at Saquash on Vancouver Island's northeast coast in 1836 and in 1852 coal mining began at Nanaimo. Gold mining, however, dwarfed the importance of coal after the gold rushes started in 1858. When the major gold deposits had been mined out in the 1880s, prospectors moved east from the Cariboo and **Fraser River** regions, following the Canadian Pacific Railway route and exploring the Columbia and Kootenay valleys. Discoveries of silver and copper at **Nelson** in 1886, gold and copper at **Rossland**, copper at Boundary Camp and **Greenwood** in 1891, and silver, lead, and zinc at Slocan in 1891 and **Kimberley** in 1892 led to the founding of major mining-based communities throughout the Kootenays. Between 1896 and 1901 a number of smelters were put into operation in the Kootenays to process the minerals found at these and other mines.

During this period, coal production also expanded significantly, with the coastal region dominating. New coal mines were also opened in the East Kootenays. The coal mined was mostly used by the railroads for fuel and by the newly built smelters for coking coal.

Between 1900 and 1935, gold production continued to decline. Copper, zinc, silver, and lead grew in importance. The major zinc, silver, and lead mining in the province was dominated by one mine—the Sullivan Mine at Kimberley.

In the late 1950s, the mining industry underwent profound change. Post-World War II demand for industrial minerals increased and substantial amounts of capital for exploration and development became available. Technological improvements led to large-scale production of lower grade ores and the appearance of open-pit mines in the province, where previously most mining was carried out underground. Production from the open-pit mines was most often sold to overseas buyers in large quantities as part of long-term supply contracts.

Also in this period the first natural gas in B.C. was discovered at Pouce Coupe in 1948 and oil at Boundary Lake in 1955. These discoveries generated unprecedented growth in the oil and gas industry, concentrated in the Peace River area.

The trends that emerged in the 1950s intensified during the 1960s and 1970s, with more and larger open-pit operations replacing the small high-grade underground mines. More mines, primarily open-pit operations, opened in northern B.C. and large-scale coal-mining operations opened in southeastern B.C. Much of this coal was shipped to Japan.

By the late 1970s, coal, copper, iron ore, oil, and natural gas dominated the export-oriented mineral production, while sand, gravel, and cement were produced in large quantities to serve the domestic construction industry. This trend continues today.

Coal is B.C.'s most valuable mineral product, valued on average at between $750 million and $950 million annually, and constitutes about 26 percent of the province's total mineral and petroleum production in terms of value. Copper, petroleum, and natural gas are the province's other most valuable mining products. In total, the province's mining industry is valued at about $3.6 billion per annum.

In terms of value this makes the mining industry the third largest sector in the province's economy—after forestry and tourism. Considering there are only about twenty-seven major mines in operation in the province this is a large contribution from a very concentrated industry. B.C. also has only three remaining primary mineral processing plants: a lead and zinc smelter in **Trail**, an aluminum smelter in **Kitimat**, and the Canadian Occidental Petroleum sulphur plant north of Fort St. John.

B.C. has an abundant energy resource base and is self-sufficient in all energy sources except oil. Production of petroleum and gas is valued at about $830 million annually, with crude oil accounting for about $250 million of this total.

As is true of most natural resource extraction industries, employment levels within the mining industry continue to shrink in B.C. as mines close or workers are displaced by technology. Only about fourteen thousand British Columbians are still employed in mining. They are, however, the highest paid group in the province, averaging over $900 a week.

Mission Indian Friendship Centre Powwow. *See* **Annual Events and Celebrations.**

Mountain Standard Time

The Kootenay region has always been known for having a small, independent population. Little wonder then that one area of the Kootenays should operate on a time different from the rest of the province. Actually, the region had little say in the matter as it was a product of how time zones were designated. Canada has six zones; Mountain Standard Time is centred on the 105th meridian near Regina, Saskatchewan, and extends to include a narrow lane of eastern British

Columbia that follows the **Rocky Mountain** range. The rest of the province follows Pacific Standard Time.

When travelling in the far eastern portions of the province, move clocks one hour ahead—except in the area from, and including, Creston east to Yahk and Kitchener. Despite provincial government edicts that the province should operate from the first Sunday in April to the last Sunday in October on Daylight Saving Time (in spring it moves one hour forward, in fall one hour back), these communities have refused to conform. Consequently, during Daylight Saving Time in the rest of the province, this small area inside the Mountain Standard Time zone shares the same clock as the rest of B.C.

Mount Golden Hinde

Situated within **Strathcona Provincial Park**, Mount Golden Hinde, at twenty-two hundred metres, is Vancouver Island's highest peak and is situated roughly in the centre of the island. It is a high, pyramid-shaped mountain towering above lower granite-shouldered summits of the **Vancouver Island** Mountains. The mountain is named after the ship in which Sir Francis Drake circumnavigated the world in a three-year voyage from 1577 to 1580. After plundering Spanish ships off Mexico in 1579, the British privateer tried to reach England via an imagined polar route from the Pacific coast east to the Atlantic. It is generally believed the Elizabethan sailor only came as far north as Cape Blanco on the Oregon coast, but some historians argue arduously and somewhat convincingly on the basis of wind and current forces that Drake would have reached B.C.'s coastline.

At 2,682 metres, Mount Golden Hinde is the highest summit on Vancouver Island. (BC Parks photo 630001.1.1.15.vi)

The 1939 article by R.P. Bishop in the *B.C. Historical Quarterly,* entitled "Drake's Course in the North Pacific," presented this case strongly. Bishop was so certain Drake must have sighted this mountain as he sailed past Vancouver Island that he managed to persuade the Geographic Board of Canada to alter the summit's name from the less-romantic Rooster's Comb to Golden Hinde in the same year as his article was published. At the same time he also won approval for naming as Mount Sir Francis Drake a 2,682-metre summit adjacent to the mainland's Bute Inlet that lies on the same latitude as Mount Golden Hinde.

Mount Macdonald Tunnel

Cutting 14.6 kilometres through Mount Macdonald and Cheops Mountain, Mount Macdonald Tunnel is the longest railway tunnel in North America. Construction by CP Rail began in mid-1984 and ended in 1988, on the twelfth day of the twelfth month at twelve noon. The grade through the tunnel never exceeds one percent, overcoming a long-standing problem the railroad had with this section of the **Rogers Pass** which was steep and slow for trains to traverse through the turn-of-the-century Connaught Tunnel. One of the problems the two groups of tunnellers working from both ends toward the middle faced was ensuring they did not miss each other. Advanced laser and satellite surveying techniques were utilized to keep the two teams on line. The tunnel was part of a major $600 million railroad upgrade project in the Rogers Pass.

Mount Revelstoke National Park

Situated seventeen kilometres east of Revelstoke, Mount Revelstoke National Park was established in 1914. Most of the park's 263 square kilometres are cloaked by heavy snow between October and June. Several higher-elevation areas of the park, particularly one known as the Icebox, are covered by snow year-round. During its brief summer, the alpine meadows below the craggy summits of the Selkirk Range mountain peaks are blanketed with wildflowers. Caribou, grizzly **bears**, black bears, mountain goats, and mountain sheep are common within its boundaries. Two roads provide access to the 1,830-metre summit of Mount Revelstoke from which spectacular views of the Selkirk and Monashee Mountain ranges are afforded. The **Trans-Canada Highway** borders the park's southern edge.

Mount Robson

With an elevation of 3,954 metres, Mount Robson is the highest peak in the Canadian **Rockies**. It stands ten kilometres southwest of the **Continental Divide** and dominates the western entrance to 219,829-hectare Mount Robson

Provincial Park. A spectacular, virtually sheer escarpment on its south side falls 2,969 metres to Kinney Lake. Heavy **glaciation** on the northern slope drops steeply to Berg Lake. Considered a mountaineering challenge, Mount Robson was first ascended in July 1913 by Conrad Kain, W.W. Foster, and A.H. MacCarthy. Several routes are used by climbers today; all are considered difficult.

Mount Terry Fox

Following the cancer-related death of Port Coquitlam resident Terry Fox on June 28, 1981, before his completion of the world-famous "Marathon of Hope," the B.C. government named this mountain north of Valemount in the young man's honour. At 2,651 metres, the mountain was the highest B.C. peak remaining unnamed and within sight of a public highway: Highway 5 (the Yellowhead South Highway).

Between April 12 and September 1 of 1980, Fox, who had lost one leg to cancer in 1977, ran 5,373 kilometres, averaging forty kilometres a day, and raising $1.7 million in donations for the Canadian Cancer Society. His name and feat continue to motivate thousands across Canada to participate each year in community marathons in which pledges raise funds for cancer research and treatment.

Mount Waddington

At 4,016 metres, Mount Waddington is the highest peak found wholly within British Columbia. **Fairweather Mountain** (4,663 metres) is higher, but its southern and western slopes are in Alaska. Mount Waddington is characterized by its distinctive twin pinnacles, which are virtually sheer and connected by ridges of granite. The mountain is host to several hanging glaciers, including Teidman Glacier at about the 1,980-metre level, which is often used as a heli-**skiing** drop point and base camp area for mountaineering expeditions to the summit.

Mount Waddington is in the heart of the **Coast Mountains** south of Highway 20 and east of coastal Bella Coola. Despite its inland location the mountain was first noticed by Europeans when mountaineers Don and Phyllis Munday spotted it from a **Vancouver Island** mountain peak they were ascending in 1921. The Mundays spent the next twelve summers exploring the mountain and environs of what they called "Mystery Mountain."

The Geographic Board of Canada, however, opted to name the peak after Alfred Waddington, the English dreamer, who in the early 1860s tried to establish an alternative **Cariboo gold rush** road to the **Fraser River** route that ran from Bute Inlet overland through the Homathko Valley into the Chilcotin.

Not bothering to consult the Chilcotin peoples before starting construction, he sparked the **Chilcotin War** in which nineteen whites were killed. The Chilcotin resorted to violence partly out of a fear that the white presence would spread smallpox into their population—perhaps a valid concern as Waddington himself perished from the illness in 1872 while in Ottawa trying to convince Prime Minister John A. Macdonald to grant him a charter to build a railroad along his beloved route to the ocean. Macdonald, calling Waddington "a respectable old fool," declined.

Murals. *See* **Chemainus.**

Museums. *See* **Cultural History.**

Nanaimo Bars

According to British Columbians, one of the great unsolved mysteries of humankind is whether this province's favourite dessert brownie was actually created by someone living in the **Vancouver Island** community of Nanaimo—hence explaining this tasty delight's name. In truth, nobody really knows the origin of either the Nanaimo bar recipe, its name, or even when the bar first appeared.

Many theories have been put forward; none are proven. A cookbook put out by Laura Secord claims that the Nanaimo bar was invented by a "well-known" food company, which the book fails to name. No company has ever claimed the Nanaimo bar as its creation.

There are also claims that the recipe first appeared in a Nanaimo hospital auxiliary cookbook published in the 1950s, but no copies of this book exist, if in fact they ever did. Others claim the recipe was brought to Canada from Holland by Dutch settlers in the early 1900s, but again no evidence exists to support this theory.

Some theorists maintain the Nanaimo bar appeared as the "Chocolate Fridge Cake" in 1936 in an issue of the *Vancouver Sun* newspaper. All efforts by the newspaper to turn up this story in its archives have been fruitless. Yet another story has a Nanaimo woman entering her chocolate squares recipe in a magazine contest and naming them after her hometown. Which magazine? Which Nanaimo woman? Nobody can say.

Many Nanaimo residents and the community's Chamber of Commerce, of course, staunchly defend the position that it is a local creation. Even the Chamber of Commerce, however, is troubled by the fact that apparently for generations a very similar bar has been served up in New York City bake shops, although this sweet is seldom called a Nanaimo bar.

The city of Nanaimo supports its ownership claim by producing the following official, municipally endorsed recipe, which is released only with imperial measures.

The Ultimate Nanaimo Bar Recipe

Bottom Layer

1/2 c.	unsalted butter (European-style cultured)
1/4 c.	sugar
5 tbsp.	cocoa
1	egg beaten
1 3/4 c.	graham wafer crumbs
1/2 c.	finely chopped almonds
1 c.	coconut

Melt first three ingredients in top of double boiler. Add egg and stir to cook and thicken. Remove from heat. Stir in crumbs, coconut, and nuts. Press firmly into an ungreased 8" x 8" pan.

Second Layer

1/2 c.	unsalted butter
2 tbsp. plus 2 tsp. cream	
2 tbsp.	vanilla custard powder
2 c.	icing sugar

Cream butter, cream, custard powder, and icing sugar together well. Beat until light. Spread over bottom layer.

Third Layer

4 squares	semi-sweet chocolate (1 oz. each)
2 tbsp.	unsalted butter

Melt chocolate and butter over low heat. Cool. When cool, but still liquid, pour over second layer and chill in refrigerator.

Nanaimo Bathtub Festival. *See* **Annual Events and Celebrations.**

Nanaimo Mine Disaster

On Tuesday, May 3, 1887, almost the entire shift of 154 men working underground at the Vancouver Coal Mining Company's Number One mine in Nanaimo perished in the province's worst **mining** disaster. The shafts of the mine, originally opened in 1883, extended under the streets of Nanaimo and beneath the waters of the adjacent inlet for up to 1.6 kilometres. The mine crew was composed of European—mostly British—and Chinese labourers.

At 5:55 p.m., a sharp tremor shook the community and black smoke poured out of the Number One shaft. By the time rescue crews arrived on site, flames were spewing from the shaft. It took twenty-four hours for the underground fires to burn out, at which time it was finally possible to send rescue parties into the shafts.

For the next five days searchers brought out the bodies of the miners. They rescued only seven men, including Nanaimo mayor Richard Gibson, who had managed to take shelter in an underground mule stable. The remaining 147 miners perished, the bodies of seven never being recovered. One of the rescue workers also died from gas poisoning, bringing the death toll to 148.

A coroner's jury ruled that the explosion was caused by a poorly placed blasting charge igniting the gas known as after-damp, which is composed primarily of carbon monoxide and is emitted from coal dust. Although the jury found that proper precautions were not taken to minimize the probability of an explosion, it attributed no criminal negligence to the British mine owners or to the mine management. Number One mine closed in 1938.

National Parks

Of Canada's thirty-seven national parks, six are in British Columbia. Of Canada's ten provinces and two territories only Ontario equals this number. The national parks in B.C. are: **Glacier** and **Mount Revelstoke** in the **Columbia Mountains, Kootenay** and **Yoho** in the **Rocky Mountains, Pacific Rim** on **Vancouver Island**'s west coast, and **Gwaii Haanas** (also known as South Moresby National Park Marine Reserve) at the south end of Moresby Island in the **Queen Charlotte Islands**.

The creation of national parks in British Columbia began in the late 1800s when the federal government, with the cooperation of the Canadian Pacific Railroad, decided in a somewhat surprising-for-the-times burst of future thinking to protect the Rocky Mountains from "sale, settlement, or squatting." On June 23, 1887, Banff National Park in Alberta became the first region to be protected. Between 1887 and 1895 a further five mountain reserves were set aside under legislation called the Rocky Mountain Parks Act. Over the next thirty-five years these reserves became Yoho, Kootenay, Glacier, Mount Revelstoke, and Alberta's Waterton Lakes national parks. Pacific Rim would be declared in 1970, Gwaii Haanas in 1988 (although many management and jurisdictional details are still being resolved between the Haida **First Nations people** and the federal government). In 1985, Kootenay, Yoho, and Alberta's Banff and Jasper parks were declared a joint World Heritage Site by UNESCO because of their combined representation of the Rocky Mountain landscape.

National parks are protected by legislation from all forms of resource extraction use, such as forestry, agriculture, mining, and sport hunting. All activities must be consistent with park resource protection. Land and resource management is concentrated on preserving the natural physical environment and allowing it to evolve according to the forces of natural ecological evolution. Only where human actions have disrupted the process of natural change or where human lives or vital facilities are endangered is there active intervention by parks' staff.

Preservation of the parks' natural state tends to conflict with making these lands accessible and open to recreational use by people. To balance these two goals a zoning designation system is incorporated into park management. There are five zones by which park land and water areas are ranked according to their ecological fragility and ability to handle human use. In Zone One all access is prohibited. Zone Two has a high degree of restricted access. In neither of these zones are vehicles allowed. In Zones Three and Four, increasing visitor facilities and more activities are permitted. Zone Five designates townsites, visitor centres, and park administration offices.

In the 1993 federal election, Liberal Party Leader Jean Chretien pledged that if he were elected prime minister British Columbia would get a new national park—**Clayoquot Sound**. At the time, B.C.'s provincial government and the province's **forest industry** scoffed at the idea of this ancient temperate **rainforest** being protected by federal action from their joint plans to log the region. When the Liberals formed the federal government with a stunning majority win, further discussion of the idea by Prime Minister Chretien or cabinet colleagues abruptly ceased. Logging operations in Clayoquot Sound proceeded with no intervention from the federal government.

Native Art; Native Basketry and Weaving; Native Land Claims; Native People of Canada; Native Religion. *See* **First Nations'** listings.

Nature Trust of British Columbia

In 1971, on the 100th anniversary of British Columbia's joining confederation, the federal government presented a $10 million gift to the province. Of these funds, the federal government set aside $4.5 million in the National Second Century Fund to serve as seed money in financing the operations of The Nature Trust of British Columbia, a private charitable corporation dedicated to the conservation of areas of ecological significance.

Hailed as one of the most imaginative and productive ventures in wildlife conservation anywhere in Canada, the trust has sought out and acquired conservation properties with a total area of more than thirty-five hundred hectares. The lands the fund either purchases or receives as gifts are leased on a pro forma basis to the provincial environment ministry, the Canadian Wildlife Service, or other appropriate management body.

Many of the properties acquired by the trust are marshes or estuaries that serve as important **bird** and wildlife habitats. The Nature Trust is also focusing its staff and financial resources on ongoing conservation programs, including The Pacific Estuary Conservation Program and **Vancouver Island** Wetlands Management Program, which aim to conserve and manage a number of important coastal wetlands that are key Pacific Flyway bird-migration stopping points. It is also working intensively on the South Okanagan Critical Areas Program, aimed at preserving unique wetland and desert areas in the southern part of the valley that sustain rare and often **endangered species**.

Nechako River

The Nechako River was once one of northern British Columbia's mightiest. It drew its waters from the 14,000-square-kilometre Nechako Plateau that included the large bodies of **Babine**, Stuart, and Takla lakes, flowing east to converge with the **Fraser River** at **Prince George**. Nechako was a Cheslatta Carrier word meaning "big river" and along its shores this native people had lived for centuries, drawing upon its waters for fish, especially **salmon** which used it as a major spawning area.

In the early 1950s, the Nechako River was subjected to a major diversion project to provide a source of water for the Alcan aluminum smelter being constructed at **Kitimat**. Construction of the Kenney Dam backed the Nechako into a huge reservoir and more than two-thirds of its flow was diverted west to create hydroelectricity for the smelter. This water was directed through a huge tunnel to reach **Kemano**, site of the hydroelectric power plant, and then drained into Gardner Canal to reach the ocean.

The $1.3-billion Kemano Completion Project, proposed for years by Alcan to increase the volume of water diverted, would have further reduced Nechako's flow to 12 percent of its historic levels. The project was opposed by environmentalists, the **fishing industry**, many local-community groups, and area native peoples because of fears that it might irreparably damage the Nechako's

biodiversity, further eroding its ability to support salmon spawning grounds.

The original diversion flooded farmland and the villages and traditional lands of the Cheslatta Carrier. In 1952 when the diversion was complete, the *Nechako Chronicle* printed an obituary which read in part that Kenney Dam "has destroyed forever a thing of beauty and divine creation."

(*See also* **Kemano**.)

Nelson

Home to more artists and craftspeople per capita than any Canadian city, Nelson is also famous for its wealth of heritage buildings, many of which have been meticulously restored since a major community-wide project began in 1981. Some 350 heritage buildings were identified in 1977 by a provincial Heritage Conservation Branch survey. Most date back to the 1890s when Nelson was a mining town and, with a population of seven thousand, the largest city between **Vancouver** and Winnipeg. Today, its population is only a couple of thousand more.

The community's setting amid mountains and overlooking Kootenay Lake's west arm makes it an incredibly scenic community. B.C. Gold Commissioner Gilbert Sproat, who founded the community in 1887 to service a nearby silver mining operation, recognized this fact immediately and wrote: "Here, where nature was so bountiful, there might be, could we keep out newspapers and lawyers, the town of all towns for civilized habitation." Despite the intrusion of both Sproat's perceived banes to civilized habitation, many residents believe Nelson lives up to its founder's dreams.

New Caledonia

In 1806, Simon Fraser—partner, trader, and explorer in the North West Company (NWC)—named the central and highland plateau area extending from the **Coast Mountains** to the **Rocky Mountains** and from the south at Alexandria, near present-day Quesnel, north to the 57th parallel, New Caledonia. Although Fraser had never been to Scotland he thought the country west of the Rockies resembled his mother's description of the Scottish highlands. New Caledonia became a trading district of the NWC and after its 1821 merger with the Hudson's Bay Company continued to be so designated.

When the mainland Crown colony was declared in 1858 it was originally named New Caledonia. France, however, possessed a South Pacific colony of that name and it was decided having two colonies of the same name would be confusing to European powers. Queen Victoria was asked to intervene and give the new colony a name. She chose British Columbia, and on August 2, 1858, the colony was officially so named. The queen apparently made her decision based simply on the fact that Columbia appeared on all the maps and by adding British to it, the name would be distinct from the **Columbia River** region of the United States to the south. Colonial Secretary Sir Henry Pelham Clinton, Duke of Newcastle, wryly commented at the time that the name was neither "very felicitous" nor "very original." It was, however, a name that swept "New Caledonia" into obscurity and its common usage in the early- to mid-1800s to describe most of the province is little known today.

New Hazelton

This small community sixty-seven kilometres north of Smithers on Highway 16 was the site of a 1914 gunfight that remains unrivalled in western Canadian history. Seven Russian anarchists had held up a Grand Trunk Railway train here earlier in the year. The first robbery was so successful and easy they returned for a sequel. Two minutes following the hold-up, however, townspeople were alerted and ambushed the bandits. A short, furious gunbattle raged in which two hundred bullets were reportedly fired. When the smoke cleared, three of the anarchists lay dead, three were wounded, and one had managed to escape with the money.

New Westminster

Had it not fallen into economic decline with the end of British Columbia's major **gold rushes** in the late 1860s, New Westminster might still be the province's capital city. In 1859, this community on the **Fraser River** estuary was declared the capital of the new Crown colony of British Columbia. On November 19, 1866, when **Vancouver Island** was united with the mainland colony, New Westminster retained capital status. But already the gold rush was dwindling and the city was in decline. On May 25, 1868, capital-city status was shifted to **Victoria**, which was still a thriving economic centre.

New Westminster was the subject of a dispute over what it should be named, with a strong lobby advocating the name Queensborough. In 1859, Queen Victoria was called upon to provide a name to settle the matter. A terse letter from Colonial Secretary Sir Edward Bulwer Lytton stated Her Majesty had decided on New Westminster. No rationale was provided, but being a royal decision the matter was immediately considered closed. Having been named by the Queen, New Westminster quickly became known unofficially as the Royal City—by which it is still known today.

The city is now an important community in the Greater Vancouver Regional District (GVRD), and its large fresh-water port is a vital supplement to the port of **Vancouver**. In 1986, SkyTrain, the GVRD's light rapid transit system, linked New Westminster to downtown Vancouver. This development coincided with a major revitalization of the city's decayed commercial districts, especially along the waterfront. New Westminster is now considered one of the most vital and thriving commercial and light industrial areas in the Lower Mainland.

Ninstints. *See* Gwaii Haanas National Park.

Nisga'a Memorial Lava Bed Provincial Park

About 106 kilometres north of Terrace, the Nisga'a Memorial Lava Bed Provincial Park is the most recent area in the province to have been affected by volcanic eruptions. In about 1750, a lava flow dammed the Tseax River, blocking its northward flow to the Nass River, to create Lava Lake. Reaching the Nass River, the lava pushed the river from its channel, squeezing the steaming river water up against the north side of the narrow valley and submerging a lake. When the lava cooled, this large deposit became the Nass Lava Beds. The resulting lava plain created by the eruption is eleven kilometres long by five kilometres wide and encompasses thirty-eight square kilometres. Today, the lava plain is part of a 17,683-hectare provincial park that is jointly managed by the park and the hereditary chiefs of the Nisga'a people.

Because the lava plain was so recently created, it is largely devoid of vegetation, and original lava features, both smooth and jagged varieties, are clearly visible to hikers exploring the park. Large colonies of lichens, mosses, ferns, and larger plants are slowly revegetating the area. This is the only known place in British Columbia where such early stage revegetation of a lava plain is occurring.

When the volcano erupted, the lava flowed down upon villages of the Nisga'a people, destroying them. Nisga'a legend says the eruption was in September when the **salmon** returned to spawn. Young men of the tribe were amusing themselves by torturing the fish with burning pitch despite warnings by the village elders that this cruelty and waste would anger the spirits. Soon a spirit drum was heard beating and the volcanic cone standing over the village erupted. Only a few villagers escaped the scalding lava, which burned the surrounding forests and boiled the water in the Tseax and Nass rivers.

(*See also* **Volcanoes**.)

Nitinat Lake

On **Vancouver Island**'s west coast, near **Carmanah Pacific Provincial Park**, twenty-four-kilometre-long Nitinat Lake is in reality a tidal inlet, with conditions found in only three other places in the world: Vancouver Island's **Saanich Inlet**, the Black Sea, and a fjord in Venezuela. These deep water bodies have narrow, shallow mouths out of which water can only drain slowly. At Nitinat, this slow outflow holds in the salt water that is pulled into the inlet by tidal currents. Despite a steady inflow of fresh water from Nitinat River and other sources, Nitinat Lake consequently always has a significant salt-water component, which supports populations of sea anemones, jellyfish, and starfish.

The narrow channel attracts constant thermal winds that average fifteen to twenty knots, leading to the area becoming a popular windsurfing destination rated by several sport magazines as the second-best windsurfing destination in North America, after Oregon's Columbia River Gorge region.

Nootka Sound

At Nootka Sound, near the end of March 1778, Royal Navy Captain James Cook became the first European to land on the coast of what would become British Columbia. Four years earlier, Spanish explorer Perez Hernandez approached the sound but was driven off by storms. Upon landing, Cook was greeted by a party of Nuu-chah-nulth belonging to the Mowach'ath tribe, who traded sea otter pelts, lumber, food, and animal feed for a variety of metal items Cook and his crew thought they could spare. During this meeting, Cook apparently confused directional instructions from the natives to "go around the harbour" as a declaration of what they called themselves and so erroneously ascribed the name Nootka to them. The name proved pernicious and it was not until 1978 when the west-coast tribes officially adopted Nuu-chah-nulth ("All along the mountains") as their name that Nootka began to fall into disuse.

Three deep inlets—Tahsis, Tlupana, and Muchalat—penetrate far inland from near the mouth of the sound. Muchalat extends sixty-five kilometres inland almost to **Strathcona Provincial Park**. The village of Yuquot on Nootka Island was, before European contact, an important Mowach'ath community and soon became a vital fur-trading centre. But by the late 1790s the sea otter population was virtually exterminated and smallpox epidemics had decimated the native population. Today, the community is almost deserted.

One of B.C.'s most **endangered species**, the sea otter is slowly being re-established in Nootka Sound with promising results.

Ocean Falls

Between 1909 and 1981, Ocean Falls was a thriving lumber and pulp-and-paper milling town. Today, this nearly uninhabited town on the coast, west of Bella Coola in Fisher Channel, reflects the growing decline of **population** in isolated west-coast locations—a change brought by increased concentration of forestry and fishing operations into large, centralized processing plants.

Between 1909 and 1954, Ocean Falls was a quintessential company town, dependent on Pacific Mills' pulp-and-paper mill for its livelihood. During that time even the community's light bulbs bore the company's stamp. In 1954, the mill was sold to Crown Zellerbach (Canada). In 1972, the mill's imminent closure was announced. The New Democratic government of the day made the town's survival a *cause célèbre* for its political policies and purchased the town and mill from the company the following year.

Although the mill continued operation, it was a constant struggle for it to sustain economic viability. In 1981, provincial government policy agendas again determined the community's fate when the now-ruling Social Credit party closed the mill, citing its unprofitability and that ownership of such operations ran counter to a hands-off economic policy. In 1986, the provincial government put the final nail in the mill's coffin by auctioning off all equip-

The B.C. coastal community of Ocean Falls was one of the province's most notorious company towns. (BCARS photo G-03799)

ment and even some salvage from the abandoned residential and business buildings.

A handful of people continue to live in the community today, eking out livings as guides for fishing and hunting expeditions, or from small independent business ventures.

It is interesting to contrast Ocean Falls—a community with no history prior to 1909—to other coastal settlements such as Bella Bella and Bella Coola that have also experienced modern declines in populations after brief periods of economic fortune. These communities survive today principally because they are historic settlements of coastal native peoples, who continue to try and sustain their communities in the face of the economic pressures that have been gradually eroding the mainland coastal population base.

Octopus. *See* **Puget Sound Octopus.**

Official Bird; Emblem; Flag; Flower; Motto; Shield; Stone; Tartan; Tree. *See* **Symbols.**

Ogopogo

Ogopogo is a legendary aquatic monster believed by many to inhabit Okanagan Lake. The stories of the monster's existence date back to the earliest **First Nations people** to enter the **Okanagan Valley**. To the Salishan, Ogopogo was known as "snake in the lake." Chinook natives called it "wicked one" and "great beast in the lake." Ancient **petroglyphs** represent it as being a snake-like monster with a head that can be variously described as that of a sheep or a horse. This description closely matches that of "Nessie," the Orm of Loch Ness in Scotland. Ogopogo's English-language name derives from a palindrome (a phrase that reads the same backward as forward) from a comic nineteenth-century English music-hall number, "Ogopogo Song."

There is a common element to stories of sighting—the monster appears as several humps swimming through the water with an undulating motion. In recent years, Ogopogo hunters have come from around the world to prove the monster's existence. High-resolution and infra-red photography, sonar detectors, deep-water diving equipment, and small submarines have all been deployed in these failed quests. Every year, however, recreational boaters and people on the lakeshore report sighting Ogopogo. Most sightings are made at night, by star or moonlight.

First Nations people believed Ogopogo lived in an underwater cave at Squally Point, adjacent to Rattlesnake Island on the eastern shore of Okanagan Lake, directly opposite Peachland. It is here the greatest number of contemporary sightings also occur.

Ogopogo is not alone. Lake serpents have been sighted in at least twenty-three other interior lakes, including Osoyoos, **Shuswap**, Harrison, Moberley, and **Kootenay**. There is also supposedly a monster living in the Lower Mainland's **Cultus Lake** and Cadborosaurus ("Caddy" for short) in the **Saanich Inlet** area on **Vancouver Island**. Some even claim that Ogopogo has relatives in Okanagan Lake, giving rise to the pluralization of its name—Ogopogi.

Biologists say none of these lakes, not even 352-square-kilometre Okanagan, could provide sufficient food to support such a large creature. Such facts, however, did not prevent the B.C. government declaring Ogopogo a protected species under the provincial wildlife act after bounty hunters, hoping to cash in on a reward offered by the Okanagan-Similkameen Tourist Association for positive proof of its existence, started talking about capturing Ogopogo with nets and other methods that might have caused the creature harm.

Okanagan Connector (Highways 5A and 97C)

The 106-kilometre Okanagan Connector links the **Okanagan Valley** to the **Coquihalla Highway** at Merritt. From Merritt to Aspen Grove the connector follows Highway 5A south; it then veers directly east on Highway 97C to cross Pennask Summit (elevation 1,728 metres) and enter the Okanagan Valley south of **Kelowna**, near Peachland.

The $225-million highway project, completed in 1990, slashes directly through a fragile alpine environment that before its construction was little touched by humanity, except as rangeland for cattle grazing. To reduce the highway's impact on wildlife, a $10.5 million protection system was implemented. This included construction of the longest—one hundred kilometres—chain-link fence in North America, designed to prevent deer, moose, and cattle getting onto the highway. Twenty-five wildlife underpasses and one overpass were also constructed to enable wildlife to travel freely through the region without being endangered by highway traffic.

The connector is not a scenic route; like the Coquihalla Highway it was designed to provide a short, fast route from the Okanagan to the Lower Mainland. There are hardly any pullouts and high cement protective barriers limit views. In winter, the long, straight uphill stretches often become slick with ice and, combined with common dense fog, the route can be hazardous.

Okanagan Lake Floating Bridge

The Okanagan Lake Floating Bridge's 640-metre pontoon structure was North America's first floating bridge. It crosses Okanagan Lake at one of the narrowest points and provides the only vehicular connection between the lake's eastern and western shores. The bridge was completed in 1958 after two years of construction. Princess Margaret presided over the opening ceremonies.

Okanagan Pocket Desert

Experts generally agree that Canada has no true desert, but no sooner is this agreed than some of these same experts start defending the Okanagan pocket desert as qualifying for true desert status. Extending along the eastern shoreline of Osoyoos Lake at the **Okanagan Valley**'s southernmost point, the pocket desert covers approximately twelve thousand hectares—most of it located on the Osoyoos Indian Band land.

The debate over whether or not this is a true desert revolves around whether the area can be identified as the northern tip of American Great Basin Desert, which extends south to Mexico, or whether it is a unique anomaly with many desert-like attributes. Among these attributes is annual precipitation of twenty centimetres (exactly the maximum precipitation level usually found in deserts), and summer temperatures reaching 44° Celsius. Primary vegetation here is greasewood, various sages, rabbitbrush, and low-growing prickly pear cactus.

The pocket desert is home to the largest concentration of birds of prey in Canada, including many hawks, turkey vultures, and the endangered burrowing owl (*see* **Endangered Species**). Species found virtually nowhere else in Canada include the Great Basin spadefoot toad (so named because it uses spade-like appendages on its hind legs to bury itself in the hard clay-baked soil during hot days), kangaroo rats, several species of tiger beetles, praying mantises, and a bird called the sage thrasher, whose only Canadian habitat is the Okanagan-Similkameen region.

A one-hundred-hectare area at the pocket desert's northern end has been protected as the Federal Ecological Reserve (Pocket Desert). This reserve is 7.5 kilometres north of Osoyoos. The reserve is the focal point of a project to save the burrowing owl population from extinction, due to loss of habitat caused by the extension of irrigation into the desert land for agricultural purposes.

Okanagan Valley

Spilled along the floor of Okanagan Valley is the remains of a large glacial lake. Most of this remnant is contained in the 128-kilometre length of Okanagan Lake. The valley's other lakes—Swan, Kalamalka, Wood, Skaha, Vaseaux, and Osoyoos—were also originally part of this lake created about nine thousand years ago when the Pleistocene-era ice-age retreated from the valley. Okanagan Lake is between two and five kilometres wide; the valley itself is only nineteen kilometres at its widest point and 160 kilometres in length. Narrow bench lands, bordering most of the lakes, merge dramatically with the steep mountains of the **Columbia** and **Cascade** mountain ranges that wall the valley on its eastern and western flanks. The lake system drains south through the Okanagan River into the **Columbia River**.

When the ice retreated it left behind large alluvial deposits of gravel, silt, and sand that provided a rich agricultural environment. The rainshadow effect of the Cascade Mountains created a hot, sunny, dry climate. About two thousand hours of sunlight fall upon most of the valley annually and it receives only about thirty to forty centimetres of precipitation.

Interior Salishan settled the valley and its name is probably a Salishan word translating as "place of water." With European settlement, the valley became first an area of ranches and then a thriving **fruit** and vegetable farming region. Farming remains a major cornerstone of the region's economy, rivalled only by forestry and **tourism**. Although the first commercial planting of grapes occurred near Kelowna in 1926, it was not until the 1970s that commercial grape growing and wine making began to thrive. **Wineries**, ranging from small farm-gate outlets to high-quality estate operations and large commercial enterprises, are spread throughout the valley; the largest concentration being from immediately south of **Kelowna** to Osoyoos.

The Okanagan Valley is the third most populous part of British Columbia, following the Lower Mainland and Greater Victoria. Although occupying only about 3 percent of the province's total land mass it is home to about 8 percent of B.C.'s population (about 262,000). This population growth has placed intense pressure on the agricultural land in the valley and many farms have been lost to housing or to commercial and industrial development.

The valley's sunny summers, sandy beaches, and beautiful lakes draw thousands of tourists annually. In the fall, winery tours are a major attraction. There are also three major ski resorts—Silver Star, Big White, and Apex—in the valley, which combine with smaller operations to attract many skiers during winter months.

Oolichan

A silver-coloured smelt that is native to the British Columbia coast, oolichan (also known as candlefish and alternatively spelled as eulachon) remains a prized source of edible oil to the Nisga'a people of the Nass River region near **Prince Rupert**. The oil produced from these fish was a major commercial product for which other Pacific Coast **First Nation peoples** traded with the Nisga'a.

For centuries the Nisga'a have established fish camps in early spring at the mouth of the Nass River, situated immediately to the south of the Alaska Panhandle, adjacent to the **Alaska-Canada Boundary**, for the annual oolichan harvest and oil production. Extracting oil from oolichan is an exact science. Large pits are dug adjacent to the water's shore and lined with clay excavated from the riverbed. Fires are then built in the pits and huge wooden vats suspended over the blaze. As the fish are netted they are dumped into the vats and boiled for eighteen hours. The oil rising to the surface of the vat is skimmed off. It's a pure, non-fishy-tasting oil that is used both in its natural state and to make a form of grease. For the Pacific coast peoples this was a vital dietary supplement and culinary aid. Oolichan provided a major source of Vitamin D, and was used for medicinal purposes and for enhancing food flavours in much the same way as butter is used.

Because of their oily composition, oolichan are a slippery fish that when held close to a fire will ignite sputteringly into flame.

Opera. *See* **Cultural History.**

Pacific Grey Whale

Once on the verge of extinction, the Pacific grey whale population has now returned to what many researchers believe was its pre-whaling-days average of about twenty thousand. Virtually all Pacific greys swim the length of B.C.'s coast twice annually. From October to December they migrate south from the Bering and Chukchi seas to Baja, California. From February to mid-May they return north. The spring migration offers the best whale-sighting opportunities, as the whales are closer to shore than in the fall. The **Pacific Rim National Park** communities of Ucluelet and Tofino claim to be the best base in the province for whale-watching expeditions.

Although removed in 1994 from the U.S. **endangered species** list, there is concern that if a return to whaling of greys is allowed the population may again be imperilled.

(*See also* **Killer Whales**; **Whales**.)

Pacific National Exhibition (PNE). *See* **Annual Events and Celebrations.**

Pacific Rim National Park

Established in 1970, Pacific Rim National Park stretches for 105 kilometres along the rugged west coast of **Vancouver Island**. This is the only national park in B.C. lacking a continuous border—it is divided into three segments interspersed with private and provincial Crown land. The park also encompasses some 22,300 hectares of ocean. Total size of the park (ocean included) is 51,300 hectares.

The three areas of the park consist of: Long Beach, a thirty-kilometre sweep of surf-pounded sand and rock south of Tofino; the **Broken Group Islands**, which are accessible only by boat and encompass more than one hundred islands at the mouth of Barkley Sound; and the seventy-two-kilometre **West Coast Trail** running from Bamfield to Port Renfrew. The West Coast Trail section is open only to **hiking**.

Because of its accessibility, the Long Beach section of the park is the most heavily used. Thousands of visitors come here annually. In winter, the attraction is the mighty storms that batter and lash the coastline. Spring draws whale watchers hoping to sight the twenty thousand **Pacific grey whales** that migrate past these shores on their way north. Summer and early fall, the beach itself is the primary feature.

Paddling

With much of its twenty-seven thousand kilometres of ocean coastline and twenty thousand square kilometres of freshwater rivers and lakes accessible to canoeists and kayakers, British Columbia is considered one of the world's best areas for paddling. In most regions of the province excellent opportunities can be found for paddlers of all skill levels.

Ocean paddlers, however, should be well aware of the level of experience required for all paddling routes, as the coastal waters of B.C. are exposed to strong winds that can rise rapidly. Further ocean threats are many areas of rip tides, and strong currents even in sheltered-looking waters. Paddling in most open coastal waters requires a high level of paddling experience. Novice paddlers usually confine themselves to the more sheltered waters of the straits between **Vancouver Island** and the mainland, where winds and waves are less severe.

Some of the best areas for ocean paddling in B.C. are the **Broken Group Islands** and **Nootka Sound** on Vancouver Island's west coast; the **Queen Charlotte Islands**—especially **Gwaii Haanas National Park**; the many islands surrounding Saanich Peninsula; and the waters around the majority of the **Gulf Islands**.

River and lake paddling on Vancouver Island is best at **Nitinat**, Upper Campbell, and Buttle lakes. On the mainland, the **Bowron Lakes** provide one of the world's best wilderness paddling routes. **Kinbasket Lake**, near Revelstoke, is also a popular wilderness lake, as is **Babine Lake** near the community of Burns Lake in the northwest part of the province.

Paralytic Shellfish Poisoning

Eating contaminated shellfish can cause serious illness, even death. Much of British Columbia's coastal waters are prone to shellfish contamination from paralytic shellfish poison and sewage contamination. Shellfish contamination is particularly common near centres of human habitation or industrial operations that discharge pollutants into the ocean.

Paralytic shellfish poison (PSP), also known as red tide, and sewage contamination affect only bivalve molluscs. These are shellfish with two shells, such as oysters, mussels, clams, and rock-, swimming- and weathervane-scallops. Other shellfish, such as shrimp, prawns, crabs, and abalone, are not affected. Finfish are also safe from contamination.

Eating raw shellfish taken from B.C. waters should only be done if the water is known to be free of either sewage or PSP contaminants. Sewage contamination bacteria can be destroyed if the shellfish is well cooked. Cooking, however, has no effect on paralytic shellfish poisoning.

The first symptom of paralytic shellfish poisoning is numbness or tingling of the lips and tongue, followed by a spread of numbness to the fingers and toes. These symptoms are followed by a loss of muscular coordination terminating in paralysis, as well as an inability to breathe. Treatment includes induction of vomiting, taking laxatives, and drinking a solution of baking powder or baking soda. Immediate medical attention should be sought if shellfish poisoning is suspected.

Among the bivalve species, the butter clam retains PSP for long durations, sometimes more than a year. The poison usually concentrates in the siphon (neck) and gills. As a precaution, when butter clams are steamed open, the siphon, gills, and liquid released during the steaming process should be discarded.

To reduce the risk of PSP and sewage contamination, the federal Department of Fisheries and Oceans (DFO), which has jurisdiction over the province's tidal waters, routinely closes parts of the coastline to bivalve mollusc harvesting. The following areas are closed year-round: any Pacific Ocean waters within 125 metres of a wharf, dock, platform, or other structure used for vessel moorage, or any permanently anchored floating structures, including float homes, barges, platforms, and vessels. Anyone planning to harvest bivalve molluscs should contact the nearest DFO office to ensure the area is not under a harvesting ban.

Parks. *See* **National Parks; Provincial Parks.**

Parliament Buildings. *See* **Legislative Buildings.**

Peace Arch. *See* **Border Crossings.**

Peace River

The headwaters of the 1,923-kilometre-long Peace River lie in British Columbia's Rocky and Omineca mountain ranges. The river flows eastward into Alberta and eventually winds north to drain into the Slave River, becoming part of the Mackenzie River system. A valley cut over millennia by the river provides an unusual linkage between British Columbia and Alberta, as this is the only wide gap through the barrier presented by the **Rocky Mountains**. As a result, British Columbia's Peace River valley region derives much of its climatic and geographic influence from the Canadian prairies, rendering it unique from the rest of the province. The region experiences more extreme winters than anywhere else in the province, although its long hot summers and lengthy frost-free period combine with the rich Peace River valley soil to make the region one of B.C.'s major **agricultural** areas—centred on grain farming.

In the 1960s, the Peace River Canyon Dam and W.A.C. Bennett Dam were constructed by the B.C. provincial government as part of a hydroelectric mega-project. The Bennett dam, one of the largest earth-filled structures in the world, opened in 1967. It is two kilometres wide and 183 metres high. Most of the dam is constructed from glacial moraine debris that was left behind in the valley when the ice retreated thousands of years ago. About fifteen thousand years ago this same debris blocked the Peace River until it found a new path around. By hauling the materials to the dam-site it was possible to use them once again to block the river's flow. The dam backed the Peace River up to form the province's largest lake and reservoir—Lake Williston. This lake is 362 kilometres long.

Petroglyphs and Pictographs

Prehistoric carvings incised, abraded, or ground with stone tools upon cliff walls, boulders, and flat bedrock surfaces are known as petroglyphs. Prehistoric paintings, often with imagery similar to that found in petroglyphs, using red ochre usually applied by a finger on rock surfaces are called pictographs. Both forms of rock art are found throughout most of North America, but within British Columbia pictographs are more common in the interior and petroglyphs very common on the coast and **Vancouver Island**.

Nuu-chah-nulth pictographs at Sproat Lake on Vancouver Island.
(Royal BC Museum photo PN 11733)

In the coastal part of the Pacific Northwest, more than five hundred petroglyph sites have been recorded by archaeologists, making this region one of the world's most notable rock art areas. Many of these petroglyphs are found in B.C., where they are usually cut into sandstone, or in some instances pecked into hard granite boulders.

What is known about the reasons ancient **First Nations peoples** made petroglyphs and pictographs is primarily speculative, based on linking the images to First Nations religions, concepts of the spirit world, and cultural symbolisms.

Usually petroglyph and pictograph art portray human forms, animal forms, or geometric designs. One of the most common is a circle face—a pair of single or concentric circles believed to represent eyes. Sometimes a third circle is included to represent a mouth. Human figures in various shapes and poses, **whales**, fish, and strange human-like forms that are believed to represent mythical figures are also common.

Most rock art is found near ancient village sites, at the mouths of streams, or within sight of the ocean.

It is believed that some rock art was created as part of winter religious ceremonies or to record the activities of secret societies. Others may mark the location of either good or dangerous fishing and hunting areas. Some probably relate local historical incidents, indicate property rights of tribes and families, or mark tribal hunting and fishing territories. Still other rock art appears to record the dreams, rituals, or spirit aids of shamans. In some cases the rock art seems to be little more than the ancient equivalent of graffiti.

Dating of rock art is complicated by the fact that there is little chance to use radiocarbon analysis on them due to a lack of carbon in most of the art work. The Milliken petroglyph in the **Fraser Canyon**, however, was successfully dated as being more than seven thousand years old and a carving at Namu on the west coast of the mainland is about six thousand years old.

The two most accessible petroglyph sites are both found on Vancouver Island. Petroglyph Provincial Park, south of Nanaimo, contains petroglyphs believed to be about ten thousand years old. The images represent humans, **birds, wolves,** lizards, sea monsters, and supernatural creatures. There are several other petroglyph sites in the Nanaimo area. Sproat Lake Provincial Park outside Port Alberni on Highway 4 has prehistoric petroglyphs in the park's southeast corner. Pictographs are less easily found on the coast, but there is a site in **Cape Scott** Provincial Park near Experiment Bight.

Some of the most intriguing pictographs in Canada are found in the interior of B.C. In park settings, pictographs are located in Marble Canyon Provincial Park near **Lillooet**, in **Wells Gray Provincial Park**, near the hot springs of **Kootenay National Park**, and at Big Rock in **Tweedsmuir Provincial Park**. The pictographs at the Kootenay National Park hot springs suggest the springs were used as a gathering place for both plains and mountain First Nations peoples. Ochre beds are found in the north end of the park and peoples from the Great Plains areas of Alberta are known to have come here to collect materials to use in their pictograph art.

Physiography

Approximately 75 percent of British Columbia stands three thousand metres or more above sea level—it is a province dominated throughout by mountains, summits, and ranges, which are always visible on at least one horizon. Between the mountains are substantial areas of lowland and plateau country and it is in these areas that most human habitation is centred.

How British Columbia is divided up by physiographers varies from source to source depending on the complexity of criteria used. At its simplest, the province can be described as lying within two of the five major physiographic subdivisions of Canada—the Canadian Cordilleran Region and the Interior Plains Region. The Canadian Cordillera is mostly mountainous and includes all of the mainland west from the eastern margin of the foothills of the **Rocky Mountains**, as well as encompassing **Vancouver Island** and the **Queen Charlotte Islands**, which are part of the mostly underwater **Insular Mountains**. Only 10 percent of the province—the northeastern corner, dominated by the

Peace River Valley—lies east of the Rocky Mountain foothills. This region of primarily flat plateaus, prairies, plains, and lowlands are part of the Interior Plains Region.

This broadstroke depiction of B.C.'s physiography can be enhanced by breaking the 90 percent of the province contained in the Canadian Cordillera section into three subgroupings. From the West Coast, including all offshore islands and extending approximately three hundred kilometres inland, is a northwesterly trending mountain system that encompasses the **Coast Mountains** and southern **Cascade Mountains** and is called the Western System. This system extends north from the U.S.-Canadian border to Alaska. The tallest peaks in B.C. are contained in the Coast Mountains and the overall geography is as rugged and spectacular as the Rocky Mountains.

Inland from the Western System lies the massive sprawl of the **Interior System**. This is a broad region of rolling forest and grasslands, averaging altitudes between six hundred and twelve hundred metres. Located north of the 55th parallel (B.C. extends from the **49th parallel** to the 60th parallel), this region is primarily mountainous—dominated by the Skeena, Hazelton, Cassiar, and Omineca ranges. A narrow band just below Yukon Territory lies within the Yukon Plateau. South of the 55th parallel is the large **Interior Plateau**, which extends south to the border and east to the **Columbia Mountains**. East of this range is the last feature of the Interior System, the **Rocky Mountain Trench**. This trench, walled on the eastern side by the Rocky Mountains, is the longest valley in North America.

The final partition of the Canadian Cordillera in B.C. is known as the Eastern System. It encompasses the Rocky Mountains and Rocky Mountain foothills of B.C. To the southeast of Dawson Creek at Kakwa River, the Rocky Mountains cut westward, becoming entirely contained in B.C. to link up with Yukon Territory's Mackenzie Mountains at the Liard Plateau, which is a series of rounded and flat-topped summits spreading south off the tail-end of the Mackenzie Mountains. The small segment of land lying east of this section of the Rockies is known as the Alberta Plateau—that part of the province lying within the Interior Plains Region.

In geological terms, British Columbia's physiography is adolescent. Folds and thrusts of the earth's surface, volcanic eruptions and outpourings of lava, and the grinding force of **glaciation** combined to give the province its violently varied landscape. As recently as fifteen thousand years ago most of B.C. was thickly covered by the advancing ice sheets of the Pleistocene Age that piled up to depths exceeding fifteen hundred metres in many places. Coastal regions were largely freed from the grip of ice twelve thousand years ago; some northern and extreme mountain regions emerged from the ice sheets as recently as seven thousand years ago. Glaciers remain a prominent feature of B.C.'s landscape and a powerful force of erosion. Streams, wind, and chemical decomposition combine with ice as the major forces of erosion at play on the province's topography.

These erosive forces are more effective in the province's eastern areas as the Rocky Mountains and other ranges there are composed of relatively splintered and porous bedrock—prone to **avalanches**, shattering, and slough-ing. The massive dome-like Coast Mountains are composed of almost mono-lithic granite, so are more resistant to erosion. As a result, scree deposits at the foot of peaks are uncommon around the base of the Coast Mountains.

Pleasure Boating

The British Columbia **coastline**'s network of long inlets and more than sixty-five hundred islands and islets combined with a rich tapestry of marine, sea mammal, and bird life make the province one of the best pleasure-boating locations on the North American west coast. Little wonder then that in an average year more than 250,000 pleasure craft ply B.C.'s coastal waters. All along the coast the provincial government has established a number of marine parks accessible only to boaters. These are most common in the **Strait of Georgia** between **Vancouver Island** and the mainland.

Due to their more sheltered waterways and vast number of inlets and bays, the best areas for power boating or sailing are the Strait of Georgia, the south-ern **Gulf Islands**, and **Desolation Sound**. For experienced sailors, a trip up the west coast of Vancouver Island is known as a tough, exhilarating adven-ture. Also recommended are the waters of the **Queen Charlotte Islands**, Jervis Inlet, and Princess Louisa Inlet.

Anyone pleasure boating in B.C. waters should be well acquainted with coping in stormy seas and keep informed about weather conditions, as these can change suddenly and dramatically. This is particularly true for boaters operating outside of the more sheltered waterways between Vancouver Island and the mainland. Every year a number of pleasure boats and fishing boats are sunk or wrecked on the coastline's largely rocky shores and reefs after being caught in an unexpected storm.

Point Ellice Bridge Disaster

On May 26, 1896, one span of the Point Ellice Bridge crossing from **Victoria** to Esquimalt collapsed, resulting in fifty-five deaths. The bridge was a metal, four-span structure built in 1885 at a cost of $11,827. From its opening there were serious doubts about its load-bearing capacity. The disaster occurred on the holiday celebrating Queen Victoria's birthday; consequently, the streetcars

*Car Sixteen (foreground) was dragged from the waters of Victoria's inner harbour
shortly after the centrespan of the Point Ellice Bridge collapsed beneath the trolley
on May 26, 1896. Fifty-four passengers aboard the trolley died.
(BCARS photo G-4578)*

were packed with celebrants. Car Sixteen, which plunged into the waters below the bridge, was believed to have 150 passengers on board at the time.
Fifty-four of the occupants perished; another man riding alongside on a bicycle was also killed.

Subsequent investigations determined that the maximum weight the bridge
could be expected to bear was ten tons; Car Sixteen and its passengers probably weighed twenty-one tons. Eventually, following several years of litiga-
tion, the City of Victoria paid more than $150,000 in settlement claims result-
ing from the disaster. The remains of the ruined bridge were dynamited in July
1900. The present, and fifth, Point Ellice Bridge was constructed in 1957.

The Point Ellice Bridge collapse remains the worst streetcar disaster in
North American history and Canada's second worst bridge disaster. Only the
August 29, 1907, Quebec Bridge disaster near Quebec City in which seventy-
five bridge construction workers died eclipses it.

Police Forces

Police protection throughout most of British Columbia is provided by the Royal
Canadian Mounted Police (RCMP), organized into three forces. Only twelve
municipalities have their own independent police forces.

The RCMP Federal Force, composed of about 840 officers, is responsible
for handling federal criminal law cases, policing international airports, providing protective policing (such as security for visiting diplomats), and operating the Indian Policing Program.

Municipalities with populations under five thousand and all unincorporated, usually rural, parts of the province are policed by the RCMP Pro-

vincial Force. This force has about 1,500 officers. Approximately 19 percent of the **population** of B.C. lives in areas policed by the RCMP Provincial Force, but the vast majority of the province falls within its jurisdiction.

The RCMP Municipal Force provides policing to fifty-five municipalities that comprise about 52 percent of the province's population. This force has about 2,225 members.

Twelve independent municipal forces serve a population of just under one million, about 29 percent of the population. The independent forces have a combined total of about 1,925 police officers. Communities with independent forces are: Central Saanich, Delta, Esquimalt, Matsqui, **Nelson**, **New Westminster**, Oak Bay, Port Moody, Saanich, **Vancouver**, **Victoria**, and **West Vancouver**.

It costs about $566 million for the province's sixty-six-hundred-strong police force to provide protection services to its citizens.

In an average year approximately seventy-one thousand people are charged with Criminal Code offences. About 30 percent of these will be charged with violent crimes, 50 percent with property crimes such as break and enters, and 20 percent with other crimes such as arson and vandalism. Approximately 26 percent of people charged with crimes are young offenders between the ages of twelve and seventeen. About 85 percent of adults charged are male, as are 80 percent of the young offenders.

Police are more successful in solving crimes of violence than any other form of crime. About 71 percent of all violent crimes are solved, compared to only about 17 percent of property crimes and 32 percent for other crimes. Nearly 80 percent of all homicides are solved.

Political History

British Columbia's political history has traditionally been polarized between a strong rightist element and a middle to leftward movement that has tended to be moderate when compared to other world social reformist and leftist political movements. The province's electoral history has been marked by two-party struggles that so polarize the population that other political parties seldom can establish more than a tentative toehold within the Legislative Assembly.

Prior to the introduction of the federal party lines of Liberal and Conservative to the province with Richard McBride's election as the first Conservative premier in 1903, anything approaching traditional party lines was little known in B.C. politics. Rather, politicians and power groups tended to cluster around someone they would put forward as their leader on the basis of personality, reputation, and perceived ability to influence the economic leaders of the community. This would lead to political candidates running for office in ridings affiliating themselves with a specific candidate they had selected as their choice for premier. The electoral candidates supporting John Herbert Turner in the election of 1895, for example, were known collectively as Turnerites. This tendency of B.C. provincial politics, especially the politics of rightist movements, to solidify around a quasi-cult of personality has persisted into modern B.C. political history.

It was in the 1920s that political parties became sharply split among right, centre, and left political and social movements. In the elections of the 1920s and 1930s, Conservatives represented the right, Liberals the centre, and the left was represented by a hodgepodge of Labour, Progressive, and Socialist parties. The Labour party, drawing many of its leaders from trade union organizers who had gained their experience in Great Britain's union struggles, managed to elect members to the Legislative Assembly throughout this period. Power, however, alternated between Conservative and Liberal governments and these parties consistently garnered the majority share of all votes.

In 1933, with the country and the province firmly in the grip of the Great Depression, the rightist Conservative Party was virtually wiped out, finishing behind the new Cooperative Commonwealth Federation (CCF), which won seven seats and 31 percent of the vote. The Liberals won the election, however, and continued to hold power for the next eight years, although only by forming the only coalition governments in B.C. history.

The time of the coalition governments ended in 1952 when a new party led by W.A.C. Bennett broke away from the Conservative Party and called itself Social Credit, after a similar party in Alberta. This party won a minority government in 1952, but went on to hold power for twenty years. This period coincided with the province's great economic boom and expansion of **population** and services into the interior.

In the 1960s, the New Democratic Party (formerly the CCF) emerged as the official Opposition and the Liberal and Conservative parties virtually disappeared from the provincial political landscape, as the electorate polarized between the right-wing Social Credit and the leftist NDP. In 1972, the NDP defeated the Social Credit with the election of Dave Barrett as premier. In the late 1960s and early 1970s these two parties defined their platforms thusly—Social Credit as favouring free enterprise and government restraint, including the provision of social programs; NDP as being moderately socialist, believing in government economic and social involvement. Each party claimed roughly one-half of the electorate as providing its support, with the fluctuation of percentage shares in the electoral ridings proving critical to winning elections. Generally, Social Credit could hold power as long as it succeeded in capturing sufficient rural ridings and a small number of urban ridings composed of an electorate that was in the upper income brackets. Losing support in either of these sectors ensured an NDP victory based on its support in the more urbanized ridings with a lower- to middle-income electorate.

When the NDP government succeeded in alienating the labour movement during its time in office, it lost sufficient support to hold onto power and Social Credit consequently returned as the government in 1979—led by W.A.C. Bennett's son, William Bennett. Bennett was re-elected in 1979 and 1983, but resigned before the next election. William Vander Zalm led the Social Credit (often acronymed the Socreds) to an election victory in 1986. Vander Zalm's involvement in a number of scandals, combined with a scandal-ridden cabinet and backbench, discredited the Socreds so badly during its five-year tenure that in 1991 the NDP (under the leadership of Michael Harcourt), swept to a vast majority win. This win was punctuated by the virtual elimination of the Social Credit Party from the province's political landscape in favour of a return of the Liberal Party as the official Opposition. The Social Credit Party subsequently collapsed into such disarray and suffered so many defections from its few remaining legislative representatives to other parties that it is unlikely ever to reclaim a significant role in the province's politics.

Following the 1991 election the rightist movements in B.C. showed signs of polarizing between the Liberal Party, which assumed the more moderate positions of the traditional Social Credit Party, and an emergent and strident anti-government involvement and conservative moral values political movement called the Reform Party. The provincial Reform Party was not officially aligned with the federal Reform Party, which arose during this same period and shared many of the provincial party's positions.

The NDP government of this period tried to build an atmosphere of political consensus and stability throughout the province. The rise of the Reform Party, however, was symptomatic of a trend among the right-supporting percentage of the population—concerned by mounting government debt and increasingly distrustful of politicians and government social welfare systems— to drift increasingly further to the right, pulling both the Liberal and the NDP party, seeking to hold onto its share of the electorate, along in its wake.

Population

When British Columbia joined confederation in 1871, its population was estimated at forty thousand people, of which about twenty-five thousand were **First Nations peoples**. By 1992, total population had grown to about 3.5 million—approximately 12.2 percent of Canada's total population. By 2016, the province's population is expected to reach 4.9 million.

B.C. is the fastest growing province in Canada, averaging annual growth rates of about 2.4 percent compared to a national average of 1.1 percent.

Between 1980 and 1990, migration of people to the province accounted for 62 percent of population growth, with natural increases due to births within the provincial population contributing the remaining 38 percent. In the early 1990s the increase of population through migration rose rapidly to an average of 74 percent. Most of this increase was from interprovincial migration, rather than immigration to the province from outside Canada. In 1992, for example, 41,240 people migrated to B.C. from other provinces and the territories, while 29,050 immigrated to B.C. from outside Canada.

Migrants to B.C. tend to be younger, on average, than existing residents. They bring with them a higher average level of education, with a larger share holding university degrees than is true of the resident B.C. population. They also tend to have a higher level of occupational skills, with a greater proportion being in managerial and professional occupations.

The age structure of B.C. will continue for several more generations to be shaped by the post-World War II baby boom and subsequent drop in birth rates. In B.C., as throughout Canada, the baby boom has caused an enormous population bulge that moves up the age scale as the baby boomers grow older. In 1992, for example, people aged twenty-five to forty-four years old accounted for 33.4 percent of the population, compared to 30.9 percent ten years earlier. This increase was primarily due to migration of baby boomers to the province from other parts of Canada.

The portion of the population that is over the age of sixty-five continues to rise in numbers as well. Between 1982 and 1992, this segment of the population rose from 11 percent to 12.9 percent. When the baby boomers reach this age group, it will grow even faster.

The consequences of an aging population are numerous and will become even more so as the percentages rise more dramatically. Demand for products and services used by the elderly will soar. Social service expenditures are projected to shift with a greater proportion going to **health care** and less to **education**.

Another factor in B.C.'s population growth patterns is the disproportionate allocation of people across the province's landscape. Population growth is almost entirely concentrated in three regions—the Lower Mainland, **Vancouver Island**, and the Thompson and **Okanagan** valleys in the southern interior. These three regions account for more than 86 percent of the province's population, but less than 25 percent of its land mass. The Greater Vancouver Regional District has a population density averaging six hundred people per square kilometre, compared to about 3.5 people per square kilometre for all British

Columbia. Nowhere in these three regions do population concentrations number fewer than ten people per square kilometre.

The centralization of B.C.'s population is expected to continue, as it results from economic influences that show no signs of changing. Other provincial regions are primarily dependent on resource-based industries, which are shrinking in the size of operations and, through modernization, reducing overall **labour forces**. Meanwhile, service-oriented industries are increasing in size and in importance to the provincial **economy**. These industries are concentrated in the three most populated regions for the very reason that that is where the population they serve is based and expanding.

Post-Secondary Education

British Columbia's post-secondary **education system** consists of: four universities, four university colleges, twelve colleges, four institutes, and the Open Learning Agency (OLA).

The province's universities are the University of British Columbia (UBC) in **Vancouver**, Simon Fraser University (SFU) in Burnaby, the University of Victoria (UVic), and the University of Northern British Columbia, opened in 1994 at **Prince George**. These institutions provide the majority of degree-level university education in B.C.

There are also four university colleges which, in collaboration with the universities, offer selected courses of study leading to a bachelor's degree granted by one of the universities. These institutions also offer career technical, vocational, and adult basic education. University college main campuses are: University College of the Fraser Valley in Abbotsford, Malaspina University-College in Nanaimo, University College of the Cariboo in **Kamloops**, and Okanagan University College in **Kelowna**.

Regionally based colleges provide a wide range of programs. All colleges offer courses in the four main fields of academic, career technical, vocational, and adult basic education. These colleges' main campuses are: Camosun College in **Victoria**, Capilano College in North Vancouver, College of New Caledonia in Prince George, Douglas College in **New Westminster**, East Kootenay Community College in Cranbrook, Kwantlen College in Surrey, Langara College and Vancouver Community College in Vancouver, North Island College in Courtenay, Northern Lights College in Dawson Creek, Northwest Community College in Terrace, and Selkirk College in **Castlegar**.

Four institutes provide specialized instruction in technologies and trades, art and design, law enforcement and public safety, and marine training. These institutes' main campuses are: The British Columbia Institute of Technology (BCIT) in Burnaby, Pacific Marine Training Institute in North Vancouver,

The Justice Institute of British Columbia in Vancouver, and Emily Carr Institute of Art & Design of Vancouver.

For people unable to attend regular college, institutes, or university classes, the Open Learning Agency, headquartered in Burnaby, offers the opportunity to earn university degrees, take college programs, and receive workplace training. The OLA uses a variety of non-traditional methods, including television, to deliver education and training.

In all, about 149,500 students are enrolled in the province's post-secondary education system each year. Some 63,300 of these are attending university, 57,200 colleges, 15,300 institutes, and 13,700 the OLA.

Potlatch

The potlatch was historically a cornerstone of Northwest Coast **First Nations peoples**. Through potlatch ceremonies, the status, rank, lines of privilege, and power were established and confirmed. Wealth in the form of utilitarian goods such as blankets, carved cedar boxes, canoes, food, fish, and prestige items including slaves and coppers (pieces of copper hammered into the shape of a shield that were among the most valued potlatch items) were bestowed on others or sometimes destroyed. All transactions were performed with great ceremony and ritual.

Potlatches celebrated initiations, mourned the dead, or marked the investiture of chiefs in a continuing series of often competitive exchanges between clans and rival groups. Great potlatches could be years in the planning and preparation and sometimes lasted several days. The ceremony entailed fasting, spirit dances, theatre performances, and gift distribution. Potlatches were an important but not common ceremony in the life of a west-coast tribe. Seldom would one chief host more than four potlatches during his life. They served, however, to confirm the social order of a culture that had no clearly established political structure.

By 1884, missionaries and Indian agents were besieging Ottawa with complaints that potlatch ceremonies were shameless, wicked, pagan celebrations that prevented west-coast peoples from being effectively converted to Christianity and taught the Victorian-aged European values of thrift and frugality. The federal government accordingly amended the Indian Act to outlaw potlatches, the winter dances of the northern peoples, and the spirit dances of the Salishan. Protests from natives were dismissed and the law was rigorously enforced until its repeal in 1951.

During this period underground ceremonies were reported, but they were small and carried out furtively for fear of prosecution. In 1922, however, high-ranking Kwakwaka'wakw (formerly Kwakiutl) chief Dan Cranmer called what some historians say was the largest potlatch ever at **Alert Bay**. Openly defying the law, chiefs came from islands and inlets throughout the province's West Coast. They wore their traditional regalia, danced their dances, sang their songs, and received splendid gifts that Cranmer had secretly gathered for years in preparation for the event. The local Indian agent responded by calling in the RCMP and the chiefs were given an ultimatum. Those who surrendered their potlatch regalia and gifts could go free; those who refused would be jailed. Despairing, many complied—the material confiscated was mostly turned over to the National Museum of Canada. Chief Cranmer refused and was imprisoned, becoming a hero and inspiring native pride in their heritage.

The repeal of the anti-potlatch law in 1951 came too late to prevent the infliction of serious damage to tribal identities and social organization—damage that is still only gradually being healed as native tribes slowly re-establish their sense of community and unique culture. Potlatches are again held today, but they are smaller affairs than in the past and are usually not marked by the largesse that typified the traditional events.

In 1980, pressure on the National Museum led to the return, conditional on their preservation in local museums, of the potlatch artefacts seized at Chief Cranmer's ceremony. The native peoples of Cape Mudge on Quadra Island and Alert Bay constructed two buildings dedicated to their heritage and undertook custody of the artefacts. At Kwagiulth Museum in Cape Mudge, more than three hundred potlatch items are displayed along with **totem poles** and other ceremonial relics. At Alert Bay, the U'mista Cultural Centre is home to the remainder of the collection.

Powell River

The small pulp-and-paper mill community of Powell River is the largest and most northern centre on British Columbia's **Sunshine Coast**. It was founded when the mill was constructed here in 1910. The original neighbourhood, called the Townsite, is home to some thirty commercial buildings and four hundred Victorian-style homes that give the milltown a pleasant ambience.

Internationally, Powell River is famous in choral group circles for its renowned choral festival, Kathaumixw (Coast Salishan word for a "gathering of peoples"), which is held biennially and attracts choristers from around the world.

Powell River is also becoming a popular destination for scuba divers and has taken to billing itself "The Dive Capital of Canada." There are some twenty major **diving** sites here, including Octopus City, where the unusually large **Puget Sound octopus** is found, and The Hulks, an area where old ships were sunk near the mill to form a breakwater.

Powell River, from which the community derives its name, is the world's second shortest river. Only five hundred metres in length, it flows out of fifty-one-kilometre-long Powell Lake into the ocean.

Prince George

Located almost at the centre of British Columbia, Prince George is the government, service, distribution, transportation, educational, and cultural heart of the province's central and northern interior region. In 1994, Canada's first autonomous university to be opened in twenty-five years—the University of Northern British Columbia—started offering classes and degrees. The university is aiming to become a leader in the areas of First Nations, environmental, international, northern, and women's studies.

After metropolitan **Vancouver**, metropolitan **Victoria**, and **Kelowna**, Prince George is B.C.'s most populous city.

Prince Rupert

Prince Rupert is the site of British Columbia's most northerly deep-water port and is a major shipping, rail, and highway terminus for the export of the province's northern resource products to world markets. It is eight hundred kilometres closer to Japan and other Asian markets than **Vancouver**, making it one of the province's vital shipping outlets. The **B.C. Ferry Corporation** runs sailings year-round between Port Hardy on **Vancouver Island** and Prince Rupert. This ferry route is part of a popular tourist loop that allows travellers to visit much of the province without backtracking by taking the ferry one way and driving the mainland highway routes the other way.

Provincial Bird. *See* Symbols.

Provincial Court. *See* Judiciary.

Provincial Emblem; Flag; Flower; Motto. *See* Symbols.

Provincial Parks

Approximately 6.5 million hectares of British Columbia comprise the provincial park system's 370 parks, 36 recreation areas, one wilderness conservancy, and 131 **ecological reserves**. Although it is often stated that parklands account for about 6 percent of B.C.'s 94.78 million hectares of land, the figure is undoubtedly lower because provincial park land inventories include inland and coastal water areas that are protected. No calculation of the actual terrestrial terrain found in the parks has been recorded.

Of the province's incredibly diverse physiographic landscapes and ecosystems, slightly more than 50 percent are represented within B.C.'s parks. These include caves, alpine meadows, mountain peaks, **rainforests**, extinct **volcanoes**, historic towns, Pacific **islands**, as well as the nation's highest **waterfalls**.

The province's parks are visited by about twenty million people per year.

(*See also* **Barkerville; Bugaboo Glacier Provincial Park and Alpine Recreation Area; Cape Scott; Carmanah Pacific Provincial Park; Cathedral Provincial Park; Cultus Lake; Height of the Rockies Wilderness Area; Khutzeymateen Valley Provincial Park; Kitlope Valley; Nisga'a Memorial Lava Bed Provincial Park; Spatsizi Plateau Wilderness Provincial Park; Strathcona Provincial Park; Tatshenshini-Alsek Wilderness Provincial Park; Tweedsmuir Provincial Park; Wells Gray Provincial Park.**)

Provincial Shield; Stone; Tartan; Tree. *See* **Symbols.**

Publishing. *See* **Cultural History.**

Puget Sound Octopus (*Dofleini octopus*)

British Columbia's ocean **coastline** is home to the world's largest species of octopus, known as the Puget Sound octopus. This eight-armed octopus ranges in weight from twenty to sixty kilograms, and can range between three and four metres across. Its tentacles can be as thick as a large man's bicep and its suckers the size of a mandarin orange.

Dofleini octopus constitute a major portion of the province's annual $438,000 octopus catch of about 140 tonnes. The octopuses are captured either by traps or underwater divers. Most of the trapping of octopuses results incidentally from commercial fishermen who have set traps for prawns and crabs. On an annual basis, there are only about twenty divers commercially capturing octopuses. The octopuses are usually sold as bait for the halibut fishery, although there is a growing market for smoked octopus that is primarily exported to Asian nations.

Divers harvest the octopus by hand as it is illegal to shoot or spear them. The harvester grabs the octopus from above and pulls it rapidly off its anchoring point and then drags it to the surface. Freed from its hold on an anchoring point, the octopus is incapable of using its tentacles as a powerful bullwhip or to entangle and hold down the diver—either of which tactics can cause injury or death to the diver.

Queen Charlotte Islands

The Queen Charlotte Islands, adjacent to **Prince Rupert**, comprise about two hundred islands clustered in a scimitar-shaped archipelago that is 250 kilometres long and up to 84 kilometres wide from east to west. The islands are separated from the west-coast mainland by Hecate Strait, which varies from 45 to 130 kilometres in width. Graham, to the north, and Moresby, to the south, are the largest islands. Graham contains most of the islands' small **population** (about six thousand) in two communities—Masset and Queen Charlotte City.

Most of the islands, covering an area of 9,596 square kilometres, are uninhabited, as is the majority of Graham and Moresby islands. Isolated and storm-swept, home to ancient temperate **rainforests**, blanketed on the west coast for about two hundred days a year by fog and drizzle, the Queen Charlottes are a unique, mystical part of British Columbia. Having escaped the last ice age that receded only fifteen thousand years ago from the rest of the province, flora and fauna life here is more ancient than elsewhere in B.C. It is home to the largest bald eagle population in the province, has the highest density of Peale's peregrine falcons in the world, has North America's largest black **bears**, and serves as a nesting ground for about 25 percent of all B.C.'s seabirds. About half of the province's sea lions also live here. All native land **mammals** and three **bird** species are subspecifically unique. A yellow daisy (*Senecio newcombei*) is only found in the Charlotte's alpine meadows; several alpine mosses usually found only in the Himalayas are also present.

Archaeological evidence reveals that the islands have been inhabited for at least ten thousand years. According to Haida legend, Rose Spit, which extends from the northeast corner of Graham Island, was where the trickster Raven opened a clamshell ten thousand years ago that contained the Haida people and released them to life on Earth. European explorer Juan Josef Perez Hernandez sailed by the islands in 1774 and traded with the Haida, but it was Captain James Cook who first landed in 1778. It is estimated that about seven thousand Haida lived on the islands at the time, but by 1915 smallpox epidemics brought by white missionaries and traders had decimated the population, reducing it to fewer than six hundred. Today, the Haida constitute one-sixth of the islands' population and there are two Haida communities—Old Masset and Skidegate, both on Graham Island.

The entire southern end of Moresby Island encompasses **Gwaii Haanas National Park** (also known as South Moresby), which has saved this section of the island from the heavy clearcutting fate that destroyed the **forest** on most of the island's northern lands. The northeastern portion of Graham Island is part of 72,640-hectare Naikoon Provincial Park, which includes stretches of unspoiled rainforest, low bogs, and dunes backing long, stretching beaches.

Just north of Masset, on the northern shore of Graham Island, 554-hectare Delkatla Wildlife Sanctuary is the first major landfall for weary southbound birds migrating on the Pacific Flyway. Up to 113 different species have been identified here.

Logging, fishing, **tourism**, and increasing demand for Haida native arts and crafts form the economic backbone of the islands. As is often the case on B.C.'s West Coast, there has been significant friction here between logging and tourism/environmentalist groups over the future of island development and resource exploitation. The declaration of Gwaii Haanas in July 1988 was hailed as a major victory by the pro-environmental preservation forces, as it preserved about 15 percent of the Queen Charlottes' land mass from further logging or **mining**.

Quesnel Lake

They hoped to discover that this Cariboo lake east of Williams Lake was the deepest in the world, but in the spring of 1994 researchers conducting an acoustic-sounding survey discovered Quesnel Lake was only 530 metres deep. That was deep enough to make it the world's deepest known fjord lake but it did not displace Great Slave Lake at 614 metres from its status as the deepest lake in the western hemisphere. Lake Baikal in eastern Siberia, which contains one-fifth of all the planet's fresh water, is the world's deepest lake—1,619 metres—and also, covering 31,500 square kilometres, its largest.

Fjord lakes, such as Quesnel, are created by glaciers scouring a valley bottom. They are typically long and narrow. **Kootenay** and Okanagan are also British Columbia fjord lakes.

Race Rocks

West of **Victoria**, opposite the rural bedroom-community of Metchosin, Race Rocks and its historic **lighthouse** are British Columbia's most southerly point. They are just eight kilometres from the international boundary. The rocks are a historic hazard to shipping and are named for the speed with which tidal currents run past them.

Radium Hot Springs

South of Golden on Highway 95, Radium Hot Springs came under National Park administration in 1920 with the creation that year of **Kootenay National Park**. The Kutenai peoples had enjoyed the 45.5° Celsius average surface-temperature mineral hot springs for centuries before Europeans happened on them. In 1915, they were renamed Radium from Sinclair Hot Springs because it was believed the water was highly radioactive (a belief that given the time's scientific comprehension of radioactivity risks in no way lessened their usage, as the presence of radon was believed to increase the water's healing capabilities). In reality, the radiation levels emitted by the hot springs equals that given off by the average watch dial.

Rafting

About thirty outfitters in British Columbia offer white-water rafting trips and expeditions down some of the province's longest and wildest rivers. The most popular rivers for rafting trips are the **Fraser** (with running **Hell's Gate** considered one of the most exciting rides in the province), **Thompson**, Tatshenshini-Alsek, Chilko, Chilcotin, Kootenay, and **Stikine** rivers. Trips range in length from one day to two weeks.

After a series of river-rafting fatalities in 1988, stringent provincial safety regulations were introduced. All rafting companies now carry a provincial licence and face stiff penalties and insurance liability if they endanger their clients by running rivers in conditions deemed too dangerous.

Railways

British Columbia has approximately sixty-eight hundred kilometres of main-line track operated by BC Rail, CN Rail, CP Rail, Southern Railway of British Columbia, and the Burlington Northern Railway. All these railway companies are involved in extensive freight-hauling operations. In addition, CP Rail operates a railcar barge service to **Vancouver Island** and CN Rail provides aquatrain service from **Prince Rupert** to Whittier, Alaska.

BC Rail, a provincial government-owned operation, provides passenger service between North Vancouver and **Prince George**. The *Royal Hudson* steam excursion train, running from North Vancouver to Squamish during summer months, is also owned and operated by BC Rail.

Great Canadian Railtour Co. Ltd. operates the *Rocky Mountaineer*, a seasonal railtour service, running during daylight hours between **Vancouver** and Banff-Calgary or Jasper. The train stops overnight in **Kamloops**.

VIA Rail Canada Inc. provides limited passenger service within British Columbia. VIA services are provided on CN Rail lines, from Vancouver via Jasper to Edmonton and eastern Canada and from Jasper to Prince Rupert. VIA Rail also provides services on CP Rail's Esquimalt and Nanaimo Railway line, between **Victoria** and Courtenay. This latter service has a long and controversial history as the various companies operating the passenger service have consistently sought to close it due to a lack of profitability, but public pressure on government and the rail corporations has resulted in its continued operation. How much longer the Vancouver Island rail passenger service will be sustained is always in question.

Rainforests—Ancient Temperate

Temperate rainforests are predominantly evergreen forests receiving at least one thousand millimetres of rain per year distributed over a minimum of one hundred days. They are extremely rare. Western North America contains about two-thirds of the world's temperate rainforests—the remaining forests are found primarily in Australia, New Zealand, Norway, and Chile.

The temperate rainforests of North America surpass tropical rainforests, such as the Amazon, in tree size and total forest biomass (literally the weight of living matter in a prescribed area). The average lifespan of most trees within the temperate rainforests is three hundred to eight hundred years, but some are far older.

British Columbia's rainforests have two distinct parts. There is a northern and a southern forest. The dividing line cuts across **Vancouver Island**'s northern tip over to the mainland coast.

The northern forest is primarily composed of western hemlock to the Alaskan border where Sitka spruce becomes dominant. In the southern part the forest is more mixed. While it is still predominantly western hemlock-based, the southern rainforest is intermixed with western red cedar and balsam, selective stands of Sitka spruce, and scatterings of Douglas-fir. With few

Carmanah Pacific Provincial Park contains one of the finest remaining examples of the ancient Sitka rainforests. (Mark Zuehlke photo)

exceptions, the remaining rainforests of any significant size in southern British Columbia grow along Vancouver Island's west coast.

Almost all the province's ancient temperate rainforests are coastal. These forests are among the last of a rapidly disappearing habitat. After the Ice Age only 0.2 percent of Earth's land area was coastal temperate rainforest. Today 90 percent of these forests are gone. Of the 10 percent remaining, about one-quarter lies within B.C. Much of this forest is threatened by logging.

(*See also* **Carmanah Pacific Provincial Park**; **Clayoquot Sound**; **CORE**; **Environmental Conflict**; **Forest Industry**; **Forests**; **Kitlope Valley**.)

Ranches. *See* Douglas Lake Cattle Company; Gang Ranch.

Rapids. *See* Paddling; Rafting.

Rattlesnakes

The only poisonous snake in B.C. is the western rattlesnake found in the southern interior dry-belt region, especially the **Okanagan Valley**. Few rattlesnake dens (communal hibernation caves and shelters beneath rocky outcroppings) survived modern development, so the snakes are relatively rare. The rattler is a lethargic species, preferring to wait for its prey to wander by rather than actively hunting. It feeds primarily on rodents, other small **mammals**, and **birds** after killing them with venom released from fangs during a bite.

Its distinctive rattle is a warning to larger creatures that they are straying close to its hiding place. The buzzing sound is produced by rapid vibration of its tail; the rattle is composed of unmoulted, modified scales, each of which once capped the tail's tip.

Rattlesnakes rarely bite humans unless provoked or accidentally stepped on. The bite can cause painful swelling, muscular paralysis, and tissue destruction. Only in rare instances, usually when medical attention is not provided quickly after the bite, will a rattler strike prove fatal.

Generally speaking, back-country hikers are most at risk of encountering a rattlesnake, but can reduce the danger by taking certain precautions. These include wearing stout, high-topped boots, and carrying a pole to rustle brush before passing through it. The noise this produces alerts a rattler so that it can either rattle a warning or slither away to escape the hiker's approach.

Rattlers are most likely to be encountered in Okanagan Mountain Provincial Park near **Kelowna**, Kalamalka Lake Provincial Park near Vernon, and the rock bluff and sage country around Oliver and Osoyoos.

Red Tide. *See* **Paralytic Shellfish Poisoning.**

Reifel Bird Sanctuary

The largest number of rare **birds** in B.C. are found at Reifel Bird Sanctuary, one of North America's major waterfowl habitats located ten kilometres west of Ladner, south of **Vancouver** on Highway 99, on the northern tip of Westham Island. Among the rare birds are black-crowned night herons and the very rare Temminck's stint—an Alaskan peep seldom seen outside western Alaska. More than 230 species of birds have been recorded within the Canadian Wildlife Service-owned sanctuary. At nearby Roberts Bank, facing the sanctuary, about twenty thousand immature snow geese winter after leaving their nesting grounds on Wrangel Island in the former Soviet Union. Best birding at the sanctuary is between October and March.

Religion

British Columbia has a population that practises a great diversity of religions, although the majority believe in Christianity. Approximately 603,000 British Columbians are Roman Catholic, 420,000 United Church, and 328,500 Anglican.

After Christianity, Sikh is the second most practised religion with about 74,550 followers. This is followed by Buddhism, which has about 36,500 believers, and Jehovah's Witness with about 33,650 members. There are 18,000 Hindus, approximately 16,000 Jews, 5,000 Unitarians, and 3,500 Baha'is.

The **Doukhobor** Christian faith is steadily declining, with only 3,700 practising Doukhobors remaining, down significantly from 1961 when there were slightly more than 10,000.

In the 1991 federal census, ninety-five British Columbians listed their religion as Satanist, the first time anyone in the province had responded in this manner on a census.

Reptiles

Although there are about six thousand reptile species in the world, only twenty-one—seventeen of which are native species—are found in British Columbia. Of these, the short-horned lizard is believed to have been extirpated from its small range in the southern **Okanagan Valley** and the western **rattlesnake** is on the provincial **endangered species** list. Reptile species in B.C. are concentrated primarily in the southern interior grassland valleys, such as the Okanagan and Thompson valleys. The northern alligator lizard is found in isolated rocky outcroppings of southern **Vancouver Island**.

Native B.C. reptile species are: western pond turtle, painted turtle, green sea turtle, Reeves' turtle, leatherback sea turtle, short-horned lizard, western skink, northern alligator lizard, rubber boa, sharp-tailed snake, western yellow-bellied racer, gopher snake, common garter snake, western terrestrial garter snake, northwestern garter snake, night snake, and western rattlesnake. The snapping turtle, red-eared slider turtle, and asiatic turtle have been introduced, as has the European wall lizard.

Revelstoke Dam

One hundred and forty-six kilometres south of **Mica Dam**, just north of Revelstoke, is Revelstoke Dam. This concrete dam with an earth-filled wing was built by **BC Hydro** in the 1980s, beginning operation in 1985. Standing 175 metres above the Columbia riverbed, it is one of the world's largest and most modern hydroelectric developments. Although constructed on the Columbia River, the Revelstoke Dam was not built as part of the **Columbia River Treaty** dam-construction project. It backed up the Columbia River to create Revelstoke Lake.

Ripple Rock

Possibly the most original solution to removing a marine hazard befell Ripple Rock on April 5, 1958. Standing just north of Campbell River in the busy Seymour Narrows section of the **Strait of Georgia** shipping lane, collisions with the rock had, since 1875, claimed twenty large ships and more than one hundred smaller vessels. Estimated loss of life had been tallied at 114.

During eighty-three years of Pacific coast marine-history, many a sailor

At 9:33 a.m. on April 5, 1958 Ripple Rock, long a hazard to Strait of Georgia shipping traffic, was destroyed in the largest non-nuclear peace-time explosion in history. (BCARS photo D-08490)

had cursed the rock and called to the heavens to destroy it—precisely what the federal government set out to do. The first attempt in 1943 was botched despite an investment of $1 million. In 1955, however, a thirty-month sapper project began at nearby Maud Island. A 152-metre shaft was drilled and then from this depth a 722-metre tunnel was dug from the island to the rock. Two holes were bored from the lower depth into the rock's core. These were stuffed with nearly 1.25 million kilograms of Nitramex 2H explosive.

A five-kilometre danger zone was cleared of all human population and at 9:33 a.m. on April 5, 1958, the explosive was ignited. It was the largest non-nuclear peace-time explosion in recorded history. (The greatest non-nuclear explosion of all also occurred in Canada at Halifax on December 6, 1917, when the French munitions carrier *Mont Blanc* exploded following a collision and levelled 2.5 square kilometres of Halifax's industrial north end, killing more than sixteen hundred people and injuring about nine thousand out of a city-population of fifty thousand.) Final cost of the Ripple Rock blast was $3.1 million to rid the strait of 360 million kilograms of the top of Ripple Rock. Marine traffic in the Strait of Georgia now sails over the submerged remnants of the rock with impunity.

Rivers

The importance of rivers to the geography, **physiography**, human settlement, and natural resource development of British Columbia cannot be underestimated. With more than 75 percent of the province elevated above three thousand metres it is the valleys that have been eroded by rivers and through which they flow that provide vital routes of travel for the majority of humans and wildlife. Were it not for the rivers much of the province would remain largely inaccessible to human development.

Almost all human settlement since earliest times within the province has been located on the shores of rivers or along the coast where river mouths open to the ocean. The majority of the province's small pockets of arable land are found in river valleys and on the deltas at river mouths. Most **highways** and **railways** wind through the province by following one river valley to another, climbing over intervening mountain passes only when absolutely necessary.

The rivers of B.C. number in the hundreds and in some isolated areas not all tributary streams have been mapped or discovered. British Columbia's longest river is the **Fraser River** (1,368 kilometres); Canada's longest river—the 4,241-kilometre Mackenzie River—has its headwaters in the province's northeast. The Fraser River is Canada's fifth longest.

Rivers in B.C. have relatively short lengths because most flow from inland areas to the Pacific Ocean and so have less distance to travel than those draining the Canadian plains or more easterly regions. There are five major drainage basins in B.C. A vast basin that is drained by ten rivers is the Coastal Drainage Basin, which runs down the coastline in a narrow band that seldom extends east of the **Coast Mountains** or the **Cascade Mountains**. The Fraser River has the largest individual drainage basin, carrying water from the **Rocky Mountains** all the way to the West Coast and draining most of the central and southern interior. The **Columbia River** drains most of the southernmost parts of the province. The Mackenzie River's headwaters drain approximately ten percent of B.C.'s northeasternmost region, and a small sliver of the northwest corner is drained northward by the Yukon River. These last two areas are, according to researchers, being encroached by the coastal drainage basin rivers, which are slowly eroding their way into headwater areas of the two northward-flowing rivers and siphoning off flow toward the Pacific Ocean.

Because the province's three main drainage basins all flow to the Pacific Ocean, almost two-thirds of the province's land is drained to this ocean, the rest going to the Bering Sea via the Yukon River and the Arctic Ocean via the Mackenzie River. Although the drainage of water into the Pacific accounts for only 10.2 percent of Canada's total land mass, the heavy westerly outflow of water coming from the province's glaciers and snowpacks totals about 23.5 percent of total Canadian water flow. When the Yukon and Mackenzie drainage basin areas lying within British Columbia are factored in, the province produces almost 30 percent of all water flow in Canada.

(*See also* **Water**.)

Rocky Mountains

The Rocky Mountains run almost the entire length of British Columbia from the **49th parallel** to about 45 kilometres south of the province's border with Yukon Territory. Their British Columbian section is twelve hundred kilometres long. For most of this stretch, they are flanked to the west by the distinctive **Rocky Mountain Trench**, except for a narrow break at the McGregor Plateau. On the east, the Rockies are flanked by the Rocky Mountain Foothills and beyond that by the Interior Plains (*see* **Physiography**).

The southern portions contain the main ranges of the Rockies and the **Continental Divide**, where Pacific watersheds back onto Atlantic and Arctic sources.

The Rockies are a major physiological and psychological barrier between the province of British Columbia and the rest of Canada. When British Columbians wish to differentiate themselves from other Canadians they tend to refer to themselves as being everyone west of the Rockies and that those on the other side are "easterners." (It is interesting to note that in its more common usage, the term "easterners" is used to distinguish anyone living east of Manitoba from those who live in western Canada.) When British Columbians discuss the flow of trade, or social and cultural affiliation, and possibly political ties south into the United States to encompass California, the eastern border for this fanciful community of mutual interest is usually the Rocky Mountains.

In the southern portion of the B.C. Rockies only two major rail and highway routes cut through narrow passes to connect the majority of the province's population with the rest of the nation. There are barely more than five road routes cutting through the Rockies from the east into the rest of British Columbia.

During the Pleistocene Age the Rockies underwent extreme **glaciation**. Ice sheets shrouded the mountains to elevations of twenty-four hundred metres in the north and up to two thousand metres in the south. Yet the mountains were higher than the ice and, consequently, other than for the Queen Charlotte Islands, this is virtually the only region of the province that has large sections of land that have never been glaciated. The glaciation that did carve the mountains produced its distinctive alpine features that make it uniquely comparable to portions of the European Alps.

The Rockies exert a major influence over the province that extends well beyond their physical occupancy of land area. From the ice and snow deposits on their slopes flow the headwaters of the **Fraser**, **Columbia**, and other B.C. **rivers** that provide the province with its vast **water** supply. The enormous wall of stone presented to the east by the Rockies also shelters most of the province from the harsh weather of the Interior Plains that extends only into about ten percent of that part of B.C.'s northeasternmost territory lying east of the Rocky Mountains, where the range doglegs west to reach its terminus just south of the Yukon border. In this region, the Rockies reach up to a maximum elevation of only 2,542 metres. The summits are rounded, often completely covered by **forests**, and show little trace of the press of glaciers that scoured them down to mediocrity. Aside from a few **mining** operations, this sparsely inhabited area is largely undeveloped.

Human habitation of the Rockies appears to date back only about four thousand years when the Kutenai and other **First Nations peoples** entered the region and used the passes to trade and hunt with the plains peoples. European explorers first ventured through the Rockies in 1793, when Alexander Mackenzie came through via the **Peace River**. The southern portion of the Rockies wasn't seriously explored until 1882 when the Kicking Horse Pass was selected as a route for the Canadian Pacific Railway to breach the mountains and proceed west through British Columbia to the Pacific Ocean.

The Rocky Mountains today are home to some of the nation and the province's most spectacular **national parks** and resort communities, and attract millions of tourists from around the world annually. Mining and forestry communities also subsist in some of the narrow passes through the mountains and along its flanks within the Rocky Mountain Trench.

Rocky Mountain Trench

The longest valley in North America, the Rocky Mountain Trench is a remarkable topographic feature extending from the **49th parallel** northwestward to the Liard River just south of Yukon Territory—a distance of fourteen hundred kilometres. It is incredibly narrow for the entire run, never exceeding twenty kilometres in width, occasionally choking down to a mere three kilometres. On its flanks are the wall-like slopes of major mountain ranges. To the east stand the **Rocky Mountains**; on the west in the south the **Columbia Mountains**; as it runs northward, the Omineca and Cassiar mountains. The northern half of the trench runs in a gradual curve between two walls of mountains. South of this portion, the trench is slightly more sinuous and wider, curving first eastward and then westward. Down most of its length flows the **Columbia River**. Between the southern and northern sections of the trench one major break occurs on the western flank to disrupt the wall of mountains. This occurs where the McGregor Plateau juts in from the west to reach across to the Rocky Mountains. The **Fraser River** takes advantage of this gap to flow westward from its headwaters to the Pacific Ocean.

Prior to construction of hydroelectric dams in eastern B.C. and Montana, seven major **rivers** occupied different parts of the trench. Now only the Fraser and Kechika follow original routes; the others, including the Columbia, empty into large reservoirs, such as Williston Lake, which flood much of the trench's valley floor.

The trench is bordered by many faults and is a zone of ancient crustal weakness—perhaps forming a continental margin where two major crusts meet. The faulting of this join, erosion and deposits by its great rivers, and intense **glaciation** during ice ages combined to create this unique physiographic feature.

The northern portion of the trench is scarcely inhabited or accessible. Its southern portion serves as a vital corridor for human traffic, and has done so since the first peoples entered the region little more than ten thousand years ago. Small communities, dependent on forestry, **mining**, and **agriculture** are scattered throughout the southern region. Most of the province's transportation systems coming out of the Rocky Mountains to the east and heading west to the coast pass through gaps between the mountains walling in each side of the trench.

Rogers Pass

Both railway and highway transportation interests were spurred to use the Rogers Pass route through the Selkirk Mountain range that is bordered on the west by Revelstoke and on the east by Golden, because it offered the shortest and seemingly most viable passage through the rugged mountains. The **Trans-Canada Highway** and Canadian Pacific Railway's national line passes through here today. Construction of both transportation routes, however, was a costly and complex process.

The pass was named for A.B. Rogers, who explored it in 1881 as part of a quest to find a route through the Selkirks for the rapidly approaching Canadian Pacific Railway construction project. It took Rogers two separate expeditions into the pass over two years to prove it was viable for the railroad. Railroad crews tackled the pass in early 1885 and by November 7 joined up with the eastward working rail crews at **Craigellachie** west of Rogers Pass. By the following year, snowsheds were erected in various places to protect the rails from the constant problem of **avalanches** of snow and mud. Between 1885 and 1916 more than 250 railroad workers were killed in the Rogers Pass by snow avalanches.

The worst slide came on March 4, 1910, when sixty-six men, mostly Italian and Japanese labourers, were killed in a slide that swept down on a workcrew struggling to clear tracks of snow from an earlier slide. Between 1910 and 1912 more than one hundred slides pounded down onto the tracks, most upon an eight-kilometre stretch known as The Loop, which descended from the pass's 1,382-metre summit to the base of Ross Peak. In 1913, the CPR abandoned hope of being able to keep this section of railway open reliably and decided to escape the implacable snow by burrowing underground. Work on the eight-kilometre Connaught Tunnel began the same year through the virtually solid rock of Mount Macdonald. By 1916, at a cost of nearly $10 million—$2.5 million in dynamite alone—the double-track tunnel was completed. In mid-1984 the Connaught Tunnel was bypassed by the even larger and more expensive **Mount Macdonald Tunnel**, which was completed in 1988.

In 1956, the B.C. government decided a shorter route for the Trans-Canada Highway had to be found to replace the Big Bend road section. Rogers Pass was selected. The pass was surveyed in 1958 and the following year construction began. Stretches of the 147-kilometre highway were built over the bed of abandoned sections of the CPR's original track. On July 30, 1962, the highway was finally completed. Several snowsheds had to be constructed in the infamous Loop area that had so plagued the CPR and an extensive avalanche safety and pre-emptive control system is utilized to prevent traffic being caught in snowslides.

Rossland

The small West Kootenay town of Rossland, just west of Trail, has a unique setting—it lies inside the eroded crater of a long-extinct **volcano**. Between 1900 and 1916, the nearby LeRoi Gold Mine yielded up more than $25 million in gold from the volcano's slopes, becoming the source of half the gold mined in British Columbia during this period. In 1901, LeRoi was also the scene of a bitter mine-workers' strike ended by the importation of strikebreakers and the subsequent collapse of the strike. This first major attempt at trade unionism in the Kootenay region did, however, set the stage for development of a strong union presence in the Trail-Rossland area that continues today.

In recent years Rossland has become a popular **tourism** and **skiing** destination. The surrounding rugged terrain draws mountain bikers from across North America, leading to the community sometimes being called the "Mountain Bike Capital of Canada." Nearby Red Mountain is a popular downhill ski resort—also the hill on which Olympic champion skiers Nancy Greene and Kerrin Lee-Gartner first honed their skills.

Royal British Columbia Museum. *See* **Cultural History.**

Saanich Inlet

There are only three other water bodies in the world similar to Saanich Inlet—B.C.'s **Nitinat Lake**, a fjord in Venezuela, and the Black Sea. All are distinguished by the shallowness of their mouth compared to their depth. This shallow entry point creates an area of intense environmental sensitivity. Nowhere along Saanich Inlet's mouth does the depth exceed seventy-five metres, but once past the mouth its depth plunges sharply to a maximum of 230 metres. The deeper the water, the heavier its salt content and lower the oxygen content. The salt water below the 130-metre level is so heavy that the thin trickle of incoming water off the **Strait of Georgia** is incapable of displacing any of this deeper water, which inevitably stagnates, while the upper reaches circulate with regular tidal flows. Only once a year, during the highest tidal flows in December, are currents in the Strait of Georgia and **Juan de Fuca Strait** strong enough to push salt-heavy water into the inlet. This heavier water thrusts down into the stagnant levels and displaces some of the bottom layer.

Because of this sluggish water turnover, the inlet is highly susceptible to damage from run-off and sewage pollution. For this reason, any proposed development projects planned for the steep hillsides bordering the inlet have been strongly resisted by environmentalists and have aroused much political controversy at municipal, regional, and provincial levels.

St. Elias Mountains

Lying in a curve of the Gulf of Alaska and extending northwestward from Cross Sound and Lynn Canal to Cook Inlet, the St. Elias Mountains, along with the **Insular Mountains**, constitute what is known as the Outer Mountain Area of B.C.'s western system (*see* **Physiography**). The St. Elias Mountains include some of North America's most rugged country, including the summits of **Fairweather Mountain** (B.C.'s highest at 4,663 metres), Mount St. Elias on the Alaska-Yukon boundary (elevation 5,489 metres), and Canada's highest peak and second highest in North America—Yukon's Mount Logan (6,050 metres).

In British Columbia, the St. Elias Mountains extend along the Alaska-B.C. boundary between Fairweather Mountain and Mount Jette. Their boundary with the Coast Mountains is along the Tatshenshini, Kelsall, and Chilkat rivers. Much of the range within British Columbia is covered by glaciers and snowfields. These are among the least explored sections of the province. South-eastward of the Alsek River, altitudes decline to between 1,975 metres and 2,600 metres. Here there is less snow and ice mantling slopes and peaks, but the peaks are sharply carved and streams and creeks swell with sediment from glacial melting. The valley flats of the lower Alsek and Tatshenshini rivers are more than 1.6 kilometres wide due to glacial and stream erosion. Low timberline on mountain slopes, sparse vegetation, and deposits of stagnant and receding ice attest to the fact that this section of the St. Elias Mountains is only just emerging from the glacial cloak that still covers the nearby higher regions.

Salamanders. *See* Amphibians.

Salmon

There are five types of salmon native to the Pacific waters of British Columbia's west coast. The largest of these—and the most prized game fish—is the chinook, which ranges from 1.5 kilograms to 30 kilograms. Chinook salmon exceeding 13.5 kilograms are called tyees. In the U.S., the chinook is usually known as king salmon. Chinook are distinguished from other salmon by their black gums and silver, spotted tail.

Coho salmon are the next largest, averaging 1.3 kilograms to 14 kilograms. Coho have white gums, black tongues, and a few spots on the upper portion of their silver-coloured tails. They are bright silver with a metallic blue dorsal surface.

Chum salmon usually weigh between 4.5 kilograms and 6.5 kilograms, but occasionally reach as much as 15 kilograms. They have a white tip on the anal fin, which is about the only significant telltale sign that distinguishes them from sockeye salmon.

Sockeye are the slimmest and most streamlined of the Pacific salmon. They usually weigh between 2.2 kilograms and 3.1 kilograms, but can reach 6.3 kilograms. They are silver blue, almost toothless, and have prominent, glassy eyes. Young sockeye remain in freshwater nursery lakes for a year or more before migrating to the sea.

Pink salmon have tiny scales and a tail heavily marked with large oval spots. Unlike the other salmon species, the tail of a pink has no silver in it. They are the smallest Pacific salmon, usually weighing about 2.2 kilograms, but sometimes reaching 5.5 kilograms. Pink salmon have a peculiar migratory pattern that sees them being more abundant in northern waters of the province in even-numbered years and in southern waters in odd-numbered years. They live only two years, making them the shortest-lived of the Pacific salmon.

Unlike other salmonid species in the world, all Pacific salmon die after spawning. Although they live their adult lives in the Pacific Ocean, they return to the **rivers** and lake systems of the Pacific West Coast to spawn in fresh water. Salmon always return to the same riverbed spawning ground in which they were born. If, due to either natural or unnatural causes, the river downstream of their spawning grounds is obstructed, the salmon will try to spawn below the obstruction. Usually, however, this spawning attempt fails and the salmon dies without successfully reproducing. For this reason blockages of major spawning streams can have a devastating effect on salmon populations. (*See* **Hell's Gate**.)

In recent years a small population of Atlantic salmon species have escaped from fish hatcheries and fish farms into Pacific waters. The presence of these non-Pacific salmon has raised concerns that they may threaten the Pacific salmon species by introducing exotic diseases or by cross-breeding.

For the **First Nations people** of the province's coast who dwelt traditionally along the salmon-spawning rivers of the mainland and **Vancouver Island**, salmon provided a major source of food. Their importance as a food source, combined with the spectacle of the salmon spawning ritual, led to the fish being assigned a great deal of mystical, religious, and economic importance in most B.C. First Nations' cultures.

Salmon are the most economically important wild animal group in the B.C. **economy**, providing the majority of the catch for the commercial **fishing industry** and constituting one of the province's most sought after sportfish catches.

In 1993, about one million salmon disappeared from the **Fraser River** spawning runs. In 1994, what was to have been a major **Adams River** run fizzled with only about one million of the expected 3.4 million salmon arriving at this spawning ground—for its size the richest in the world. These sudden, unexpected massive declines in the salmon spawning stock signalled that the Pacific coast salmon species were possibly threatened, and as the salmon provide about 60 percent of the west-coast fishery's value, the industry was also in danger.

The disappearance of these millions of salmon has been blamed by scientists on everything from poaching by First Nations peoples, to drastic errors in population measurement, to overfishing, to habitat loss and salmon spawning ground destruction by the **forest industry** and pollution, to the warming of Pacific waters by El Nino currents.

(*See also* **Fishing Industry**; **Salmonid Enhancement Program**.)

Salmon Farms. *See* **Aquaculture.**

Salmonid Enhancement Program

Launched in 1977, the Salmonid Enhancement Program (SEP) is a joint federal-provincial government program with the objective of restoring salmonid populations in British Columbian waters to historic levels. Seven species of the salmonid fish family are the subject of SEP projects—all five species of Pacific **salmon** occurring on the West Coast and two species of trout; steelhead and cutthroat. The federal government is responsible for enhancement programs regarding the salmon species and the provincial government for those pertaining to trout species.

Enhancement activities cover a broad range. Hatcheries, fishways, spawning channels, incubation boxes, research, habitat improvements, and educational and public awareness activities are among the tools that SEP uses to increase fish production and foster preservation of natural runs and fish habitat. Each year some two hundred B.C. streams undergo some enhancement work. There are sixteen major enhancement hatcheries operating in the province, and a total of about three hundred hatcheries in all.

The core premise of the enhancement projects is that if salmonids can be assisted through the early stages of their life, more will reach adulthood and be available to the commercial, sport, and First Nations fishery, as well as being able to propagate the species through spawning at the end of their life cycle. In the wild, only about 15 percent of newly hatched fry survive, whereas about 85 percent of salmon born in hatcheries reach juvenile age and can be released into the wild. Since 1977, more than two billion juvenile salmonids have been released from B.C. hatcheries.

The SEP-produced fish account for about 10 percent of all fish taken by the commercial fishery in an average year. Even larger percentages of the fish caught by sport fishing are from tagged SEP stock.

Despite its objective goal of doubling the salmon catches on the West Coast, salmon stocks have been steadily decreasing, leading some researchers to suggest the entire enhancement project has been a costly failure and perhaps even contributed to the rapid decline of salmon stocks. Some researchers suggest that enhanced salmon stock is actually displacing wild stocks of salmon, but that these enhanced fish are less capable of resisting disease or of propagating effectively.

Saltspring Island. *See* **Gulf Islands.**

Sandcastle Competitions. *See* **Annual Events and Celebrations.**

Sasquatch

A Salishan First Nations word, sasquatch means "wild man," or "hairy man." The name is used in British Columbia to denote the mysterious ape-like creature rumoured to live in many of the remoter regions of the Pacific Northwest.

Evidence for the existence of the sasquatch in B.C. is found in many historical First Nations myths, in passages from the writings of the explorer David Thompson, and in the 1840s painter Paul Kane's *Wanderings of an Artist Among the Indians of North America*. In modern times there is usually a spate of sasquatch sightings each year in some region of the province. Since 1960, there have been approximately two thousand to three thousand sightings reported in Canada and the United States.

The only serious evidence—other than reported sightings—to support the existence of sasquatch are various footprints that have been discovered throughout the Pacific Northwest. Unfortunately, there is always the question of whether these footprints are ingenious fakes.

Typically the footprints do have a similar pattern. They are usually between thirty-seven and forty-three centimetres in length and are far wider than would be a human foot of the same length. In most cases all toes are the same size.

The size and stride of footprints and compaction of the ground measured by anthropologists indicates that males typically stand about 2.4 metres tall and weigh about 363 kilograms. Female sasquatch are smaller at about 1.8 metres tall, and weigh about 227 kilograms.

Anthropologists who have studied the subject believe that sasquatch are not human, although they may be close relatives. It is probable, researchers say, that sasquatch are surviving members of a large ape species known as *Gigantopithecus*, of which fossil remains dating back about 500,000 years have been found in China.

The behaviour of this ape species is believed to have been such that sasquatch would live in small groups of one male and up to four females and their young. They would, however, often roam alone, returning to the group only for mating purposes. For the most part, sasquatch would be nocturnal; sleeping on piles of vegetation gathered together for a bed during the day. Researchers generally argue that sasquatch would not be aggressive toward humans, but instead would take flight from an encounter.

If sasquatch do exist, researchers say they probably live throughout British Columbia, including **Vancouver Island** and the **Queen Charlotte Islands**. At most there might be a population of about two thousand living in the region from northern California to the Yukon.

In northern California, sasquatch are called Big Foot (or bigfoot). Similar creatures have been described as living in the Himalayas and other parts of Asia, where they are known as Yeti or the Abominable Snowman.

Seamounts

Seamounts are underwater volcanic peaks rising more than one thousand metres above the neighbouring ocean floor. From the Gulf of Alaska to the Oregon Coast a cluster of large seamounts numbering more than one hundred are found. Three massive seamounts lie between 108 to 500 kilometres off the British Columbia coast. Rising from the ocean floor, the highest of these is Union Seamount which is 3,300 metres high and comes within 293 metres of the ocean surface. Union Seamount is 108 kilometres west of Vancouver Island's Estevan Point. It is an almost conical volcanic mountain.

Slightly lower than Union are the pinnacles of Cobb and Bowie seamounts. These two seamounts are unique because they are accessible to scuba divers. Cobb is 500 kilometres southwest of the entrance to **Juan de Fuca Strait**. It is a massive seamount with a base width of 32 kilometres and a rise of 2,750 metres to a 47.6-metre central spire that comes within 34 metres of the sea surface. This spire forms an oval 10.5-hectare platform that is believed to have sunk below rising seas at the end of the last ice age about ten thousand years ago. Evidence of surf erosion at varying depths down to 195 metres prove the seamount once stood well above sea level. Much of the research conducted on this seamount was carried out by researchers aboard the Canadian Hydrographic Service submersible *Pisces I* in May 1976.

Bowie Seamount is about 220 kilometres west of the **Queen Charlotte Islands** and rises from a depth of over 3,000 metres to within 37 metres of the surface. *Pisces IV* discovered evidence that this seamount once stood at least 238 metres above sea level.

(*See also* **Volcanoes**.)

Sechelt Nation

In 1988, the Sechelt Nation was the first First Nations band in Canada to achieve the right of self-government from the Canadian government. It organized as a municipality, with full taxation and administration rights accorded under municipal law.

Sechelt village on the **Sunshine Coast** is a thriving community situated on a sandbar. It is the traditional home of the Sechelt people. Sechelt is also home to the internationally recognized Festival of the Written Arts, held in mid-August, which draws writers from around the world.

Sharks. *See* **Hornby Island.**

Shellfish. *See* **Invertebrates.**

Shellfish Poisoning. *See* **Paralytic Shellfish Poisoning.**

Shipwrecks

Hundreds of ships, many of which are unrecorded, have sunk off the British Columbian coastline or been wrecked upon its rocky coastal shores. With a **coastline** largely devoid of beaches, featuring long unbroken stretches of rocky headlands, and often battered by storms that can last for days on end, the province's coast is known as one of the most dangerous for shipping in the world. In all, about eleven hundred ships have been recorded as lost in the province's coastal waters.

The west coast of **Vancouver Island** experiences some of the province's worst storms, so it is not surprising that many of the first ships lost in B.C. waters were wrecked here. At Long Beach, in **Pacific Rim National Park**, the remains of an unidentified Spanish galleon dating back to the late 1700s can still be examined.

One of the earliest wrecks found in coastal records is that of the 220-ton schooner *Lark,* lost with her crew of thirty-eight in July 1786, on Copper Island in the **Queen Charlotte Islands**.

A few ships were lost as the result of being attacked and burned by the province's coastal **First Nations people**. In July 1794, the schooner *Resolution* met this fate in the Queen Charlotte's Cumshewa Inlet. On March 22, 1803, the American trader *Boston* was reportedly burned off Vancouver Island and her crew killed. In 1811, the American ship *Tonquin* exploded mysteriously during a battle between natives and the ship crew near Clayoquot Sound. According to later evidence given by a native witness, one of the crewmen deliberately detonated the ship's powder magazine in order to kill as many of the natives as possible. The majority of shipwrecks, however, in British Columbia during the late 1700s and early 1800s resulted from storms, poor navigation, and shipboard fires; historically and even today the primary reasons for shipwrecks.

The worst sinking in terms of loss of life in B.C. waters occurred on January 22, 1906, when the steamship *Valencia* foundered on the west coast of Vancouver Island and 117 of the estimated 154 crew and passengers aboard perished.

As most ships travelling the province's coastline opt to sail down the Inside Passage between Vancouver Island and the mainland because of its more storm-sheltered waters, it is probably not surprising that the narrow waterways of the **Strait of Georgia** have taken the heaviest toll in shipwrecks.

About 333 ships have sunk in the strait. The single most dangerous spot on the coastline was **Ripple Rock** in the Strait of Georgia, which, until it was blown up in 1958, claimed approximately 120 vessels and 114 lives.

The north coast of the province, including the mist-shrouded Queen Charlotte Islands, are known to have claimed at least 294 ships.

As many of the ships lost in B.C. waters either foundered against the rocky shorelines or eventually washed up on shore as wrecks, there are literally hundreds of sunken ships that are today popular **diving** sites.

Each year, too, a few more ships are added to the inventory of underwater wrecks. Despite the existence of an extensive network of navigational aids such as **lighthouses**, the **Canadian Coast Guard** responds to about two thousand distress calls every year and some of these ships are inevitably lost, sometimes with their entire crews. In recent years, ships lost at sea have often been small fishing vessels caught in unexpected storms.

Shuswap Lake

The odd four-armed shape of this lake (usually referred to as a ragged-H or ragged-X) in B.C.'s interior gives Shuswap Lake a shoreline of about one thousand kilometres, much of which is unpopulated. Surrounded by Monashee Mountains and Shuswap Highland peaks ranging up to twenty-two hundred metres, the lake has many beaches and small coves, which make it one of the province's most popular boating lakes. A fleet of about 350 houseboats operates out of Sicamous, giving rise to this community's claim to be the houseboat capital of Canada.

Skagit Valley

In the 1970s the Skagit Valley on the Canadian side of the border was to have been flooded by a reservoir resulting from a dam built to back up the Skagit River for hydroelectric purposes. The valley, situated south of Manning Park off Highway 3, was a remote, beautiful wilderness area of dense forests and rushing streams. When the plan was announced, it appeared the provincial government was going to allow the flooding of Canadian territory in return for financial compensation, but soon the government found itself tangling with a small ad-hoc environmental movement that demanded the valley be saved and preserved as a **provincial park**. The debate dragged on for years and public support for saving the Skagit grew with each passing month. Finally, the American plan to flood the Skagit was refused by the provincial government and the valley is now protected within the 32,570-hectare Skagit Valley Provincial Recreation Area.

Skeena River

The 580-kilometre-long Skeena River is the second-largest river (after **Fraser River**) lying entirely within British Columbia. Its headwaters are in the northern interior and it flows southwest to meet the Pacific Ocean at **Prince Rupert**, draining fifty-four thousand square kilometres along the way. Skeena was, and remains today, an important river to the **First Nations peoples** who have lived near its shores for at least eight thousand years. Its waters provided the region's primary transportation route and the rich variety of fish found in it served as a dietary mainstay.

The 580-kilometre-long Skeena River winds a course through the lowlands below the peaks of a mountain formation known as the Seven Sisters. (BCARS photo I-11659)

The lower reaches of the Skeena between Hazelton and Prince Rupert were used by European settlers as a steamship route almost immediately upon their arrival in the area in 1866. By 1914, however, the second transcontinental railroad was completed along its shores and the steamship era ended. Highway 16, which also hugs Skeena's shoreline for this stretch, was constructed in 1944. With the highway's completion the area opened up for more development, although the isolation and harsh winters have kept the region's **population** relatively small.

Skiing

Approximately 75 percent of British Columbia stands more than three thousand metres above sea level and the majority of the rest of the province consists of high-elevation plateaus. The rugged, mountainous terrain provides ideal conditions for downhill skiing and heli-skiing. The province's plateaus, valleys, and valley slopes are excellent for cross-country skiing. Much of the province receives heavy snowfalls, particularly on the mountains, so the ski season typically runs from early November to early March. At the same time, reasonably mild climates in the southern portions of the province result in few winter days when temperatures are so severe that outdoor activities are limited.

There are thirty-five full-facility downhill ski areas in B.C., plus a number of smaller hill operations that have limited facilities. About thirty cross-country skiing destination resorts and trail systems also exist. Throughout the province there are additional cross-country trail networks that have been developed by local clubs, many of which are open to the public at no, or minimal, charge. Heli-ski and powder cat-skiing operators are scattered throughout the province, with a concentration of these operations focused on the **Columbia Mountain** and **Rocky Mountain** ranges, and at **Whistler**/Blackcomb in the **Coast Mountain** Range.

For downhill skiing the most famous locations are Whistler/Blackcomb and Grouse Mountain in southwestern B.C., Red Mountain and Whitewater in the Kootenays, Big White and Silver Star in the **Okanagan Valley**, and Mount Washington on **Vancouver Island**. Whistler/Blackcomb is the province's most well-known and well-developed ski resort, considered by many to offer some of the finest skiing and resort facilities in North America.

The most famous cross-country skiing is found at Mount Washington, at Whistler, at Manning Park in southwestern B.C., at Lac le Jeune in the **Thompson River** area near **Kamloops**, and at 108 Mile and The Hills in the Cariboo.

Snakes. *See* **Rattlesnakes; Reptiles.**

Sointula

In December 1901, Finnish political refugee philosopher and playwright Mattii Kurikka established on the south shore of Malcolm Island, situated off **Vancouver Island**'s east coast adjacent to Port McNeill, a utopian community he named Sointula. In Finnish, Sointula means "place of harmony." Kurikka envisioned the community as being a socialistic, independent economic unit based on logging, fishing, and **agriculture**. By 1902, there were 127 Finnish followers of Kurikka living at Sointula and a small sawmill was in operation. Most of the residents were refugees of another kind—Finnish immigrant workers fleeing the dangerous conditions of the coal mines operated by James Dunsmuir in the Nanaimo region.

The socialist utopia was short-lived. Torn by internal dissension, debt, and a fire, it was disbanded in 1905. Kurikka died in 1915 at the age of fifty-three. About half the population left the island, but the small community of Sointula remains distinctly Finnish in character with many of the original settler's descendants still living there.

South Moresby Island National Park. *See* **Gwaii Haanas National Park.**

Spatsizi Plateau Wilderness Provincial Park

A virtually unadulterated wilderness, Spatsizi Plateau Wilderness Provincial Park is one of Canada's largest parklands. It is extremely isolated, lying three hundred kilometres north of Terrace and fifty kilometres east of Highway 37, which runs from just west of Hazelton to Watson Lake in Yukon Territory. The nearest communities are Iskut and Dease Lake, both with populations barely over 250. Access into the park is usually by floatplane or packhorse out of Iskut.

There are more than 140 species of **birds** in Spatsizi, including horned larks, gyrfalcons, and all three B.C. ptarmigan species. Woodland caribou, grizzly **bears**, stone sheep (dark version of Dall's sheep), and white mountain goats are common. The area contains a red sandstone formation on one mountain that sloughs off deposits of red iron-oxide, which the white mountain goats often roll in, dying their coats red. This gave rise to the region's name Spatsizi—which is a Dene word for "red goat."

Gladys Lake Ecological Reserve is found in the Spatsizi. One of the province's largest such reserves, it is set aside for the protection and study of stone sheep and mountain goats in a natural setting.

Spiders. *See* **Invertebrates.**

Stanley Park

On a peninsula between English Bay and Burrard Inlet in the heart of **Vancouver**, Stanley Park covers 405 hectares and is one of North America's largest and most impressive city parks. The creation of this park in 1888 showed remarkable foresight on the part of Vancouver's municipal politicians of the day who petitioned the federal government two years earlier to lease the land to the municipality for park use. The federal government, which was holding the land as a military reserve, granted Vancouver a lease for a dollar a year.

Today the park is home to the Stanley Park Public Zoo, the Children's Zoo, Vancouver Aquarium, the ten-kilometre Stanley Park Seawall (a broad non-vehicular route encircling the entire park's waterfront), numerous beaches, and dense forests.

Stein River Valley and Watershed

The headwaters of the Stein River contain the last unlogged watershed in British Columbia that is within close proximity of a heavily populated area (it is 160 kilometres from Vancouver). The river hugs the eastern border of the **Coast Mountains**. Within its watershed are three small glacier systems, four major lakes, about 520 square kilometres of alpine meadow, and **forests** ranging from ponderosa pine to Douglas fir, cedar, and spruce. The river descends from elevations of 2,935 metres in the high mountains to drain into the **Fraser River** near Lytton. Along the way the river drops down spectacular waterfalls, passes through pristine lakes, and funnels into a steep gorge with walls rising 1,220 metres.

Since the mid-1980s, the Stein River has been the subject of intense controversy surrounding land-use issues. Forestry and **mining** companies want to log and mine the rich resources; environmental groups and the **First Nations peoples** of the Lytton area want the Stein preserved as the Stein Tribal Heritage Park. The provincial government has waffled back and forth, declining to make a definitive decision and negotiations drag on.

To ensure people had the opportunity to visit the region before it could be disturbed by logging or mining, natives and environmentalists worked together to cut the seventy-five-kilometre-long Stein Heritage Trail, which follows the river from its Fraser River mouth to the headwaters high in the Coast Mountains.

Stikine River

With its headwaters in **Spatsizi Plateau Wilderness Provincial Park**, the Stikine River flows 539 kilometres in a wide arc north and then west through the Stikine Plateau and then south through the **Coast Mountains** to join the Pacific Ocean near Wrangell, Alaska, on the Alaskan Panhandle, where the river creates a wide delta that is a major salmon-spawning ground.

Stikine is a Tlingit word for "great river." This name derived in part from the Tlingit's respect for the river's power majestically manifested by the Grand Canyon, which is situated northeast of Telegraph Creek. The ninety-six-kilometre Grand Canyon is Canada's largest canyon. The Stikine compresses into narrows between its towering three-hundred-metre volcanic walls to become an unnavigable torrent. Much of the rest of the Stikine is riven with stretches of whitewater, leading to its designation as one of the best whitewater **rafting** rivers in the world.

Strait of Georgia

The Strait of Georgia is a body of water lying between **Vancouver Island** and the mainland, running south from Quadra Island adjacent to the island's community of Campbell River. The strait is a basin between the **Coast Mountains** and Vancouver Island mountains that was cut by glacial movement. Artefacts of Coastal Salishan tribes prove their presence on these waters ten thousand years ago. Strait of Georgia is heavily used by commercial, fishing, and pleasure boat traffic because the presence of Vancouver Island to the west provides a sheltered north-south route along an extensive stretch of the province's **coastline**. The strait is also a major centre for the Pacific **salmon** fishery. Six deepsea ports draw heavy commercial shipping usage into the strait.

Strathcona Provincial Park

Created in 1911, Strathcona Provincial Park in central **Vancouver Island**, west of Campbell River, was the province's first **provincial park**. It is also Vancouver Island's largest provincial park. Its easternmost point is only thirteen kilometres from the sea at Comox Harbour, while its southwest corner reaches tidewater at the head of Herbert Inlet, on Vancouver Island's opposite shore. The park encompasses 2,310 square kilometres, with elevations ranging from sea level to twenty-two hundred metres at the summit of **Mount Golden Hinde**. The landscape is highly diverse, including dense rainforests, glacial ice sheets, and alpine meadows. Della Falls, at 440 metres the second-highest waterfall in Canada, also lies within the park boundaries.

Strathcona is home to one of the island's few remaining colonies of Roosevelt elk, and has significant **wolf** and **cougar** populations. Although Strathcona is a provincial park, special forestry and **mining** licences have been proposed to allow limited natural resource extraction within its boundaries. These have been highly controversial proposals, strongly opposed by environmental groups. To ensure the protection of specific environmental areas from resource-development encroachment, some 122,500 hectares of the park have been designated as Nature Conservancy Areas in which any development is forbidden.

Sunshine Coast

The 130-kilometre-long Sunshine Coast extends from Langdale to Lund. Although a mainland coastal region, it is accessible only by ferry or boat, which gives the area a distinctly island feel.

The Sunshine Coast earns its name by averaging twenty-four hundred hours of sunshine annually and being touched by only ninety-four centimetres of precipitation. Its coastline is characterized by deep inlets and fjords broken by reaches of long sandy beach. The sheltered fjords and inlets are ideal for **aquaculture**. A popular tourist region, the summer population swells by twenty-five percent to about thirty-two thousand people.

Supreme Court. *See* Judiciary.

Swiftsure Yacht Race. *See* Annual Events and Celebrations.

Symbols

British Columbia has a number of official symbols and emblems that serve to represent the province both at home and abroad and reflect its natural and historical heritage.

The province's shield, designed by Reverend Arthur Beanlands, was approved by King Edward VII in 1906. It shows the Union Jack on the upper third, symbolizing the province's origin as a British colony. A gold half-sun stands at the bottom as if setting, symbolizing B.C.'s position as the most westerly province of Canada. The shield is supported on either flank by a ram and a stag.

B.C.'s motto is engraved on the shield, *Splendor sine occasu*, meaning Splendour Without Diminishment.

The provincial flag, duplicating the shield in the shape of a rectangle, was adopted by the provincial government in 1960.

The Pacific dogwood tree became the province's official emblem in 1956. The official flower is the Pacific dogwood's large, white blossoms, which appear in the spring. This native tree is now protected by law.

After a government-sponsored popularity poll was conducted in 1988, the Steller's jay was declared the province's official bird. The red cedar, traditionally used by **First Nations peoples** for **totem poles** and dugout canoes, is the official tree.

A nephrite jade of dark green, known as B.C. jade, is the official stone and is used extensively throughout the province for jewellery. Commemorating yet again the province's links with Britain, B.C. has an official tartan, consisting of 128 types of threads, which was recorded in 1969 in the books of the Court of the Lord Lyon, King of Arms in Scotland.

Symphony. *See* Cultural History.

Takakkaw Falls

Situated just west of the Continental Divide in **Yoho National Park** east of Field, Takakkaw Falls is the highest **waterfall** in Canada and the world's sixteenth-highest. Takakkaw drops a total height of 503 metres, with its greatest uninterrupted leap spilling down 366 metres from a U-shaped upper valley into the Yoho River below. Measured by vertical drop, Takakkaw is the highest waterfall in North America; it is nearly ten times the height of Niagara Falls. The falls are fed by snow and ice melt from Daly Glacier in the **Rocky Mountains**. The name Takakkaw comes from the Cree language and means "it is magnificent."

Tatshenshini-Alsek Wilderness Provincial Park

The extreme northwestern corner of British Columbia falls completely within the boundaries of the Tatshenshini-Alsek Wilderness Provincial Park founded in 1994. Covering 958,000 hectares, Tatshenshini occupies virtually all of the small knob of the province that separates the Alaska Panhandle from Yukon Territory. It encompasses some of the wildest and most pristine wilderness remaining in B.C.

Included in the park are many of the peaks of the **St. Elias Mountains** and about 350 glaciers forming part of the largest non-polar icecap on Earth.

The park derives its name from the major river (Tatshenshini) which flows through it to drain into the Alsek River within the park boundaries. The Alsek flows into Alaska and on to the Pacific Ocean. Tatshenshini is a mighty river, carrying more water than the Colorado River with which it has often been compared by environmentalists due to the two rivers being long endangered. Before the designation of all of the Tatshenshini-Alsek watershed as a Class 'A' **provincial park**—meaning there can be no development of any kind within the park boundary—Tatshenshini was considered, after the Colorado, as the second most endangered river on the continent.

When the Tatshenshini runs into the Alsek, their combined waters pass through an area of intense geological activity. Here, glaciers calve house-sized blocks of ice that slide into the river.

The parklands support a large grizzly bear population and Canada's only known population of glacier **bears**—a colour variant of black bear with an unusual genetic blue-black pigmentation. Half of British Columbia's population of Dall sheep also live within the park boundaries. (*See also* **Mammals**.)

Tatshenshini River is the centrepiece of a spectacular 260-kilometre river journey that attracts some eleven hundred river rafters annually. The river is rated one of the seven best white-water **rafting** and kayaking trips in the world (it was first kayaked from head to mouth in 1976) with the Alsek River section of the run passing through a series of glacier ice-choked rapids.

Linked up with existing Canadian and U.S. national parks in the adjoining parts of the Yukon and Alaska, the park is part of one of the largest international protected areas in the world—8.5 million hectares. In December 1994 this combined region was declared a United Nations Educational, Scientific and Cultural Organization (UNESCO) World Heritage Site, becoming the world's largest international world heritage site.

Technical Schools. *See* **Post-Secondary Education.**

Thompson River

The headwaters of the **Fraser** and Thompson rivers nearly meet deep in the **Rocky Mountains** near the Yellowhead Pass, leading from British Columbia to Alberta at Jasper. But the steep mountains between them channel both rivers along opposite flanks of the Rockies. The Thompson, therefore, flows for 489 kilometres south and then west into the province's interior before finally converging with the Fraser River at Lytton. Earlier, at **Kamloops**, the main track of the Thompson, known from its headwaters to Kamloops as the North Thompson River, is joined by a lesser stream that flows from **Shuswap Lake** to Kamloops called the South Thompson River. From Kamloops to Lytton the two form the Thompson River.

Along all its length, the Thompson river system created by the two divergent flows is noted for its green-blue water that is instantly lost when it meets the dark, muddy-brown water of the mightier Fraser River. For most of its journey to Lytton the Thompson passes through the rich timber country of the eastern Cariboo, but from Kamloops its banks are bordered by large, dry barren terraces and benchlands. Both the CPR and CNR transcontinental **railway** lines follow the Thompson River from Kamloops to Lytton—the CPR bordering the South Thompson all the way from its headwaters at Shuswap Lake.

The river system was named after explorer and mapmaker David Thompson by fellow-explorer Simon Fraser, who mistakenly believed Thompson travelled the rivers during his explorations of British Columbia between 1808 and 1811.

Tidal Waves. *See* **Tsunamis.**

Time Zones. *See* **Mountain Standard Time.**

Toads. *See* **Amphibians.**

Totem Poles

Totem poles served as historical and genealogical records, and memorials for the northwest-coast **First Nations peoples**. There were six principal types of poles—memorial or heraldic poles, grave figures, house posts, house-front or portal poles, welcoming poles, and mortuary poles. The poles were carved with crests and figures that generally reflected the lineage of a clan or family and both the art on the pole and the pole itself were considered important lineage property.

The images of animals carved on the poles included the beaver, bear, wolf, shark, whale, raven, eagle, frog, and mosquito. Also represented in the carvings were supernatural figures—monsters with animal features, human-like spirits, and legendary ancestors. After the coming of Europeans, some poles included images of white men.

Totem poles were skilfully carved from red cedar and were painted black, red, blue, and sometimes white and yellow. The paint was derived from natural mineral and vegetable pigments. **Salmon** eggs were chewed with cedar bark to form the binder for the ground pigment.

Haida clan poles at Skidegate in the Queen Charlotte Islands.
(BCARS photo I-15825)

The poles varied in size. House-front or portal poles were usually the largest, ranging up to more than one metre in width at the base and reaching heights of over fifteen metres. These poles were generally faced toward the shores of rivers or the ocean fronting the village and houses.

With the arrival of Europeans in British Columbia, the variety of totem art grew rapidly, due to native carvers acquiring broader access to ranges of paint colours and steel tools that allowed more intricate and refined carving techniques. By the 1830s, carving of large totems was commonplace, the totem's size and complexity of art serving to demonstrate the social standing of the family or clan.

This renaissance of totem carving, however, was followed by a period of decline in the art form that lasted from 1884 to the 1950s as a result of the federal government making **potlatches** illegal. As most totems were erected during potlatches, and the carving of totems was intertwined with the potlatch ceremony and celebration, the art form itself was suppressed by government authorities.

The anti-potlatch law was dropped in 1951. This coincided with efforts by several museums, art galleries, and tribal councils to foster preservation of First Nations arts, leading to a revival in totem pole art that continues today. By the late 1960s, totems were again being erected at potlatches held by the First Nations peoples of the B.C. Pacific coast.

Tourism

In an average year about twenty-four million overnight tourists travelling in the province pump approximately $5.5 billion into British Columbia's **economy**. Tourism accounts for 105,000 direct and 185,000 related jobs, making it one of the province's largest employment sectors.

About $2.8 billion, or 51 percent of total tourism revenues, is generated by British Columbians holidaying away from home, but within the province. British Columbians also account for the majority—approximately 16.2 million—of the total tourists in an average year.

Tourists coming from the rest of Canada and the United States arrive in roughly equal numbers. In 1992, for example, 3.4 million U.S. tourists came to B.C., along with 3.3 million tourists from the other Canadian provinces and the territories. Of the American tourists, one-sixth were from California.

Every year, about 880,000 tourists come to Canada from outside North America, constituting only about 3.7 percent of total tourist traffic. These tourists, however, generate about 8.7 percent of tourism revenues.

The three major non-North American nations from which tourists come to visit B.C. are Japan, the United Kingdom, and Germany, and the number of visitors from these three nations grows significantly each year. In 1993, for example, 219,700 Japanese tourists visited B.C., an increase of 7.6 percent over the previous year. German tourism in the same period was up by 21.1 percent from 1992, with about 103,500 visitors. Visitors from the United Kingdom numbered 127,100, an increase of 8.2 percent.

During their travels in British Columbia the majority of tourists apparently visit at least one **provincial park**, which average more than twenty million visits a year.

Based on accommodation revenues, the two areas experiencing the greatest overall growth in tourist trade are the Nechako and Cariboo regions, previously areas that were little known for their tourist draw. This leads some experts to suggest that tourists are increasingly seeking out attractions that are outside traditional tourism haunts and also are looking for more wilderness and outdoor-recreation-related tourist pursuits.

At the same time, tourism growth within **Vancouver** and other Lower Mainland destinations is concentrated on visitors who opt to stay in the larger, more expensive hotels that have 250 or more rooms.

Tourist Infocentres

The provincial government, working with local municipalities throughout the province, has created a large, integrated Travel Infocentre Network so that there is extensive information and visitor service facilities available to help tourists visiting almost any area of British Columbia. The province directly operates three information centres—one on Highway 99 at the Canada-U.S. Border, south of Vancouver; one at **Mount Robson**, on Highway 16 in Mount Robson Provincial Park; and one at Field, on Highway 1 in **Yoho National Park**. This last facility is operated in partnership with Parks Canada and Alberta Tourism.

In addition, about 145 communities in B.C. operate Travel Infocentres. Most of these facilities are conspicuously placed to be visible from adjacent highways and most are staffed or managed by government-certified travel counsellors.

Trail

More than a third of the population of Trail works at the massive Consolidated Mining and Smelting of Canada Ltd. (Cominco) smelting complex whose 120-metre-tall smokestacks dominate this small city. The presence of the smelter makes it one of the province's key industrial cities despite its isolated location in the southern reaches of the Kootenays.

The smelter is the world's largest zinc and lead smelting complex, processing some 300,000 tonnes of zinc and 135,000 tonnes of lead annually from ore shipped to it from around the world.

Opened in 1895, the smelter's workforce was drawn heavily from Italian immigrants who had mining and smelting experience. Today the city retains a 30 percent Italian ratio. In 1961, Trail became internationally famous when its amateur hockey team, appropriately named the Trail Smoke Eaters in reference to the famed smoke belched forth by the smelter in those pre-anti-pollution treatment days, captured the world hockey championship.

(*See also* **Mining Industry; Rossland.**)

Trans-Canada Highway (Highway 1)

By 1910, Canadians across the nation were calling for the construction of a sea-to-sea **highway** that would span the nation. It would take until 1962 for the highway to become a reality; much of the delay involved the complex engineering task of building a route through the mountains of British Columbia. On July 30, 1962, the highway was officially opened at the final point completed—the **Rogers Pass** in the eastern part of the province. Of the highway's 7,821 kilometres, more than 3,000 remained unpaved at this time.

Major construction of the highway started in the summer of 1950 with an infusion of $150 million in federal funds. This was half the estimated cost of construction; the provinces were expected to pick up the other half of the cost for construction within their territory. Ultimately, the federal contribution would rise to $825 million by the project's conclusion. The highway would finally be completed six years later than scheduled. Although opened in 1962, final paving and construction of the highway was not completed until 1970 and the total cost was more than $1 billion.

Transit. *See* BC Transit Authority.

Triathlons. *See* Annual Events and Celebrations.

Tsunamis

At 7:36 p.m. on Good Friday, March 27, 1964, an intense earthquake originated near the west side of Unakwik Inlet about 102 kilometres east of Anchorage, Alaska. It was one of the strongest **earthquakes** ever recorded on the North American continent, registering 8.5 on the Richter scale. The earthquake caused a major uplift over 250,000 square kilometres of sea floor adjacent to the Alaska coast. This sudden rising of ground thrust water upward to create a series of tsunamis that raced across the Pacific Ocean surface. Less than four hours later the first waves reached the west coast of **Vancouver Island**.

The villages of Hot Springs Cove and Zeballos were the first to be hit and both suffered major wave and flood damage. Shortly after, a wave swept up Alberni Inlet and slammed into the shoreline of Port Alberni. This wave caused only minor damage but served as a warning to the residents to evacuate coastal areas of the community. No sooner was the evacuation hastily completed than a massive seven-metre wave rolled in and devastated the community's shoreline. Because of the evacuation there were no deaths, but damage to ships, and residential and industrial property totalled $10 million. Houses were thrown up to three hundred metres from their foundations, cars upended and crushed, boats capsized. Logs moving at speeds in excess of thirty-two kilometres per hour were driven into buildings. Fifty-eight buildings were destroyed, 320 others suffered extensive damage.

The seven-metre wave was the largest tsunami ever officially recorded in British Columbia. Tsunami waves produced by the same earthquake, however, that struck Shields Bay on the west coast of the **Queen Charlotte Islands** were estimated to be over nine metres higher than the low-tide level. Damage here was light because the bay was home at the time to only a small logging camp.

Tsunamis are caused by underwater earthquakes, underwater **landslides** and shoreline slumps into the ocean, and submarine volcanic eruptions. They are rare. Between 1900 and 1970, for example, only 176 tsunamis were recorded over the entire Pacific Ocean. Of these, thirty-five caused damage and only nine caused widespread destruction.

The only known death in B.C. resulting from a tsunami wave occurred on June 23, 1946, near Mapleguard Point opposite the southern end of Denman Island in the **Strait of Georgia**. A wave of about 1.2 to 1.5 metres generated by a 7.3 Richter magnitude subduction earthquake, with an epicentre near Mount Washington on Vancouver Island, struck the shore here and killed a man standing on the shoreline. The earthquake also broke underwater telegraph cables.

(*See also* **Earthquakes**.)

Tweedsmuir Provincial Park

Covering 981,000 hectares of wilderness, Tweedsmuir Provincial Park is B.C.'s largest. The park is bordered by the **Coast Mountains** to the west and the **Interior Plateau** to the east. Whitesail Lake, part of the reservoir created from the damming of the **Nechako River**, wraps around the park's northern boundary. The park itself narrows as it runs from north to south. About a third of the way down its length, Highway 20 cuts across the park from Anahim Lake to Bella Coola on the western coast.

Tweedsmuir was established in 1936 and is named for Lord Tweedsmuir, then Governor General of Canada. The park encompasses part of the **Alexander Mackenzie Heritage Trail**.

Most of Tweedsmuir is extremely isolated, rugged, and lacking in any facilities. Its terrain incorporates high mountains, icefields, a variety of lake chains, alpine meadows, and highland plateaus. It is primarily a destination for adventure **hiking**, fishing, and **paddling**. Access to many of the park's high-mountain lakes is by floatplane. Commercial horse-packing trips are also possible. Parks brochures carry the following advice: "Outdoor recreation opportunities are almost unlimited, but those who are not prepared to be completely self-sufficient or who do not wish to employ a professional guide should not contemplate a visit." For the less adventurous hiker, there are several trail systems accessible from Highway 20, including a hike into 253-metre Hunlen Falls.

Underwater Volcanoes. *See* **Seamounts.**

Universities. *See* **Post-Secondary Education.**

Utopian Communities. *See* **Aquarian Foundation; Cape Scott; Sointula**

Valencia Sinking

On Monday, January 22, 1906, just fifteen minutes before midnight, the passenger liner SS *Valencia* crashed onto rocks 4.8 kilometres east of Pachena Point on **Vancouver Island**'s rugged western shore. The fast, powerful, seventy-seven-metre iron steamer was bound for **Victoria** and Seattle from San Francisco with 154 passengers (many of whom were women and children) and crew.

Caught in a howling gale from the southwest, the ship was attempting to turn Cape Flattery on the Olympic Peninsula and enter **Juan de Fuca Strait**. Somehow the ship overshot the strait's mouth by more than sixty kilometres and spent more than six hours running off course before an increasingly alarmed Captain O.M. Johnson finally ordered the ship to go to "Dead Slow." Suddenly soundings being taken went from sixty fathoms to thirty fathoms.

Minutes later *Valencia* struck a rock a glancing blow, then hit another and the engine stalled. Although the crew quickly got the engine going again and backed away from the rocks, they soon discovered the ship was taking on water faster than the bilge pumps could handle. Faced with either sinking or beaching the ship immediately, Captain Johnson ordered *Valencia* run aground. She went in stern first and lodged on a reef about twenty-seven metres from a landhead of thirty-metre high sheer rock walls. Huge breakers smashed the partially beached vessel up and down on the rocks, eventually stoving in the hull and pinning the ship in place. Larger waves rushed across the deck threatening to sweep passengers overboard.

Four lifeboats, mostly loaded with women and children, were lowered and set loose into the rough seas but all were overturned and everyone aboard drowned. Attempts to fire lifelines ashore with harpoons also failed. By dawn the storm was passing and a lifeboat with six male volunteers (the remaining women all now refusing to go into the lifeboats) was launched. Another boat with nine men was also released. The first safely reached a beach and the men aboard made their way on foot to Cape Beale **lighthouse**, where the lightkeeper wired a distress message to Victoria. The other boat was swamped but the men aboard managed to swim safely to shore.

Several ships, responding to the distress call, came into the area but could not draw alongside the foundering *Valencia* because of the continuing high breakers. By early morning, *Valencia* started to break into sections and most of the deck flooded. Many of the survivors climbed into the rigging of its two masts. Crew aboard the vessels standing offshore watched helplessly as one by one women and children weakened, lost their grip on the rigging lines, and fell into the sea.

As it became obvious the other ships could not help the survivors escape, renewed attempts were made to launch lifeboats. None of the women would join the men who decided on this desperate attempt, nor would they allow the children to be taken. Nine men went in the first liferaft, nineteen in the second. The raft with nineteen men aboard was rescued and all saved, the one with nine aboard drifted for two days before washing ashore on Turret Island in Barkley Sound where two survivors were eventually rescued.

Shortly after these two rafts were launched *Valencia* broke up and the foremast toppled into the sea along with fifteen men, women, and children who all died, including Captain Johnson. As the storm abated the ships scoured the surrounding water for survivors, and life-saving parties began arriving by overland routes. When the final toll was compiled, 117 lives were lost and only thirty-seven survivors (all men) were rescued.

In a grim footnote, No. Five lifeboat was found drifting in Barkley Sound in 1933, apparently lost at sea for twenty-seven years. Possibly this lifeboat was the source of repeated mariner tales of sightings off the west coast of a lifeboat manned by skeletons. It may also have confirmed native fisherman Clanewah Tom's claim to have explored a sea cave five months earlier containing a lifcraft with skeletons aboard.

The wreck of *Valencia* on a **coastline** in which many other ships had foundered on the rocks led to construction of a good trail to aid shipwreck victims in reaching safety and to speed the ability of rescue teams to get to the coast. The Lifesaving Trail, also known as the Shipwrecked Mariner's Trail, was officially designated a public highway on December 20, 1911. This trail would later become the **West Coast Trail**.

(*See also* **Shipwrecks**.)

Vancouver

The largest city in British Columbia and Canada's third-largest metropolis, Vancouver has water bodies on three of its sides. Burrard Inlet separates the city from North and **West Vancouver** on its northern boundary. The **Strait of Georgia** forms Vancouver's western border, and the north arm of the **Fraser River** separates the city from its southern satellite communities. Vancouver City's **population** is 471,872 (1992 provincial government estimate) but this figure misrepresents the city's true size and dominant position in relation to the rest of the province. The city is an economic and service centre that is the fulcrum around which more than half of the province's population is based. Of B.C.'s 3.35 million residents (1992), 1.885 million live in what the provincial government terms the Lower Mainland/Southwest region, which encompasses primarily the Greater Vancouver Regional District and Lower Mainland communities to Hope at the foot of the **Cascade Mountain** range. This area comprises only 4.2 percent of the province's land area, yet 55.9 percent of its people live here.

Greater Vancouver is the hub for most financial, educational, tourist, transportation, cultural, and industrial activity in the province. The majority of British Columbia provides the resource exploitation source to fuel the socioeconomic engine of Vancouver. With each passing year, Vancouver's influence on the province is growing as population growth and migration continue to increase the concentration of British Columbians in this small area. Between 1982 and 1987 the region's population grew by 10.2 percent; from 1987 to 1992 it swelled by another 17.3 percent. By comparison, most other regions of the province, except **Vancouver Island** and the **Okanagan Valley**, had either declining or static populations.

The concentration of people into the Greater Vancouver region results from declining resource-based economies in other parts of the province and the growth of service-oriented economic activity which is concentrating in urban areas. Retirement populations are also fuelling this growth.

The Greater Vancouver Regional District (GVRD), sometimes referred to as Metropolitan Vancouver, encompasses Vancouver, **New Westminster**, North Vancouver, Richmond, Surrey, Port Coquitlam, White Rock, Langley, Port Moody, the districts of Burnaby, Coquitlam, Delta, North Vancouver (both a district and city), Langley (also district and city), West Vancouver, villages of Anmore, Belcarra, and Lions Bay, and the three electoral areas of University Endowment Lands, Ioco, and Bowen Island. As prices for land and housing rise incrementally in relation to proximity to Vancouver's core, population growth has sprawled outward in search of less expensive and less concentrated housing. Consequently, Vancouver and Toronto (Canada's largest metropolis) tie for first place in having the longest average commuting times per capita—one hour. Vancouver, however, has a less developed metropolitan transit system, with only the SkyTrain providing any rapid-transit options for commuters.

Vancouver's development into Canada's third-largest city has followed the kind of rapid growth usually associated with **mining** boomtowns that rise and fall just as quickly. Discovered by Spanish navigator Jose Maria Narvaez in 1792, several months before Captain George Vancouver (after whom the city would be named) arrived in Burrard Inlet, Europeans didn't settle here until 1862. That year, John Morton, William Hailstone, and Sam Brighouse, all of England, staked out a claim to all lands lying between modern-day Burrard Street and **Stanley Park**, English Bay and Coal Harbour—virtually the entire lands of today's Vancouver City. They started a brickmaking factory in anticipation of the community's rapid growth as a mining centre but the nearby coal deposits fizzled and so too did their operation.

White settlement in the area was sporadic until the 1880s, when the Canadian Pacific Railway decided to extend its westernmost terminus to Burrard Inlet to take advantage of it as a deepwater shipping harbour. On April 6, 1886, the provincial legislature gave the rapidly growing town its name and official municipal status. The Klondike Gold Rush of 1896 and pre-World War I economic expansion started the young city on what has been a largely uninterrupted upward economic and population spiral ever since.

In the 1960s, the city's inner core started undergoing a major rebuilding that gives it today's distinctive skyline of highrise office and hotel towers. This development also coincidentally parallelled the rapid growth of the city's ethnic and racial diversification. In 1951, fully three-quarters of Vancouver's population were of British ethnic origin. By 1979, however, 40 percent of elementary school children spoke English as a second **language**. Most of these children were of Chinese, Italian, or East Indian descent. Throughout Vancouver's history there have been many incidents of racial intolerance, especially towards Asian peoples. (*See* **Chinatowns** and **Japanese Canadian Relocation**.) The ethnic diversification of Vancouver continues at a rate higher than elsewhere in the province.

Two of the province's four universities are located in Vancouver—the University of British Columbia and Simon Fraser University. It also has several regional colleges, and the B.C. Institute of Technology. (*See* **Post-Secondary Education**.)

The city is the province's cultural and athletic sports centre. Vancouver is home to the province's largest and most successful theatre and musical groups, and film production companies. It is the venue for most major international entertainment performances coming to the province, and has the highest concentration of museums, art galleries, and other cultural attractions. Within the GVRD are hundreds of parks, the largest being Stanley Park, right in the city's heart. The National Hockey League's **Vancouver Canucks** hang their skates here and the Canadian Football League's **British Columbia Lions'** home turf is at **BC Place**.

(*See also* **Cultural History**.)

Vancouver Canucks

Although since 1970 a member of the National Hockey League (NHL), the Vancouver Canucks hockey team has played continuously in **Vancouver** since 1946 when they faced off as one of the Western Hockey League teams. The team owners, the Medicor Corporation of Minneapolis, paid $6 million in 1970 to gain membership in the NHL, hoping to boost lagging attendance figures. The Canucks faced off in their first NHL season game on October 9, 1970, in the three-year-old, 15,564-seat Pacific Coliseum. They went on to a sixth-place finish in their seven-team division.

In 1974, the team was purchased by a consortium of Vancouver businesspeople. That same year the Canucks posted a strong regular season performance, finishing atop the Smythe Division with 86 points in 80 games. In 1982 they made an unexpected advance through the play-offs to win a berth in the Stanley Cup final, but lost in four straight games to the New York Islanders. They were back in the Stanley Cup again in the 1993–94 season for a full seven-game contest against the New York Rangers, but lost the final game. After this defeat, Canuck fans responded by holding a riot in the city's downtown core that resulted in much property damage and two deaths.

Vancouver Island

The largest island on North America's west coast, Vancouver Island covers 31,284 square kilometres. It is approximately 460 kilometres long from north to south and ranges between 50 and 80 kilometres wide. The island is separated from the mainland by the **Strait of Georgia**, and Queen Charlotte and Johnstone straits to the north. **Juan de Fuca Strait** curves around its southwestern and southern sides to divide it from the Olympic Peninsula of Washington State.

Vancouver Island's west coast is extremely rugged, cut by many fjord-like inlets that are bordered by mountains rising to elevations averaging six hundred to one thousand metres but reaching up to as much as twenty-two hundred metres at **Mount Golden Hinde**. These mountains and their foothills were historically densely forested by ancient woodlands. The eastern shoreline of the island is gentler, with relatively wide shelves extending from beaches to the eastern slopes of the Vancouver Island Mountains. Not surprisingly, most of the island's population is concentrated on these narrow shelves following the eastern coastline and dominating the southern tip where **Victoria** is located.

The island's entire coastline is 3,440 kilometres long and the many sheltered inlets, coves, and bays along its coast were used by **First Nations people** as early as ten thousand years ago for fishing-based settlements. Buried under a great glacial ice flow until fifteen thousand years ago, the island was missed by most British Columbia mammal populations—by the time they appeared it was separated from the mainland by straits too wide to cross. There are only about thirty-three mammal species here, ranging from **bats** to black **bears**, **cougars** and **wolves**, marmots and squirrels. Among **mammals** that are missing are coyotes, foxes, moose, and chipmunks.

In the surrounding saltwater, about twenty-eight marine mammal species are found including **killer whales**, endangered sea otters, **Pacific grey whales**, seals, porpoises, and dolphins. The island is astride the Pacific Flyway. Each spring and fall hundreds of thousands of **birds** pass over the island in their north and southward migrations. About 150 species stop on the island each spring as part of their southward migration.

Historically, Vancouver Island's economic base has been forestry, fishing,

mining, and **agriculture**. Most of the island communities continue to depend on these for economic survival—especially forestry and fishing. Heavy logging since the 1950s has, however, created a serious shortage of timber supply and many sawmills and logging operations are either in decline or have shut down entirely. The **fishing industry**, too, has been experiencing difficulty as west-coast fish stocks decline. **Tourism** and the continued growth of Victoria, the province's capital, as a service centre have been unable to offset the economic losses in resource industries.

The conundrum of how to continue to support the survival of communities based on resource extraction at the same time that ecological protection of old-growth **forests** and preservation of wildlife and fish stocks is considered of prime importance to many (especially urban islanders) continues to spark many controversies over future economic development of the island.

Vanderhoof

Ninety-seven kilometres west of **Prince George** on Highway 16, Vanderhoof is ten kilometres east of the geographical centre of British Columbia. A cairn alongside the highway marks the spot, which is otherwise unremarkable.

Vanderhoof, a small cattle ranching and forestry town, claims Canada's largest camp-in air show (there's too little accommodation to put up the visitors in hotels or motels), attracting about twenty-five thousand people annually for the July event.

Vegetation

British Columbia's varied **physiography, climate**, and history of **glaciation** have resulted in development of a complex plant cover throughout the province. **Forests** dominate the vegetation but there are also extensive grasslands, wetlands, scrub, and tundra.

In coastal areas, the non-forest vegetation is typically understorey growth beneath the timber stands. Mosses dominate. Ferns, salal, blueberries, huckleberries, and devil's club grow mostly in openings where some light manages to reach the forest floor. The coastal region also includes the drier, rainshadow area of the **Strait of Georgia**. Here, on the southeastern side of **Vancouver Island**, in the **Gulf Islands**, and on part of the mainland coast the vegetation is unique. Here, **Garry oak ecosystems** are common. The meadows and grasslands of this system are dominated by annual grasses, sprinkled with many spring flowers such as camas, sea-blush, blue-eyed Mary, white fawn lily, and satinflower.

Some parts of the coast feature extensive wetlands of bogs or coastal muskeg. In the north coastal lowlands, for example, there is an expanse of muskeg in a landscape of low hills covered by scrub forests and bogs full of stunted tree growth.

Plant life is sparse on the coast's rocky headlands and beaches, but amid the rocks can be found hairy cinquefoil, roseroot, mist-maidens, coast straw-berry, and chocolate lily. The upper reaches of cobble beaches support clumps of lime grass, beach pea, giant vetch, and springbank clover. The coast's few sand beaches support searocket, beach-carrot, and beach pea at the driftwood level. Farther up the beach, dune grasses are common, along with paint-brush and lupines. These beaches are typically backed by dense salal.

Tidal marshes border estuary and protected bay and inlet shorelines. In the marshes, grasses and sedges dominate, along with Pacific silverweed, springbank clover, and checker-mallow. Salt-tolerant vegetation, such as glasswort and sea arrow-grass also grow here.

The grasslands of the interior are dominated by bunchgrass, primarily bluebunch wheatgrass and fescues. Sagebrush is the most common shrub, especially at lower elevations. Rabbit-bush and antelope-bush are also found. Growing in most grassland areas of the province are such species as bitterroot, mariposa lily, prickly-pear cactus, sage buttercup, yellow bell, brown-eyed Susan, and fleabanes. **Knapweed** infestations plague large parts of the prov-ince's grasslands and are crowding out many of the natural flora species.

In the forest areas of the dryland interior the primary understorey is com-posed of pinegrass, yielding to more scrub brush and mosses in the higher, denser forests.

There is an interior wet belt region in the Columbia and Kootenay areas. The vegetation here is similar to that found on the coast. Understorey species beneath the dense timber stands vary greatly and include yew, devil's club, various berries, ferns, queen's cup, false azalea, and false sarsaparilla.

In the northern boreal forest above 56° north latitude extensive growths of tamarack are found in the bogs and swamps, which also support unusual veg-etation species, including several species of orchid. Dry pine forests in this region are usually undergrown by lichens or spruce-feathermoss. There are also areas of grassland. In the northern subalpine environments, shrub fields, wetland growth, and fescue grasslands are interwoven in the treeless valley floors.

B.C. has an extensive alpine zone that occurs throughout the province. This area has a wide variety of shrub, herb, bryophyte, and lichen growth. In the meadows a diverse range of flowering species occurs, including glacier lily and mountain daisy. At the highest elevations, few species of flowering plants survive. Most vegetation is composed of moss campion, purple saxifrage, and sandworts.

There are approximately 2,850 vascular plant species and subspecies, 1,000 bryophytes (mosses and liverworts), and 1,600 lichen species present in B.C. Of the vascular plants one species is known to be extirpated from the province, 238 are on the provincial environment ministry's Red List (legally designated, or being considered for legal designation, as endangered or threatened) and another 378 are on the Blue List (considered sensitive or vulnerable).

Victoria

The provincial capital, Victoria is situated on the extreme southern tip of **Vancouver Island** and is bounded on three sides by water. Although dwarfed by Greater Vancouver's **population**, Greater Victoria, with about 300,000 people, is British Columbia's second-largest city.

Victoria has a spectacular physical setting. Across the broad waters of **Juan de Fuca** and Haro straits, the Olympic and **Cascade Mountain** ranges, plus the volcanic peak of Mount Baker all rise up majestically on neighbouring Washington State's mainland. The city itself stretches across beach-fronted lowlands broken by low hills and bordered to the west by fjord-like **Saanich Inlet**.

In 1838, when Captain W. H. McNeill anchored offshore he was moved to write of the area: "The place itself appears a perfect 'Eden' in the midst of the dreary wilderness of the Northwest coast, and so different in its general aspect, from the wooded rugged regions around, that one might be pardoned for supposing it had dropped from the clouds into its present position." It is a feeling that persists today.

In a province in which most communities feel as new as they are likely to be, Victoria shows its age to advantage, especially in the downtown core where brick and stone commercial buildings dating back to the pre-1900s indelibly link the city to its historic roots as a **government**, trade, and service centre. Chosen by Hudson's Bay Company chief factor James Douglas in 1843 as a site for settlement in anticipation of the company's being forced to abandon forts south of the **49th parallel** with the U.S.-Britain boundary settlement, a small trading fort named in honour of the reigning British queen was soon in operation. The **Fraser River** gold rush of 1858 accelerated growth and in 1862 Victoria was incorporated as a city. Three years later the British Admiralty established a naval base in Esquimalt Harbour, which continues today to be an important Department of National Defence base—CFB Esquimalt.

Until 1866, Victoria was the capital of the Colony of Vancouver Island, but lost its capital status that year when the colony was united with the mainland and **New Westminster** was designated the capital. The loss of capital status rankled residents, as the city was at the time the most populated and influential centre in British Columbia. Two years later, as New Westminster's fortunes withered, the capital was shifted to Victoria and has remained there ever since, despite sporadic outbursts of agitation for its return to the mainland by first New Westminster and later **Vancouver**. In 1893, Premier Theodore Davie decided to stifle further debate on this issue by replacing the existing government buildings with palatial legislative buildings. Opened in 1897, the B.C. Legislative Buildings cost a, for the times, astounding $923,000. After that outlay of money from the government coffers further talk of shifting the capital was effectively muzzled, although to this day the debate occasionally resurfaces.

Being the province's governmental centre has dictated much of Victoria's growth in social and economic terms. Today, more than 17 percent of its population are public servants, working either for the provincial or federal governments, and 40 percent of the work force are employed in the service industry. The other key element of its economy is **tourism**—more than three million tourists visit the city annually.

Until recently, Victoria also had the highest proportion of retirees per capita in Canada, but has now fallen behind Halifax and other Canadian communities in this regard. It is, however, growing rapidly—doubling its population in the past thirty years and predicted to increase by another 25 percent by the year 2010 if continued development remains largely unrestricted.

Status as the provincial capital and the predominance of a well-educated and urbanized population has also led to the community being home to many cultural and social amenities that normally would be missing from a city of its size. Victoria has a professional symphony, professional opera company, several professional and semi-professional theatre troupes, and a large concentration of the province's writers and artists. The Royal B.C. Museum, Maritime Museum of B.C., Art Gallery of Greater Victoria, the British Columbia Archives and Records Service, and the University of Victoria provide cornerstones to the city's cultural life. (*See also* **Cultural History**.)

In 1994, Victoria hosted the 15th Commonwealth Games and many of its sport and recreation venues were expanded or new facilities added for the athletic events. Hosting the games constituted part of a strategy to continue building the city's reputation as an international destination for tourism and events.

One fly-in-the-ointment for this ambition has been the city's persistence in dumping its raw (after cursory screening) sewage into Juan de Fuca Strait, a practice which has led to much controversy that has attracted international attention and led to cancellation of some conventions in protest. City engineers maintain, however, that the sewage is flushed at such a depth that the strait's strong currents immediately dissolve it and there is consequently minimal environmental impact.

A more immediately troubling problem facing the community is the economic challenge arising from cutbacks by both provincial and federal governments that affect its government-dependent work force. Several divisions of the Department of National Defence operations here started closing or being moved to other locations in 1994 and the provincial government continues a program of staff attrition to try and reduce its mounting debt problems. Its small resource- and manufacturing-based work force also continues to shrink as companies involved in the once-thriving marine and harbour industries close, raising the spectre of an increasingly unsustainable working harbour falling into dereliction that will come under growing pressure for residential development use. Facing the prospect of exploding population growth in the early years of the new millennium, Victorians are increasingly mindful of, debating, and trying to plan for the city's future growth and economic development.

Vineyards. *See* **Wineries.**

Volcanoes

Although no volcanoes in British Columbia are believed to be approaching geologic readiness for eruption, the province does lie within the same volcanic belt that contains Alaska's famed Ring of Fire and the massive volcanic cones of the Pacific Northwest United States, including Mount St. Helens, which erupted in 1980. In Alaska there are more than eighty potentially active volcanoes, several having undergone minor eruptions since 1980. Several Alaskan volcanoes could potentially undergo massive eruptions.

British Columbia's **physiography** has been significantly influenced by volcanic action and many mountains are former volcanic cones. Coastal and northern regions underwent the most intensive changes due to volcanic action, with river valleys, such as the Nass, being reshaped or dammed by lava flows and massive ash deposits.

In about 1750, the last volcanic eruptions in British Columbia ended at what today is the site of **Nisga'a Memorial Lava Bed Provincial Park** near Terrace. No active volcanoes remain in the province, but some researchers believe that several volcanoes in the Nass and Iskut river regions of the British Columbia's northwestern corner may only be dormant—several probably having erupted in only the last few hundred years.

Hoodoo Mountain on the north side of the Iskut River, near the southernmost edge of the Alaska Panhandle, is believed by some scientists to be the most likely volcano in the province to be merely in a dormancy phase, rather than being extinct. With an elevation of about 1,980 metres it retains the virtually classic cinder cone shape of an active volcano. Its crater is filled with ice and snow, but surrounding valleys are clogged with lava and ash deposits that in recent geological time (several hundred years ago) diverted streams.

(*See also* **Seamounts**.)

Water

Fresh water, in the form of about twenty-four thousand lakes, **rivers**, and streams, cover 1.9 percent (1.807 million hectares) of British Columbia's total land mass to make the province one of the most water-rich areas in the world. Almost one-third of all the freshwater run-off in Canada is contained within the province's borders. This run-off, however, is concentrated in only a few rivers.

The largest is the **Fraser River**, which drains nearly 25 percent of the province. The Liard, **Stikine**, Nass, **Skeena**, **Peace**, and **Columbia** are the other primary rivers draining run-off. For the most part these rivers are isolated from the province's **population** concentrations, so although water rich, much of that water is too far away to be much used by the province's population or industry.

As a consequence of the province's water distribution versus population concentration, areas such as the Greater Vancouver Regional District and the Capital Regional District (including **Victoria**) have experienced the need for water rationing. Fully 25 percent of B.C. regional districts cite water availability as a future constraint on economic development.

This problem is exacerbated by the fact that long-term data indicates that average annual streamflows in southern sites, where the population is centred, is decreasing while increasing in northern sites. Similar trends have been observed in snowpack water storage. This is believed to be a result of global warming reducing summer precipitation levels and simultaneously increasing summer evaporation.

In Canadian terms, British Columbians are not heavy water users, but are incredibly wasteful in international terms. Average water use in B.C. accounts for only 6.5 percent of Canada's total consumption, but this figure fails to take into account that more than 60 percent of national consumption goes to thermal power generation—while most B.C. power is generated by hydroelectric plants that do not remove water from stream beds. At an international level, the average Vancouverite uses about 950 litres of water daily compared to average individual consumption in Africa of 20 litres.

Most water consumed in B.C. goes into manufacturing use. Of the 2.755 million cubic metres of water consumed annually in B.C., 51 percent is consumed by manufacturing, 22 percent by agricultural operations (including some water that is used for human consumption), 22 percent by municipal water plants (mostly for human consumption), 3 percent by the **mining industry**, and only 2 percent by thermal power plants.

(*See also* **Rivers**; **Waterfalls**.)

Water—Drinking

Most of British Columbia's urban and semi-urban areas are serviced with good supplies of drinking water drawn from local water reservoir, stream, and lake sources provided to individual residences through underground piping systems. To ensure that the water is safe for drinking, the majority of communities purify it with chlorine. Some communities also add fluoride to the water system. In recent years, concerns about the purity of urban water systems has led to increased use of bottled water for drinking purposes.

Rural residences, such as farms and acreages, most often draw water from individual wells tapping into groundwater supplies or rely on water storage tanks. About 600,000 British Columbians depend on groundwater supplies for their water. Approximately 9 percent of the province's total water consumed comes from groundwater sources. Communal wells are relatively rare. When they do exist, the water is usually fed directly to each residence via a piping system.

The streams and lakes of British Columbia should generally be considered as unsafe for untreated drinking purposes. Since the early 1990s the spread of various intestinal parasites, the most prevalent being *Giardia lamblia,* which causes giardiasis or "beaver fever," has rapidly infiltrated even many of the province's most remote rivers and lakes. Giardiasis causes diarrhoea, cramps, bloating, weight loss, and stomach gas. Severe cases are complicated by vomiting and dehydration. The disease's acute stage is usually only a few days, but it is an intensely uncomfortable affliction. After this period, however, those infected continue to carry the parasite and can contaminate other water sources unless they receive medical treatment to eliminate the parasite from their body. The disease is spread by people through poor hygienic practices, and by animals, including dogs and beavers (hence "beaver fever"). Generally, unless water is clearly identified as being safe to drink, sterilization procedures should be taken whenever drawing water from B.C. streams, lakes, or wells.

For the province with the greatest water wealth in Canada, British Columbia also has the most problem with water-borne illnesses, averaging about two hundred cases for every 100,000 population. This compares to a Canadian average of about 145 cases per 100,000. Giardiasis outbreaks account for about 60 percent of these illnesses.

Waterfalls

Of waterfalls with the highest vertical drop in Canada, British Columbia is home to six, including four of the five highest. The highest is **Takakkaw** (503 metres), followed by Della (440 metres), Twin (274 metres), Hunlen (253 metres), and then Alberta's Panther (183 metres). The measures shown here are based on the distance from when the water goes over the crest and drops vertically or near vertically to the fall's base. Most waterfalls are backed by a series of violent rapids leading to the crest. This distance is not factored into these measurements.

In a province strewn with mountains that have been splintered and lifted by geological faults and **earthquakes**, and gouged by glaciers as recently as fifteen thousand years ago, it is not surprising that B.C. has literally thousands of waterfalls ranging from continuous flowing, high ones such as those listed above to intermittent run-off falls dropping only a few metres.

In geological terms, all waterfalls are transient because their erosive power will eventually lead to self-destruction when they finally erode away the surface beneath them to attain a more gradual angle between their upper reaches and the base below.

(*See also* **Helmcken Falls**; **Takakkaw Falls**.)

Weeds. *See* Eurasian Watermilfoil; Knapweed; Vegetation.

Wells Gray Provincial Park

Commonly recognized as one of North America's great wilderness parks, Wells Gray Provincial Park covers 529,748 hectares, mostly high in the Cariboo Mountains. Accesses are from Clearwater and Blue River on Highway 5 between **Kamloops** and Jasper, and from 100 Mile House in the Cariboo region.

The park was heavily glaciated by past ice ages and was once a highly volcanic region—two forces that have combined to give the park a terrain of rugged valleys cut by river torrents draining out of the Clearwater watershed that plunge down numerous **waterfalls** (including **Helmcken Falls**). The park is also scattered with numerous lakes, dense **forests**, alpine meadows, glaciers, extinct **volcanoes**, lava beds, mineral springs, and steep mountain peaks. About 170 species of **birds** and more than fifty **mammal** species have been identified within park boundaries—including the largest population of mountain caribou in southern British Columbia. In winter the area is subject to heavy snowfalls and severe cold; summer temperatures are hot with powerful thunderstorms common. The park is popular with outdoorspeople in all seasons. Winter cross-country **skiing** is considered to be among the best in the province. The rest of the year the park attracts thousands of hikers, paddlers, and anglers. The extensive river and lake system is an internationally popular canoeing destination.

West Coast Trail

About nine thousand people hike the seventy-two-kilometre West Coast Trail annually, making this the province's most famous and popular backcountry **hiking** trail. The trail tightly hugs the western coastline of **Vancouver Island** from Port Renfrew north to the northwest end of Pachena Bay, three kilometres from Bamfield. It takes five to seven days to complete the hike and hikers must be prepared to cope with heavy rain, dampness, mud, and the threat of hypothermia and exhaustion from what, in poor weather, can be a gruelling endurance test.

The trail is open to hikers from May 1 to September 30. To hike the West Coast Trail, hikers must register with Parks Canada's **Pacific Rim National Park** offices. Only fifty-two hikers per day are allowed to start out on the trail, because overuse was threatening to cause irreparable damage to both the trail and surrounding habitat.

The southernmost portion of the trail is through second-growth forest, but beyond this stretch most of the hike passes through the ancient temperate **rainforest** of the Walbran, **Carmanah**, and other valleys out of which streams run that must be crossed. Beaches are scattered all along the route.

Original construction of the West Coast Trail began in 1906 after the wreck of the passenger vessel SS *Valencia,* the worst shipwreck in B.C. history, along this coastline. It was constructed by the federal government as a lifesaving trail to enable rescuers, as well as survivors of **shipwrecks**, to move over the area's harsh coastal terrain. The area by this time had become known as the Graveyard of the Pacific, because so many ships had foundered on its rock shelves. To date, about sixty ships have been lost on this section of Vancouver Island's west coast since 1854, including the MV *Vanlene*, which ran aground in 1974, spilling oil on the beaches of Cape Beale, just north of Pachena. For years the lifesaving trail was maintained by solitary linemen keeping the trail open and fixing the telephone line that was strung along its path.

West Vancouver

A mecca of mansions and wealth, West Vancouver has the distinction of having the highest per capita incomes in British Columbia and in the mid- to late 1980s the highest per capita incomes in the nation. Lying across Burrard Inlet from **Vancouver**, it is a small, idyllically pretty mountainside community of about forty thousand. Eighty percent of its labour force is linked to the commercial district of Greater Vancouver by the **Lions Gate Bridge**, which they commute across each workday. The city is twenty kilometres long and five kilometres wide at its broadest point. Along the upper ridgelines stretches the elite British Properties neighbourhood, home to many of Greater Vancouver's rich and famous.

Despite the city's posh reputation, most of its residents deny living here out of a desire to dwell in an enclave of wealth and privilege; rather they contend it is the ambience, the small-town atmosphere, the country-like feel that makes West Vancouver an enticing escape from the frenzy of Vancouver's downtown core where many of West Vancouver's residents spend their working days.

Whales

The present population of about 275 resident and one hundred transient **killer whales** constitutes only a fragment of the whale population that used to ply the waters off the B.C. coast. Excessive hunting by whalers decimated the original whale population, which included humpbacks, **Pacific grey whales**, Baird's beaked whales, and thirty-metre-long blue whales—the largest animal ever known.

Although the whales were victims of hunting expeditions throughout human habitation of the Pacific coast, they were not subjected to intensive hunting until 1905 when advances in whale gun and processing technology accelerated the kill levels. Between 1905 and 1972 more than thirty thousand whales were killed off the shores of Washington State and British Columbia. Whaling stations operated in Barkley Sound and Kyuquot Sound on Vancouver Island's west coast from 1905 to the late 1920s. Following World War II, a modern operation was established in Quatsino Sound on **Vancouver Island**, which was active in whale killing until it closed in 1967 due to the declining whale population.

In 1972, the federal government declared a halt to all whaling operations based in Canadian ports, but by that time there were only three such operations, all on the Atlantic coast. All whaling within Canada's territorial waters was subsequently banned.

But the damage was done to most of the whale populations on the West Coast. To date, only the Pacific grey whale has managed to return to historical levels. Humpback whales are rarely seen in B.C. waters and many other species are extinct.

Whistler Resort

International ski magazines routinely recognize Whistler Resort, one hundred kilometres from the boundary of Greater **Vancouver** virtually due north on Highway 99, as North America's best ski resort. Two magnificent, ski-run laden peaks guarantee it—Whistler at 2,181 metres, and Blackcomb at 2,287 metres. They have a combined total of two hundred runs and twenty-seven lifts. Whistler has North America's second-longest lift-serviced vertical run—1,530 metres. Blackcomb is home to the longest such run—1,609. Blackcomb also has the longest uninterrupted fall-line **skiing** in North America.

On the edge of Garibaldi Provincial Park, Whistler is also the jumping-off point to extensive **hiking** and other outdoor recreation activities in this popular park. The easy access to year-round outdoor sports has fuelled Whistler's growth in recent years. It is the province's fastest growing municipality. The addition of many world-class hotels and golf courses has made it a popular international destination for conventions and conferences.

Whistler's development is surprisingly recent considering its proximity to the province's largest **population** base. In the early 1970s there was little more than a few scattered ski cabins built randomly around the mountains. In 1975, responding to pressure from a group of visionaries who recognized the area's potential, the provincial government established Whistler as B.C.'s first and only Resort Municipality, imposed firm development controls, and hammered out a long-range development strategy. The resort opened officially in December 1980. Since then growth has been steady and rapid, but carefully controlled.

(*See also* **Skiing**.)

Wildlife. *See* Biodiversity.

Williams Lake Stampede. *See* Annual Events and Celebrations.

Wineries

British Columbia's wine industry dates back to the 1860s when Father Charles Pandosy planted vines at the Oblate Mission south of **Kelowna**, near the shores of Okanagan Lake. But it was not until the 1960s that the province's wine industry became a significant agricultural economic sector. Throughout the 1960s and 1970s, however, the wines produced in the province were generally of a poor quality and carried equivalent names, such as Lonesome Charlie and Baby Duck.

In the 1980s, a glut of poor wines and equally poor grape varieties under cultivation led to serious economic problems for the entire industry, a trend which resulted in a decision to reorganize B.C.'s wine production operations so that the emphasis shifted from quantity of product to quality of product. By the 1990s, this shift in focus was of critical importance because of the introduction of the North America Free Trade Agreement (NAFTA) and several General Agreement on Trades and Tariffs (GATT) decisions that opened Canada's wine retail market to stiffer competition from foreign producers.

From this point on the emphasis of the industry was solely on production of world-class-quality wines, requiring the planting and cultivation of premium grape varieties. Before the introduction of the initial U.S.-Canada Free Trade Agreement in 1988, for example, there were more than two hundred vineyards growing 1,376 hectares of grapes. The following year, after massive cutbacks in the industry, only 459 hectares of vineyards remained. That number has slowly increased until today there are about 765 hectares of vines grown in 130 vineyards. The primary grape variety planted in B.C. is *Vitis vinifera*.

There are four main grape growing areas in the province: the **Okanagan**, Similkameen, and **Fraser** valleys, and southeastern **Vancouver Island**. Of these, the adjoining Okanagan and Similkameen valleys represent about 90 percent of the total grape growing area and wineries. The Fraser Valley has some vineyards and Vancouver Island is undergoing a renaissance that is seeing a number of new wineries opening and expanded vineyard plantings underway. There are more than thirty wineries operating in the province.

In B.C. there are three types of wineries that are licensed for operation: major wineries, estate wineries, and farm wineries. Major wineries, such as Calona Wines and Mission Hill Wines, are not restricted in the quantity of wine they produce. They may import grapes and juice from other countries and label the resulting wine "Bottled in British Columbia." They may or may not have their own vineyards. Most produce specific lines of wines that are made 100 percent from B.C. grapes and compete with estate and farm wineries in terms of quality.

Estate wineries produce wine made from 100 percent B.C. grapes, 50 percent of which must be grown on the winery property. All steps from crushing to bottling must be performed at the winery. By licence, estate wineries can sell up to 181,840 litres of wine per year. This amounts to approximately twenty thousand cases.

Farm wineries produce wine made from 100 percent B.C. grapes, 75 percent of which must come from their own vineyards. Farm wineries are limited to production and sale of 45,460 litres annually (about five thousand cases).

The majority of B.C. wineries are either estate or farm wineries, with the number in each category being about equal. Since 1990, B.C. wines have performed exceedingly well at international wine competitions. In 1993, for example, B.C. wines from eight wineries captured three gold, thirty-two silver, and forty-five bronze medals at seventeen international wine competitions.

Wolves

Before the arrival of Europeans, North America's largest wild dog, the wolf, inhabited the continent from the Mexican plateau to the Arctic. Perceived as vermin by European settlers, however, many of the continent's wolves were slaughtered. In British Columbia, the fact that so much of the province remained wilderness until well into the twentieth century acted to protect wolf populations until it was eventually recognized that wolves, as is true of all naturally occurring carnivores, play a vital role in sustaining the natural balance of the continent's **biodiversity**. Today, B.C.'s wolf population is one of the most well distributed and stable in North America.

There are approximately eight thousand wolves throughout the province. Until a few years ago, some areas of the West Kootenays, the Thompson-Okanagan region, and the Lower Mainland had no wolves, but the two interior regions now support small packs and individual wolf populations. The largest wolf concentrations are found in the northern part of **Vancouver Island** and in the northeastern part of the province, especially near **Fort St. John**.

Wolves are extremely shy of humans and elusive, preferring to hunt and move at night. They hunt deer, caribou, moose, and smaller game. In coastal areas, wolves have been known to feed on intertidal life and fish.

Unlike most North American predators, wolves are not solitary by nature. Instead, they sustain a complex social order by living in small packs. Most packs number about five to eight members, although packs numbering as many as thirty individuals have been sighted in the Fort St. John region. A pack consists of a dominant breeding pair, pups of the year, yearlings, and, occasionally, other related adults. Only the dominant pair will breed while the pack stays together. Litters number four to seven pups.

Packs roam over a large range in search of prey. An individual pack's territory will vary from 130 to 1,500 square kilometres. As a pack's young reach maturity they usually disperse to form a new pack, ranging up to three hundred kilometres from their birth pack. Wolves often travel thirty to forty kilometres a day in search of prey.

Work Force. *See* **Labour Force.**

Yellowhead Pass

At an elevation of 1,133 metres the Yellowhead Pass crosses the **Continental Divide** between Alberta and British Columbia twenty-five kilometres west of Jasper, Alberta. On the B.C. side to the west, Yellowhead Lake empties into the **Fraser River**, forming part of this river's headwaters.

Originally, Europeans called this passage Leather Pass, in reference to the Hudson's Bay Company using it as a route for moving moose and caribou hides to the east between 1826 and 1828. In 1862, the pass became a secondary route to the Cariboo goldfields and later was seriously considered for the first route through the **Rocky Mountains** by the Canadian Pacific Railroad before the **Rogers Pass** was deemed shorter and more feasible. In the early 1900s, the Grand Trunk Pacific and the Canadian Northern Railway used the pass, running lines in some places right beside each other. Both the Yellowhead Highway and Canadian National Railroad today use the pass, which in 1985 was designated a Canadian historic site.

Yoho National Park

Yoho is believed to be the Kutenai peoples' word for "awe." With twenty-eight towering mountain peaks reaching up to more than three thousand metres, steep, glacier-carved valleys, thundering waterfalls (of which **Takakkaw** is Canada's highest), green glacial lakes, icy peaks, crystal caves, natural bridges, hoodoos, and high alpine meadows, the name appropriately describes this thirteen-hundred-square-kilometre national park created in 1886. The park is bordered by Banff National Park to the east and **Kootenay National Park** to the south; it is part of the UNESCO Canadian Rockies World Heritage Site. Although flanked by the Alberta border it lies entirely within British Columbia.

The park has a prolific wildlife population that includes mountain goats and sheep, golden eagles, white-tailed ptarmigan, Clark's nutcrackers, pika, marmot, grizzly **bears**, moose, wolverines, marten, and elk.

CPR surveyor Tom Wilson gave the same name of Emerald Lake to two lakes in the region because of their stunning green tints. Obviously one had to be changed and the more accessible one was renamed Lake Louise in honour of Queen Victoria's daughter—yet another time when the reign of this monarch during western Canada's exploration and early development left its in-

Although Takakkaw Falls in Yoho National Park is Canada's highest waterfall,
the park contains many other spectacular waterfalls, such as Twin Falls.
(Frances Backhouse photo)

delible royal mark upon the landscape. There is also an Emerald Glacier in
Yoho that feeds both the lake and Kicking Horse River, which runs westward
from roughly the centre of the park to join the **Columbia River** at Golden.

The park is divided by the **Trans-Canada Highway** and primary access
is from the community of Field, twenty-six kilometres east of Golden. Contained within the park boundaries is Kicking Horse Pass via which both the
Canadian Pacific Railroad and the highway cut through the Rockies to link
Alberta with British Columbia. The pass came by its unusual name when Sir
James Hector was leading the Palliser Expedition through from Vermillion in
1858. They came to a river and Sir James soon found himself struggling with
a horse caught in its current. As he struggled to rescue it the horse kicked him
in the chest—and a river and a pass won a name.

Zeballos. *See* **Tsunamis.**

About the Author

Mark Zuehlke, a full-time writer since 1982, has written extensively on his native province, British Columbia. His other books include *Scoundrels, Dreamers & Second Sons: British Remittance Men in the Canadian West; The Vancouver Island South Explorer: The Outdoor Guide;* and, with co-author Louise Donnelly, *Magazine Writing from the Boonies.* He has published more than two hundred magazine articles in such publications as *The Financial Post Magazine, Canadian Business, Canadian,* and *Maclean's.*

PHOTO: ROSEMARY NEERING

Zuehlke lives in Victoria, where, among other recreational activities, he enjoys hiking and sea kayaking.